Urban Diversities and Language Policies in Medium-Sized Linguistic Communities

MULTILINGUAL MATTERS

Series Editors: John Edwards, *St. Francis Xavier University, Canada*

Multilingual Matters series publishes books on bilingualism, bilingual education, immersion education, second language learning, language policy, multiculturalism. The editor is particularly interested in 'macro' level studies of language policies, language maintenance, language shift, language revival and language planning. Books in the series discuss the relationship between language in a broad sense and larger cultural issues, particularly identity related ones.

Full details of all the books in this series and of all our other publications can be found on http://www.multilingual-matters.com, or by writing to Multilingual Matters, St Nicholas House, 31–34 High Street, Bristol BS1 2AW, UK.

MULTILINGUAL MATTERS: 159

Urban Diversities and Language Policies in Medium-Sized Linguistic Communities

Edited by
Emili Boix-Fuster

MULTILINGUAL MATTERS
Bristol • Buffalo • Toronto

Library of Congress Cataloging in Publication Data
Urban Diversities and Language Policies in Medium-Sized Linguistic Communities/Edited By Emili Boix-Fuster.
Multilingual Matters: 159.
Includes bibliographical references and index.
1. Language policy—Social aspects. 2. Urban dialects—Social aspects. 3. Multilingualism—Social aspects. 4. Language and languages—Variation. 5. Linguistic geography—Variation. 6. Sociolinguistics. I. Boix, Emili, 1956- editor.
P40.5.U73U73 2015
306.44'6091732–dc23 2015009682

British Library Cataloguing in Publication Data
A catalogue entry for this book is available from the British Library.

ISBN-13: 978-1-78309-390-8 (hbk)
ISBN-13: 978-1-78309-389-2 (pbk)

Multilingual Matters
UK: St Nicholas House, 31–34 High Street, Bristol BS1 2AW, UK.
USA: UTP, 2250 Military Road, Tonawanda, NY 14150, USA.
Canada: UTP, 5201 Dufferin Street, North York, Ontario M3H 5T8, Canada.

Website: www.multilingual-matters.com
Twitter: Multi_Ling_Mat
Facebook: https://www.facebook.com/multilingualmatters
Blog: www.channelviewpublications.wordpress.com

Copyright © 2015 Emili Boix-Fuster and the authors of individual chapters.

All rights reserved. No part of this work may be reproduced in any form or by any means without permission in writing from the publisher.

The policy of Multilingual Matters/Channel View Publications is to use papers that are natural, renewable and recyclable products, made from wood grown in sustainable forests. In the manufacturing process of our books, and to further support our policy, preference is given to printers that have FSC and PEFC Chain of Custody certification. The FSC and/or PEFC logos will appear on those books where full certification has been granted to the printer concerned.

Typeset by Techset Composition India (P) Ltd, Bangalore and Chennai, India.
Printed and bound in Great Britain by Short Run Press Ltd.

Contents

	Contributors	vii
	Introduction	xi
1	Mapping Urban Multilingualism in Europe: In Search of Untapped Resources in Primary Schools *Guus Extra*	1
2	Competitive and Cooperative Orientations in Language Policies: A Critical Look at the Situation of Dutch in Brussels *Philippe Hambye*	25
3	Language Diversity in Vigo: The Challenges of a Minoritized Language in a Highly Castilianized City *Iago González Pascual and Fernando Ramallo*	50
4	Helsinki as a Multilingual City *Pirkko Nuolijärvi*	67
5	Tallinn, a Multilingual City in the Era of Globalization: The Challenges Facing Estonian as a Medium-Sized Language *Josep Soler-Carbonell*	85
6	Multilingual Valencia: Linguistic Destruction and Reconstruction of an Urban Space *Miquel Nicolás Amorós and Francesc Jesús Hernández Dobon*	112
7	Multilingualism in Barcelona: Towards An Asymmetrical Multilingualism *Emili Boix-Fuster*	143

8 Language in Copenhagen: Changing Social Structures,
     Changing Ideologies, Changing Linguistic Practices   168
   Marie Maegaard and J. Normann Jørgensen

   Conclusions   186

   Index   189

Contributors

Miquel Nicolás Amorós (Valencia, 1959) Philology D. and professor of Catalan Philology at the Universitat de València, where he has held academic responsibilities and taught undergraduate and graduate courses in different academic careers since 1986. He specializes in issues of social history of the Catalan language, sociolinguistics, language assessment and management of multilingualism in educational contexts. He has also participated in several research projects and published in different languages studies such *La història de la llengua catalana: la construcció d'un discurs* (Barcelona: PAM, 1998) and *Història de la llengua catalana* (Barcelona: Ediuoc, 2011), co-authored with Antoni Ferrando.

Emili Boix-Fuster is full professor of sociolinguistics, Department of Catalan Philology, University of Barcelona, Catalonia, Spain. He regularly teaches sociolinguistics, language planning and applied linguistics. He has published, among others, *Sociolinguistics of the Catalan Language* [in Catalan] (co-edited with F.X. Vila, Ariel 1998), *Democratic Policies for Language Revitalisation: The Case of Catalan* (co-edited with M. Strubell, Palgrave, 2011) and *Languages on the Coach. Family Plurilingualism in the Catalan-Speaking Territories* [in Catalan] (co-edited with R.M. Torrens Pagès, 2012). He is editor of the academic journal *Treballs de Sociolingüística Catalana*.

Guus Extra has held the Chair of Language and Minorities at Tilburg University, the Netherlands, in the School of Humanities, Department of Culture Studies from 1981–2011. From 1998–2008, he was Director of *Babylon, Centre for Studies of the Multicultural Society*. Guus Extra has an extensive record in research and publications on second language acquisition, first language use/maintenance/loss by immigrant minority groups, and multilingualism and education, both at the national (Dutch) and the European level. He also has an extensive record in coordinating research in these domains, at both levels. He was a member of the steering committees for the Dutch Science Foundation Programme on Multilingualism and Minorities in the Netherlands (1988–1994) and for the DSF Programme on The Multicultural and Pluriform Society (1998–2002). He was also a member of the international management team for the European Science Foundation Programme on Second Language Acquisition by Adult Immigrants (1982–1988) and coordinator of the Multilingual Cities Project funded by the European Cultural Foundation (1998–2004). From 1982, he supervised 37 successfully defended dissertations and acted as a referee of research proposals and grant applications for the Dutch Science Foundation (NWO), the Dutch Royal Academy of Sciences (KNAW), the Flemish Science Foundation (NFWO), the European Science Foundation (ESF), and the South Africa – Netherlands Research Programme on Alternatives in Development (SANPAD). He spent sabbaticals in the non-European English-dominant immigration contexts of the USA (Stanford/California, 1978/1979), South Africa (Durban/Kwazulu Natal, 1997), and Australia (Melbourne/Victoria, 2006). He has given conference keynotes, guest lectures, seminars and workshops in each of these three countries, in 17 European countries, in Morocco and in Japan.

Iago González-Pascual graduated in Translation and Interpreting from the University of Vigo and in Linguistics from the University of Barcelona. He obtained an MA in Audiovisual Translation from the Universitat Autònoma de Barcelona and an MA in Applied Linguistics from the University of Vigo. He has worked as a research assistant in sociolinguistic projects and he currently works as a translator. He has also lectured in Translation. His main research interests include sociolinguistics, language planning and policy and discourse analysis.

Philippe Hambye is professor of French linguistics at the University of Louvain (UCL, Belgium). His research mainly includes works in sociolinguistics regarding variation of linguistic norms and practices in the French-speaking area, language practices in education and at work, and language policies. These works aim at discovering the role language plays in issues of legitimacy, power and social inequalities.

Francesc Jesús Hernández Dobon was born in Valencia, Spain, in August 1959. He has a PhD in Philosophy (1986), Education (1991) and Sociology (2002), Valencia University. He is a professor of Sociology of Education at Valencia University, Department of Sociology and Social Anthropology. Dr Hernàndez has been a visiting professor in universities in Latin America (Brazil, Colombia, Cuba and Uruguay) and Europe (Germany and Ireland). He has authored more than 25 books. The latest include: *Teorías sobre sociedad, familia y educación* (Valencia: Tirant lo Blanch, 2010), *Sociología de la educación* (Madrid: McGraw-Hill, 2011) and *Estructura social y educación* (Valencia: Tirant lo Blanch, 2014).

Jens Normann Jørgensen passed away on 29 May 2013. He was a professor at the Lanchart Centre at University of Copenhagen. As a linguist, he had a strong interest in sociolinguistics, multilingualism and social inequality. His work included research in diverse fields, such as dialectology, distributive sociolinguistics, educational linguistics, linguistic ethnography and language ideology. His influential ideas of languaging and polylingualism took form through his longitudinal studies of language variation and change among multilingual young people in Denmark.

Marie Maegaard is an associate professor at University of Copenhagen, Department of Nordic Research. She is a sociolinguist working mainly in the fields of language variation and change, multilingualism, dialectology, language attitudes and linguistic ethnography. She has a strong interest in the social embedding of linguistic variation, and in variation and social meaning. She has studied linguistic variation in many parts of Denmark, ranging from rural western Jutland to urban Copenhagen, and from older dialect speakers to young multilingual speakers.

Pirkko Nuolijärvi is a professor and the director of the Research Institute for the Languages of Finland in Helsinki. Her research focuses on variation in Finnish, institutional interaction and language policy. She has studied the change of Finnish, the language situation in Finland, and language variation in the public sphere as well as in the fiction in Finnish and Nordic projects. She has published several books and numerous articles in sociolinguistics.

Fernando Ramallo is a senior lecturer of Linguistics at the University of Vigo. He has published widely in sociolinguistics. Between 2000 and 2013, he was the co-editor of the journal *Sociolinguistic Studies* (Equinox, UK). Since 2013 he has been a member of the Committee of Experts for the European Charter for Regional or Minority Languages (Council of Europe). His research interests include language ideologies, discourse analysis and language policy. In recent years, his work has focused on minority language new-speakers.

Josep Soler-Carbonell (PhD in Linguistics and Communication, University of Barcelona) is a Lecturer at the Centre for Academic English, Department of English, Stockholm University, and a Research Fellow at the Institute of Estonian and General Linguistics, University of Tartu. His research focuses on aspects related to linguistic ideologies, language policy and planning, language attitudes and linguistic ethnography. His current work examines the area of university language policies, with a particular focus on the Estonian context. His research has appeared in several edited collections as well as in journals such as the *International Journal of Bilingual Education and Bilingualism*, *Multilingua*, and the *Journal of English as a Lingua Franca*.

Introduction. Cities and Diversities: A Cross-National Perspective in Medium-Sized Linguistic Communities

Emili Boix-Fuster

Language policy in urban areas has often been approached and discussed in a dichotomous and simplistic way, either from the point of view of dominant, hegemonic languages or from that of minority, minoritized and threatened languages. However, the current processes of globalization and internationalization show a more nuanced scenario with many medium-sized linguistic communities (MSLCs) striving both to maintain their languages in everyday communication and to use them in high prestige domains in competition with dominant codes. We define MSLCs, mainly from the demographic point of view, as communities that speak languages which are not international languages, nor languages with a large number of speakers, nor (at the other extreme) minority languages or languages that are not widely spoken. In demographic terms, MSLCs are conventionally defined as languages spoken by between one and 25 million people. As Vila and Bretxa (2013: 3–4) have pointed out in a recent volume on the same topic,

> the languages included in this intermediate group are far from homogeneous. They range from fully standardized languages, with a long record of written literature, to varieties that have rarely transcended the status of oral vernaculars and tend to be regarded as dialects of other languages [...]. In general terms, the majority of these languages lead a placid life. Debates about the long-term sustainability of many of these languages may often be regarded as unrealistic by speakers and specialists alike. Nevertheless, in spite of all these debates, many of these, especially but not only those that have gained the status of nation state official language, constitute vivid examples of linguistic sustainability in virtually

all domains of social life. This makes them appropriate subjects for analysis in order to make progress in the field of language policy.

Thus the modest aim of this definition is to group together a set of linguistic communities whose sustainability, viability and survival in today's globalized world appear to face common ecological problems and challenges which are often quite different from those facing other languages, and which therefore require the adoption of specific social, political and legal instruments. This volume aims to: (1) provide new data and reflections; (2) reevaluate the old dichotomous opposition between 'majority' and 'minority' languages; and (3) inculcate good practices. As Milian-Massana states (2012: 15), 'the starkness of the binary (official-working/all-other) approach to the status of languages within the EU masks a much more complex reality'.

The first MSLCs to be analysed (Milian-Massana, 2012; Vila, 2013) are those which belong to socioeconomically developed societies and enjoy healthy intergenerational transmission and a high degree of vitality, as witnessed by their use at all levels of contemporary society in both public and private domains: in government, administration, the legal system, health and at all levels of education including higher education; in daily interpersonal communication; in the written and audiovisual media, cinema, theatre, music, the book industry and popular culture; and on the Internet and in the economic and commercial domains. A fair amount of common ground has been found among these MSLCs:

(1) there is no need for language shift in order to thrive economically and socially. In other words, maintaining whatever sort of local languages there are does not necessarily hinder progress and welfare;
(2) all the MSLCs analysed use elaborate, complete languages;
(3) linguistic sustainability may not require monolingual societies. Multilingualism tends to be the norm rather than the exception; and
(4) there are low expectations as far as the learning of the MSLC languages is concerned.

However, in most cases there are significant numbers of L2 speakers: MSLCs attract new speakers, and therefore analysts have to raise the question of who is the legitimate speaker of a given language.

Further research should discuss those MSLCs which lack such traits, for example the Amazigh community in North Africa and the Kurdish community in the Middle East. So far (Vila, 2013: 197) the role of the state has been crucial: 'States are the engines that create public language policies, and they also set the frames for private language management'.

These characteristics of MSLCs give them some homogeneity in terms of the problems and challenges they face. MSLCs hold an intermediate position: they are both the head of a dog and the tail of a lion. This more down-to-earth approach enables the reader to see a more detailed view of the evolution of linguistic communities than that provided by standard research. From this book's perspective, cities play a leading, central and decisive role in language conflicts: their impact cannot be ignored. Cities allow us a more refined sociolinguistically-oriented comparative analysis and, above all, a better understanding of crucial aspects of both the vulnerability and sustainability of a given language community: why does an MSLC lead a peaceful life or why does an MSLC run the risk of disappearing?

This volume explores the language policies implemented in different urban areas, all characterized by a dynamic multilingualism. Chapter 1 maps urban multilingualism in Europe; Chapter 2 deals with Brussels (mainly French, Dutch and English); Chapter 3 analyses Vigo in Galicia (mainly Spanish, Galician and English); Chapter 4 discusses Helsinki (mainly Finnish, Swedish and English); Chapter 5 deals with Tallinn (mainly Estonian, Russian and English); Chapter 6 deals with Valencia (mainly Spanish, Catalan and English); Chapter 7 discusses Barcelona (mainly Catalan, Spanish and English); Chapter 8 analyses Copenhagen (mainly Danish and English) and, finally, the Conclusion.

Not all the chapters adopt the same focus. Most papers were presented in a preliminary version in two seminars which took place in Barcelona on 30 September and 7 October 2010 under the title 'The challenges of urban areas in medium-sized linguistic communities', coordinated by Emili Boix-Fuster and Vanessa Bretxa under the auspices of Linguamón – House of Languages and the CUSC (University Centre for Sociolinguistics and Communication) at the University of Barcelona.[1]

The participants in this workshop were given the following outlines:

(1) What is the linguistic repertoire of the city? What are the attitudes or ideologies concerning the different languages and varieties in the city?
(2) What is the bilingual and multilingual image of the city (its linguistic landscape), e.g. public and private services and signage. What are their effects on the citizen's sense of belonging and the identity of the city?
(3) In which public domains does the city decide to offer services in different languages and why?
(4) To what extent is the city a microcosm of the country and a reflection of its culture? What role does the city play as far as the sociolinguistic situation of the whole country is concerned?
(5) How does the educational sector contribute to bilingualism/multilingualism in the city?
(6) What is the demolinguistic balance in the urban environment? What is the social distribution of the languages in contact? What are the effects of immigration and population movements? Are there multilingual services for minorities and immigrants?
(7) How does the private sector face the challenge of offering spoken and written services in different languages?

(8) Is it possible to find similarities with other urban areas inside and outside the country?

The content of the chapters is as follows:

The first chapter, 'Mapping Urban Multilingualism in Europe: In Search of Untapped Resources in Primary Schools' by Guus Extra (Tilburg University, Netherlands), gives a comparative overview of six major multicultural cities in the European Union, namely Gothenburg, Hamburg, The Hague, Brussels, Lyon and Madrid. The rationale and methods of the Multilingual Cities Project are presented. These data from the project are used to create a pseudolongitudinal comparison of the processes of both intergenerational acculturation and language maintenance by means of four reported dimensions: *language proficiency*, i.e. the extent to which the home language under consideration is understood; *language choice*, i.e. the extent to which this language is commonly spoken at home with the mother; *language dominance*, i.e. the extent to which the home language is spoken better than others; and *language preference*, i.e. the extent to which the home language is spoken in preference to others. The conclusions show that:

(1) using more than one language is a way of life for an increasing number of children across Europe;
(2) mainstream and non-mainstream languages should not viewed in terms of competition;
(3) English enjoys a high status everywhere; and most importantly
(4) there is an increasing mismatch between linguistic practices at home and at school.

The second chapter 'Competitive and Cooperative Orientations in Language Policies: A Critical Look at the Situation of Dutch in Brussels' by Philippe Hambye (Catholic University of Louvain) describes the unique multilingualism of the European capital. Special emphasis is placed on the role played by Dutch, which is the receding language under the pressure of both the dominant language, French and the main international language, English, which might even play the role of lingua franca. The reader will find a discussion of the role played by social associations and societies fighting to keep the Dutch face of the Belgian metropolis alive.

The third chapter, 'Language Diversity in Vigo: The Challenges of a Minoritized Language in a Highly Castilianized City' by Iago González Pascual and Fernando Ramallo (University of Vigo), explains how Galician has been a second-class language for decades or even centuries, despised by the dominant classes as only appropriate for peasants and the uneducated. The authors describe how, since democracy returned to Spain (1978), militants in favour of Galician have fought to gain social domains for their language in all Galician cities. The results are uneven: while written knowledge of the language has increased, spontaneous oral use in everyday communications has not.

The fourth chapter, 'Helsinki as a Multilingual City' by Pirkko Nuolijärvi (Research Institute for the Languages of Finland), starts by explaining the linguistic history of Finland, focusing on its two historical languages: Finnish and Swedish. Special attention is paid to allochthonous languages other than Finnish and Swedish. Allochthonous pupils can study their language throughout their entire time at school. Finnish students who have studied a language abroad may receive instruction in that language (two hours per week) to retain their skills if they wish. The second part of the chapter presents an overview of the linguistic image of Helsinki. In the third section the author describes how in higher education and science both Finnish and Swedish tend to diminish in importance in favour of English. Finally the author considers to what extent Finland will be able to use the multilingual competence of its young people.

The fifth chapter, 'Tallinn, a Multilingual City in the Era of Globalization: The Challenges Facing Estonian as a Medium-Sized Language' by Josep Soler-Carbonell (Universities of Stockholm and Tartu, Estonia) introduces the reader to the interaction between the local, dominant and historical language (Estonian), the former colonial language still spoken by a significant minority (Russian) and English as a growing *lingua franca* in the city. The author describes in detail how the linguistic repertoire of the city is distributed unevenly in different social sectors. Above all the author shows how Estonian has striven to become not only a language of authenticity but also the default language in public domains, the anonymous language. English is increasingly a valued code on the instrumental axis, whereas the most valued code on the solidarity axis is Estonian. Finally it is stressed that the profile for Russian is being revived and that both the Russian and Estonian communities still remain highly separated.

The sixth chapter, 'Multilingual Valencia: Linguistic Destruction and Reconstruction of an Urban Space' by Miquel Nicolás Amorós and Francesc Jesús Hernández Dobon (University of Valencia), describes how Valencia is a city where the historical language, Valencian (the local variety of Catalan), has been largely substituted. Most upper, middle and even lower class speakers have adopted Spanish as their first or preferred language due to the low ethnolinguistic vitality of Valencian. The authors discuss the Valencian (i.e. Catalan) images of the city and above all describe the difficulties facing attempts to revitalize the language.

In the seventh chapter, 'Multilingualism in Barcelona: Towards an Asymmetrical Multilingualism' by Emili Boix-Fuster (University of Barcelona), the author analyses the sociolinguistic landscape of this bilingual city where Catalan, the city's 'own' language, and Spanish, the dominant language throughout Spain, compete in most domains of everyday life ranging from education to trade to leisure. So far there is no clear winner, but there is a certain tendency towards linguistic hybridism, especially among young people with a sound command of both official languages thanks mainly to the educational system. This limited hybridism does not mean a generalized linguistic mixing, but occasional or recurrent alternations to either Spanish or Catalan in everyday speech.

The eighth chapter, 'Languages in Copenhagen: Changing Social Structures, Changing Ideologies, changing linguistic practices' by Marie Maegaard and Normann Jørgensen (University of Copenhagen), begins by describing how Standard Danish has been built around the Copenhagen variety, on the basis of the heterogeneous variations of spoken Danish. The second part of this chapter explores the school reception system for foreigners. In the third part the authors report on some recent developments involving xenophobia. They then analyze the competition between Danish and English as the foremost lingua franca. One of the outcomes of this competition is that foreign languages other than English are being abandoned. This eighth chapter is followed by a general conclusion of the volume.

This book is a follow-up to three volumes already written from the perspective of medium-sized communities: A general introduction (Vila, 2013), a comparative legal analysis (Milian-Massana, 2012) and an analysis of higher education (Vila & Bretxa, 2013). All these studies are contributions from a group of specialists to a broader interdisciplinary research project entitled 'The sustainability of Medium-Sized Language Communities (MSLC) in the age of globalization: new trends, new solutions?' run by the University Centre for Sociolinguistics and Communication at the University of Barcelona (CUSC-UB),[2] the Department of Catalan Philology and the Department of General Linguistics at the same university, and sponsored by Linguamón – House of Languages and the Spanish Ministry of Science and Innovation (currently the Ministry of Education, Culture and Sport).[3] Readers interested in the framework of the studies we present here or who would like a fuller account of the criteria used to define MSLCs should consult the project's website[4] and the introduction and conclusions of the book *Survival and Development of Language Communities: Prospects and Challenges*, edited by F. Xavier Vila (Multilingual Matters, 2013).

This book thus explores the language policies implemented in seven European urban areas, providing detailed information on their current situation and on the corresponding evolution of their linguistic repertoire. The volume provides valuable insights into the dynamics of language practices which are sure to be of interest to many other urbanized societies facing the dilemmas of multilingualism as regards both neighbouring and dominant languages.

Notes

(1) The author is grateful to F. Xavier Vila and Albert Bastardas for their comments on previous versions of the introduction and conclusion of this volume.
(2) http://www.ub.edu/cusc/.

(3) The reference for the Ministry's project is: *Globalización, intercomunicación y lenguas propias en las comunidades lingüísticas medianas* [MLC Medium-Sized Language Communities] FFI2009–10424.
(4) http://www.ub.edu/cusc/llenguesmitjanes/?lang=en.

References

Milian-Massana, A. (ed.) (2012) *Language and Legal Challenges in Medium-Sized Language Communities*. Barcelona: Institut d'Estudis Autonòmics.

Vila, F.X. (ed.) (2013) *Survival and Development of Language Communities: Prospects and Challenges*. Bristol: Multilingual Matters.

Vila, F.X. and Bretxa, V. (2013) The analysis of medium-sized language communities. In F.X. Vila (ed.) *Survival and Development of Language Communities: Prospects and Challenges* (pp. 1–17). Bristol: Multilingual Matters.

1 Mapping Urban Multilingualism in Europe: In Search of Untapped Resources in Primary Schools

Guus Extra

Summary

First, a range of criteria for the definition and identification of population groups in multicultural contexts will be discussed (Section 1). In Sections 2 and 3, conceptual dimensions for the mapping of diversity in both non-European English-dominant immigration countries and in European Union countries will be addressed and compared. The rationale and methodology of the Multilingual Cities Project (MCP), funded by the European Cultural Foundation, will be discussed in Section 4, and its major outcomes will be assessed in Section 5. Three major home language surveys have been carried out as follow-up studies of the MCP: in Vilnius/Kaunas/Klaipeda (Lithuania), in Vienna (Austria) and in Dublin (Ireland). Section 6 concludes by discussing methodological considerations for the last of these home language surveys, the one performed in Dublin.

1. Criteria for the Definition and Identification of Population Groups in Multicultural Contexts

Collecting reliable information on the diversity of population groups in multicultural contexts is no easy enterprise. What is, however, more interesting than compiling numbers or estimates of the size of particular groups is to establish the criteria that are used to determine these numbers or estimates. Comparative information on population figures in European Union (EU) member-states is available from EuroStat, the Statistical Office of the EU in Luxembourg. Eurostat's data indicate an overall decrease in the indigenous population in most EU countries over the last decade and at the same time an increase in the immigrant minority (henceforward IM) figures. For a variety of reasons, however, reliable and comparable demographic information on IM groups in EU countries is difficult to obtain. Seemingly simple questions like *How many Turkish residents live in Germany compared to France?* cannot be easily answered. For some groups or countries, no updated information is available or no such data have ever been collected. Moreover, official statistics only reflect IM groups with legal resident status. Another source of disparity is the use of different data collection systems, ranging from census data to administrative registers or statistical surveys (Poulain, 2008). In addition, most residents from former colonies already have the nationality of their country of immigration. Most importantly, however, the widely used criteria for IM status – nationality and/or country of birth – have become less valid over time because of an increasing trend towards naturalization and births within the countries of residence.

For a discussion of the role of censuses in identifying population groups in a variety of multicultural nation-states, we refer the reader to Kertzer and Arel (2002). Alterman (1969) offers a fascinating account of the history of counting people from the earliest known records on Babylonian clay tablets in 3800 BC to the US census of 1970. In addition to the methods of counting, Alterman discusses at length who were counted and how, and who were not counted and why. The issue of mapping identities through periodical nation-wide censuses by state institutions is commonly coupled with a vigorous debate between proponents and opponents of the following 'ethnic dilemma': how can you combat discrimination if you do not measure diversity? (Kertzer & Arel, 2002: 23–25). Among minority groups and academic groups, both proponents and opponents of mapping diversity can be found: its proponents defend the social or scientific need for population data bases on diversity as prerequisites for affirmative action by the government in domains such as labour, housing, health care, education and media policies; opponents argue in terms of the social or scientific risks of public or political misuse of these data bases for stereotyping, stigmatization, discrimination or even removal of the 'unwanted other'. Kertzer and Arel (2002: 2) argue that the census does much more than simply reflect social reality; it plays a key role in the construction of this reality and in the creation of collective identities. At the same time, it should be acknowledged that the census is a crucial area for the politics of representation. On the basis of (home) language databases, minority groups often make language rights one of their key demands.

Decennial censuses became common practice in Europe and the New World colonized by Europeans in the first part of the 19th century. The US became the first newly established nation-state with a decennial census in

1790. The first countries to include a language question in their census, however, were Belgium in 1846 and Switzerland in the 1850s, both European countries with more than one official state language. At present, in many EU countries, only population data on nationality and/or country of birth (of the person and/or parents) are available on IM groups. In 1982, the Australian Institute of Multicultural Affairs recognized the above-mentioned identification problems for inhabitants of Australia and proposed including questions in the Australian census on country of birth (of the person and parents), ethnic origin (based on self-categorization in terms of the ethnic group a person considers him/herself to belong to), and home language use. In Table 1.1, the four criteria mentioned are discussed in terms of their major (dis)advantages.

First, Table 1.1 shows that there is no simple road to solving the identification problem. Moreover, inspection of the criteria for multicultural population groups is as important as the actual figures themselves. Seen from a European perspective, there is a top-down development over time in the utility and utilization of different types of criteria, inevitably going from nationality and birth-country criteria in the present statistics to self-categorization and home language in the future. The latter two criteria are generally conceived of as being complementary. Self-categorization and home language references need not coincide, as languages may be conceived to varying degrees as core values of ethnocultural identity in minority or migration contexts.

2. Mapping Diversity in Non-European English-Dominant Immigration Countries

Various types of criteria for identifying population groups in multicultural societies have been suggested and used outside Europe in countries with a longer immigration history and, as a result, with a longstanding history of collecting census data on multicultural population groups (Kertzer & Arel, 2002). This holds in particular for non-European immigration countries in which English is the dominant language, like Australia, Canada, South Africa and the USA. To identify the multicultural composition of their populations, these countries employ a variety of questions in their periodical censuses. In Table 1.2, an overview of (clusters of) questions is provided; for each country, the census given is taken as the norm.

Five types/clusters of questions are distinguished in Table 1.2. Both the type and the number of questions differ according to country. Canada takes up a prime position with the highest number of questions. There are only three questions that are asked in all countries, while two questions are asked in only one country. Four different questions are asked about language. The operationalization of the questions also shows interesting differences, both

Table 1.1 Criteria for the definition and identification of population groups in a multicultural society (P/F/M = person/father/mother) (Extra & Gorter, 2001: 9)

Criterion	Advantages	Disadvantages
Nationality (NAT) (P/F/M)	• objective • relatively easy to establish	• (intergenerational) erosion through naturalization or double NAT • NAT not always indicative of ethnicity/identity • some (e.g. ex-colonial) groups have NAT of host country
Birth country (BC) (P/F/M)	• objective • relatively easy to establish	• intergenerational erosion through births in host country • BC not always indicative of ethnicity/identity • invariable/deterministic: does not take into account boundary changes in society (in contrast to all other criteria)
Self-categorization/ ethnicity (SC)	• touches the heart of the matter • emancipatory: SC takes into account person's own conception of ethnicity/identity	• subjective by definition: also determined by the language/ethnicity of interviewer and by the spirit of the times • multiple SC possible • historically charged, especially by experiences of World War II
Home language (HL)	• HL is significant criterion of ethnicity in communication processes • HL data are prerequisite for government policy in areas such as public information or education	• complex criterion: who speaks what language to whom and when? • language is not always a core value of ethnicity/ identity • useless in one-person households

between and within countries over time (see Clyne, 1991 for a discussion of methodological problems in comparing the answers to differently phrased questions in Australian censuses from a longitudinal perspective).

Questions about ethnicity, ancestry and/or race have proven to be problematic in all the countries under consideration. In some countries, ancestry and ethnicity have been conceived of as equivalent. Examples are US census

Table 1.2 Overview of (clusters of) census questions in four multicultural countries (Extra & Yağmur, 2004: 67)

Questions in the census	Australia 2001	Canada 2001	SA 2001	USA 2000	Coverage
(1) Nationality of respondent	+	+	+	+	4
(2) Birth country of respondent	+	+	+	+	4
(3) Birth country of parents	+	+	−	−	2
(4) Ethnicity	−	+	−	+	2
(5) Ancestry	+	+	−	+	3
(6) Race	−	+	+	+	3
(7) Mother tongue	−	+	−	−	1
(8) Language used at home	+	+	+	+	4
(9) Language used at work	−	+	−	−	1
(10) Proficiency in English	+	+	−	+	3
(11) Religious denomination	+	+	+	−	3
Total no. of dimensions	7	11	5	7	30

question 10 in 2000: *What is this person's ancestry or ethnic origin?* and Canadian census question 17 in 2001: *To which ethnic or cultural group(s) did this person's ancestors belong?* Australian census question 18 in 2001 only involved ancestry and not ethnicity, cf. *What is the person's ancestry?* with the following comments for respondents: *Consider and mark the ancestries with which you most closely identify. Count your ancestry as far as three generations, including grandparents and great-grandparents.* As far as ethnicity and ancestry have been distinguished in census questions, the former is related most commonly to present self-categorization of the respondent and the latter to former generations. The diverse ways in which respondents themselves may interpret both concepts, however, remains a problem that cannot easily be solved.

According to Table 1.2, South Africa remains the only country where a racial question is asked instead of a question on ethnicity and/or ancestry. The paradox in South Africa is that questions on ethnicity are often considered to be racist, while the racial question (in terms of *Black/White/Coloured/Indian*) from the earlier Apartheid era has survived. Although the validity of questions about ethnicity, ancestry and/or race is problematic, at least one question from this cluster is needed to compare its outcomes with those of questions on language. Language is not always a core value of ethnicity/identity and multiculturalism may become under-estimated if it is reduced to multilingualism. For this reason, one or more questions deriving from cluster 4–6 in Table 1.2 are necessary complements to one or more questions derived from cluster 7–10.

Although, according to Table 1.2, 'ethnicity' is mentioned in the recent censuses of only two countries, all four language-related questions are asked only in Canada. Over time, a 'mother tongue' question has been replaced by a 'language' question in three out of four countries. Canada has retained the mother tongue question in addition to the home language question, which allows for comparative analyses of predictably different outcomes. The mother tongue question (7) in Canada is defined for respondents as *the language first learnt at home in childhood and still understood*, whereas questions 8 and 9 are related to the language *most often* used at home/work. Table 1.2 shows the added value of language-related census questions for the definition and identification of multicultural populations, in particular the added value of the question on home language use compared to questions on the more opaque concepts of mother tongue and ethnicity. Although the language-related census questions in the four countries under consideration differ in their precise formulation and commentary, the outcomes of these questions are generally conceived as cornerstones for educational policies with respect to the teaching of English as a first or second language and the teaching of languages other than English.

Table 1.2 also shows the importance of comparing different groups using the same criteria. Unfortunately, this is often not the case in the public or political discourse. Examples of such unequal treatment are references to *Poles vs. Jews, Israelis vs. Arabs, Serbs* and *Croatians vs. Muslims, Dutchmen vs. Turks* (for Dutch nationals with Turkish ethnicity), *Dutchmen vs. Muslims*, or *Islam vs. the West* (where does the West end, when the world is a globe?). Equal treatment presupposes reference to equal dimensions in terms of Table 1.2.

3. Mapping Diversity in European Union Countries

The data presented here come from the analysis of two comprehensive documents published by the European Commission and EuroStat (2004, 2005). In 23 out of 27 EU countries, nationwide censuses held at variable intervals are still in use. Scandinavian countries and the Netherlands rely on yearly updated administrative (municipal) registers in combination with periodical sample surveys. Other countries such as Austria, Belgium, France, Latvia, and Slovenia combine nationwide census data with administrative register data and/or sample survey data. The following parameters are used in all or many EU countries for the definition and identification of population groups:

- *(dual) citizenship or nationality*: the category of (dual) citizenship or nationality is used in all EU countries. In north-western European countries these two concepts are commonly used as synonyms nowadays; in southern, central and eastern European countries, however, these two categories are commonly used distinctively. In these countries citizenship refers to what is termed nationality or citizenship in north-western Europe, whereas (ethnic) nationality refers to what is termed ethnicity in north-western Europe. In the Czech Republic, for instance, the nationality question asks for an indication of *what nationality you consider yourself to be*, which is different from the citizenship question;

- *country/place of birth*: this is a common category in all EU countries; in some countries, this question refers explicitly to the country/place of (permanent) residence of *your mother when you were born*;
- *ethnicity*: ethnicity or ethnic nationality is asked for in 13 EU countries, three of which consider this question to be voluntary/optional;
- *language*: one or more language questions are asked in 17 EU countries, two of which consider this/these question(s) to be voluntary/optional;
- *religious denomination*: religious denomination questions are asked in 15 EU countries, six of which consider this question to be voluntary/optional.

Table 1.3 gives an overview of the *status quo* with respect to the latter three parameters across EU countries. It should be noted that collection of data on some or all of these questions in some EU countries is considered to be in conflict with privacy legislation and/or illegal, while in other countries such questions are taken to generate crucial information.

Table 1.3 shows that there is strong variability across countries in the utilization of each of these three parameters. This holds also for the operationalization of questions asked. Detailed ethnicity questions are asked in the UK and Ireland. In the UK, five categories are distinguished, i.e. *White, Mixed, Asian (British), Black (British), Chinese/Other*, in all cases with subcategories. Similar questions are asked in Ireland. Hungary lists 14 categories (plus *other*) and asks *which of these nationalities' cultural values and traditions do you feel affinity with?* Estonia lists six (plus *other*) ethnic nationalities, and Cyprus lists *Greek-Cypriot, Armenian, Maronite, Latin* and *Turkish-Cypriot*. Questions on religion are asked in terms of *belief, church, faith, religion* and/or *religious affiliation/community/confession/denomination,* and in terms of *religion/ religious denomination you were brought up in*. The latter – additional – question is only asked in Scotland, not in the UK as a whole. Table 1.4 shows an overview of the operationalization of the language questions asked for in 17 out of 27 EU countries.

Three main conclusions emerge from Table 1.4. First, European census questions on non-national languages focus on regional minority languages, not on IM languages. Second, the three most commonly asked questions on language use relate to mother tongue (11 countries), (other) language(s) spoken (frequently) (six countries) and language(s) (most frequently) spoken

Table 1.3 Identification of ethnicity, language and religion in 27 EU countries (Extra & Gorter, 2008: 19)

EU countries	Ethnicity/ethnic nationality	Language	Religion
Austria	−	+	+
Belgium	−	−	−
Bulgaria	*	*	*
Cyprus	+	+	+
Czech Republic	+	+	+
Denmark	−	−	−
Estonia	+	+	*
Finland	−	+	+
France	−	−	−
Germany	−	−	+
Greece	−	−	−
Hungary	*	*	*
Ireland	+	+	+
Italy	−	−	−
Latvia	+	+	−
Lithuania	+	+	+
Luxembourg	−	−	−
Malta	−	+	−
Netherlands	−	−	−
Poland	+	+	−
Portugal	−	−	*
Romania	+	+	+
Slovakia	+	+	+
Slovenia	*	+	*
Spain	−	+	−
Sweden	−	−	−
United Kingdom	+	+	*

* = voluntary/optional question.

at home (five countries). Third, Hungary makes the greatest investment in finding out about language use. For a complete picture, it should be mentioned that in some countries collecting home language data are in fact in conflict with current language legislation. This holds in particular for Belgium, where no census data on language use have been collected since 1947 and traditional language borders between Dutch, French and German have been allocated and fixed in the law.

Table 1.4 Operationalization of language questions in 17 EU countries (Extra & Gorter, 2008: 20)

EU countries	Mother tongue	(Other) language(s) spoken (frequently)	Language(s) (most frequently) spoken at home	Language(s) spoken with family or friends	Speak well/ average/a little	Understand/ Speak/Read/ Write
Austria	–	–	+	–	–	–
Bulgaria	+	–	–	–	–	–
Cyprus	–	+	–	–	–	–
Czech Republic	(1)	–	–	–	–	–
Estonia	+	+	–	–	–	–
Finland	+	–	–	–	–	–
Hungary	+	+	–	+	–	–
Ireland	–	(2)	–	–	–	–
Latvia	+	+	–	–	–	–
Lithuania	+	+	–	–	–	–
Malta	–	–	+	–	+	–
Poland	–	–	+	–	–	–
Romania	+	–	–	–	–	–
Slovakia	+	–	–	–	–	–
Slovenia	+	–	+	–	–	–
Spain	(3)	–	(3)	–	–	(4)
United Kingdom	–	–	–	–	–	(5)

(1) Indicate the language spoken by your mother or guardian when you were a child.
(2) Only Irish; if yes, daily within/outside the educational system/weekly/less often/never.
(3) Both language questions in the Basque County, Navarre and Galicia, for Basque/Galician.
(4) In Catalonia, Valencia and the Balearic Islands for Catalan.
(5) Only in Wales and Scotland, for Welsh and Gaelic respectively.

4. The Multilingual Cities Project: Rationale and Method

Here, we present the rationale and method of the *Multilingual Cities Project* (henceforward MCP), a coordinated multiple survey study conducted in six major multicultural cities in different EU nation-states. The project was carried out under the auspices of the *European Cultural Foundation*, established in Amsterdam, and was coordinated by a research team at *Babylon, Centre for Studies of the Multicultural Society*, at Tilburg University in the Netherlands, in cooperation with universities and educational authorities in all participating cities. The aims of the MCP were to gather, analyse, and compare multiple data on the status of IM languages at home and at school, taken from cross-national and cross-linguistic perspectives. In the participating cities, ranging from northern to southern Europe, Germanic or Romance languages have a dominant status in public life. Figure 1.1 gives an outline of the project. For the final cross-national report we refer to Extra and Yağmur (2004).

The criteria for selecting a city to participate in this multinational study were that it should be prototypical of a multicultural environment with a great variety of IM groups, and that it should offer a university-based research facility able to handle the local data gathering and analysis and the final reporting of the local results. Given the increasing role of municipalities as educational authorities in all partner cities, the project was carried out in close cooperation with researchers at local universities and local educational authorities. In each partner city, this cooperation proved to be of essential value. In sum, the rationale for collecting, analysing and comparing multiple home language data on multicultural school populations derives from four different perspectives:

- from a *demographic* perspective, home language data play a crucial role in the definition and identification of multicultural school populations;
- from a *sociolinguistic* perspective, home language data offer valuable insights into both the distribution and vitality of home languages across different population groups, and thus raise the public awareness of multilingualism;
- from an *educational* perspective, home language data are indispensable tools for educational planning and policies;
- from an *economic* perspective, home language data offer latent resources that can be built upon and developed in terms of economic opportunities.

Home language data put to the test any monolingual mindset in a multicultural society and can function as agents of change (Nicholas, 1994) in a variety of public and private domains. Taken from an educational perspective, it remains a paradoxical phenomenon that language policies and language planning in multicultural societies are often drawn up in the absence of basic knowledge and empirical facts about multilingualism.

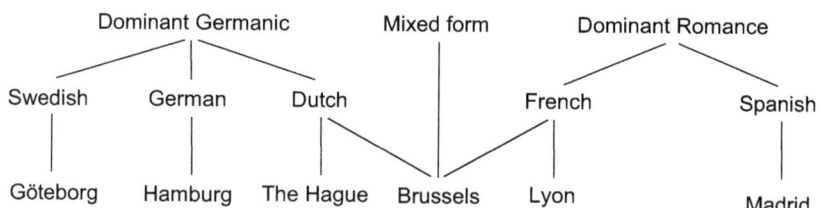

Figure 1.1 Outline of the Multilingual Cities Project (MCP)

Our method of carrying out home language surveys amongst primary school children in each of the six participating cities has profited from experiences in non-European English-dominant immigration countries with nationwide population surveys which tended to ask single questions on home language use. Unlike these questionnaires, our survey was based on multiple rather than single questions on home language use and on cross-nationally equivalent questions. In doing so, we aimed to describe and compare the multiple language profiles of major IM communities in each of the cities under consideration.

The questionnaire for data collection was designed after ample study and evaluation of language-related questions in nationwide or large-scale population research in a variety of countries with a longer history of migration and minorization processes. The design of the questionnaire also derived from extensive empirical experience gained in carrying out municipal home language surveys amongst pupils in both primary and secondary schools in the Netherlands (Broeder & Extra, 1995, 1998; Extra *et al.*, 2001, 2002). A number of conditions for the design of the questionnaire need to be met.

The first prerequisite is that the questionnaire should be appropriate for *all* pupils and should include a question for distinguishing between pupils in whose homes only the mainstream language is used and pupils in whose homes one or more other languages alongside or instead of this language are used. For the most frequently mentioned languages, a home language profile will be specified. This language profile consists of four dimensions, based on reported language proficiency, language choice, language dominance and language preference.

A second prerequisite of the questionnaire is that it should be both short and powerful. It should be *short* in order to minimize the time needed for pupils to answer it during school hours, and it should be *powerful* in that it should have an optimal and transparent set of questions which should be answered by all pupils individually, if needed – in particular with younger children – in cooperation with the teacher, after an explanation of the aims and design of the survey in class.

A third prerequisite of the questionnaire is that the answers given by the pupils can be scanned and verified as automatically as possible, given the large size of the resulting database. In order to fulfil this demand, both hardware and software conditions have to be met.

The agreed-upon questionnaire was translated into equivalent versions in Dutch, French, German, Spanish and Swedish. These versions were tested in at least one primary school in each partner city. On the basis of the suggestions of local educational authorities and researchers, the phrasing and wording of the questionnaires were adapted further. All six cities had the same questions, but one additional question on 'nationality' was added to the German questionnaire. This question was not included in any of the other cities.

The local questionnaires were printed in multiple copies. Due to the requirements of automatic processing, it was essential that printed rather than photocopied questionnaires were used. Uniformity, both in terms of content and form, was a prerequisite for data processing. Local educational authorities sent out letters to schools and/or parents asking them to give permission for their children to participate in the survey. In each city, the printed questionnaires were distributed to school directors. Both for classroom teachers and for data collection assistants, a manual in the local language was prepared to facilitate interaction with the pupils. The completed questionnaires were delivered by the schools to the researchers at the participating universities. After checks of the total set of questionnaires per school had been made, all delivered questionnaires were sent to Tilburg University in the Netherlands for data processing.

Data processing was performed centrally in Tilburg by *Babylon* researchers. Given the large size of the database, an automatic processing technique based on specially developed software (*Teleform*) and available hardware was developed and used. With these tools about 5000 forms could be scanned per day. Because some questionnaire items were filled out by hand, additional verification of these items had to be performed using character recognition software; in this way, around 4000 forms could be processed per day. After scanning and verification had been completed, the database for each city was analysed using the SPSS program. Table 1.5 gives an overview of the resulting database, derived from the reports of primary school children in an age range of 4–12 years (only in The Hague were data also collected at secondary schools). The total cross-national sample comprises more than 160,000 pupils.

In order to carry out systematic analyses of the data set, an SPSS syntax file which was developed step-by-step was used in the preparation stage. In

Table 1.5 Overview of the MCP database

City	Total of schools	Total of schools in the survey	Total of pupils in schools	Total of pupils in the survey	Age range of pupils
Brussels	117[a]	110[a]	11,500	10,300	6–12
Göteborg	170	122	36,100	21,300	6–12
Hamburg	231 public 17 Catholic	218 public 14 Catholic	54,900	46,000	6–11
Lyon	173[b]	42[b]	60,000	11,650	6–11
Madrid	708 public 411 Catholic	133 public 21 Catholic	202,000 99,000	30,000	5–12
The Hague	142 primary 30 secondary	109 primary 26 secondary	41,170 19,000	27,900 13,700	4–12 12–17

[a]Dutch-medium schools only; [b]Réseau d'Education Prioritaire only.

the analysis stage, another SPSS syntax file was used in order to achieve uniformity in the findings. The last stage of data processing was the transmission of the outcomes of the analyses in a readable format. Given the fact that the research results had to be presented in the same format in all six participating cities in the project, a cross-nationally uniform format was set up. *Excel Worksheets* and *Microsoft Graphics* within *Word for Windows* were used to present the results. Both the worksheets and the templates for figures within *Microsoft Graphics* were predefined. In this way, a uniform format for all the tables and figures was obtained, which then needed to be interpreted.

5. The Multilingual Cities Project: Major Outcomes

Distribution of languages

The local language surveys amongst primary school children have delivered a wealth of new cross-national evidence on the distribution and vitality of IM languages in the home. Apart from selecting one or more of the pre-specified languages in each of the local surveys, pupils could also opt for self-references to other home languages by filling out by hand the boxes provided for this objective (see Appendix). The resulting database consists of a huge variety of self-references (types) and the frequencies with which they were mentioned (tokens). In most cases, the pupils referred to entities that could be (re)traced as existing languages. In this context, the regularly updated database of *The Ethnologue (www.sil.org/ethnologue;* Grimes, 1996) on languages of the world proved to be very helpful. Apart from self-references to known and unknown languages, the pupils also made references to countries that could not reasonably be traced back to languages or to other/unknown categories. In general, however, the resolution level of the language question in the survey was very high, and relatively few references could not be traced back to languages. Table 1.6 gives a cross-national overview of the data under consideration.

Based on the overview of types and tokens of (re)traced home languages, the distribution of these home languages was specified in a ranked order of decreasing frequency. A common phenomenon in all participating cities was that few languages (types) were referred to often (tokens), and that many languages (types) were referred to rarely (tokens). Therefore, the most frequently mentioned home languages represent a very high proportion of the total number of occurrences/tokens in all cities.

Apart from Madrid, the late-comer amongst our focal cities in respect of immigration, the proportion of primary school children in whose homes other languages were used alongside or instead of the mainstream language ranged between one third and more than a half. The total number of languages other than Swedish/German/Dutch (The Hague/Brussels)/French/

Table 1.6 References made by pupils in terms of types and tokens

Municipality	Reference to languages		Reference to countries		Other/unknown references	
	Types	Tokens	Types	Tokens	Types	Tokens
Göteborg	75	7,598	8	40	10	20
Hamburg	90	16,639	12	229	10	92
The Hague	88	23,435	13	788	17	24
Brussels	54	12,737	9	186	7	11
Lyon	66	6,106	17	130	–	–
Madrid	56	2,619	x	x	x	x

Note: x = not specified.

Spanish ranged per city between 50 and 90. The figures were 36% of the total student population in Göteborg, 35% in Hamburg, 49% in The Hague, 82% in Brussels, 54% in Lyon and 10% in Madrid.

The outcomes of the local surveys were aggregated in one cross-national database. On the basis of the number of references made to home languages, the top 20 of the most frequently mentioned languages in each city were identified. Forty-nine languages were in the group of the top 20 list in the six cities. Out of these 49 languages, 19 were represented in 3–6 cities and 30 in only 1–2 cities. There were also unique references in the top 20 per city; most of these languages were either languages of neighbouring countries, languages of former colonies, or regional minority languages. For purposes of cross-national and cross-linguistic analyses, 20 of the most frequently mentioned languages in these cities were chosen.

Two criteria were used to select these 20 languages from the list of 49. Each language had to be represented by at least three cities, and each city had to be represented in the cross-national database by at least 30 pupils in the age range of 6–11 years. Our focus on this age range was motivated by comparability considerations: this range was represented in the local databases of all participating cities. Romani/Sinte was included in the cross-national analyses because of its special status in our list of 20 languages as a language without territorial status. Two languages had an exceptional status: English 'invaded' the local databases as a language of international prestige, and Romani/Sinte was solidly represented in Hamburg and Göteborg only. The concept of language group was based on the pupils' answers to the question whether and, if so, which other languages were used at home instead of or alongside the mainstream language. On the basis of their answer patterns, pupils could belong to more than one language group.

Eight languages were represented in 5–6 cities, while 11 languages were represented in 3–4 cities. With respect to French, Brussels is a special case, given the public and private status of both French and Dutch in this city (Verlot et al., 2003). There is a notable municipal distribution of two pairs of languages which are often in competition in their source countries, i.e. Turkish and Kurdish in Turkey, and Arabic and Berber in north African countries (in particular, Morocco). Only in Göteborg was Kurdish more strongly represented than Turkish, and only in The Hague were Berber and Arabic balanced. In our database, Kurdish hardly appeared at all in Brussels and Madrid. The same applied to Berber in Göteborg and Hamburg.

Specification of language profiles and language vitality

For all 20 language groups mentioned above, a cross-linguistic and pseudo-longitudinal comparison was made of the four reported dimensions of language proficiency, language choice, language dominance, and language preference. For this analysis, the four reported dimensions were operationalized as follows:

- language proficiency: the extent to which the home language under consideration is *understood*;
- language choice: the extent to which this language is commonly spoken at home *with the mother*;
- language dominance: the extent to which the home language is spoken *best*;
- language preference: the extent to which the home language is *preferably* spoken.

The focus of the chosen dimensions was on oral skills at home and not on literacy in order to give IM languages a fair chance of emerging in societal contexts in which the acquisition of literacy is rarely promoted, whether at home or at school. Moreover, earlier analyses have shown that the four selected dimensions are highly correlated and lead to reliable scores (Extra et al., 2002: 129). The operationalization of the first and second dimensions (language proficiency and language choice) aimed to achieve maximal scope for tracing language vitality. Language understanding is generally the least demanding of the four language skills involved, and the mother generally acts as the major gatekeeper for intergenerational language transmission (Clyne, 2003).

In the analyses, the four above-mentioned language dimensions were compared as proportional scores, i.e. the mean proportion of pupils per language group that indicated a positive response to the relevant questions. The calculated language vitality index (LVI) is, in turn, the mean value of these four proportional scores. This LVI is by definition a value-driven index, in the sense that the *chosen* dimensions with the *chosen* operationalizations are weighted *equally*. The establishment of this index makes it feasible to carry out crosslinguistic and crossnational comparisons of large databases in which equal criteria for these comparisons are used. On the basis of the LVI established, LVI scores were calculated per age group and per generation, for each language group. For all 20 language groups, language profiles were specified based on tabulated and graphic information. Tabulated information was provided on the number of pupils and the language vitality (index) per age group and per generation. For all language groups, three age groups and three generations were distinguished. The age groups consisted of children aged 6/7, 8/9, and 10/11 years old. The three generations were operationalized as follows:

- G1: pupil + father + mother born abroad;
- G2: pupil born in country of residence, father *and/or* mother born abroad;
- G3: pupil + father + mother born in country of residence.

On the basis of this categorization, the intergenerational shift can be estimated. In addition, graphic information was provided on the pseudo-longitudinal outcomes per age group on the four dimensions of language proficiency, language choice, language dominance, and language preference. In all cases, the total population of age groups was always larger than the total population of generations. This discrepancy is the result of a predictably larger number of missing values (i.e. non-responses) for generation than for age. In the former case, references have to be made to the countries of birth of the pupil, the father, and the mother; in the latter case, reference has to be made only to the age of the pupil. Language vitality indices for age and generation were calculated only if at least five children were represented in a particular group. Given the possible non-responses of children to any of the questions represented in figures and tables, all figures and tables were presented and interpreted in proportional values.

Conclusions

The findings show that using more than one language is a way of life for an increasing number of children across Europe. Mainstream and non-mainstream languages should not be conceived in terms of competition. Rather, the data show that these languages are used as alternatives, depending on factors such as type of context and interlocutor. The data also reveal that the use of other languages at home does not occur at the cost of competence in the mainstream language. Many children who addressed their parents in another language reported being proficient in the mainstream language.

Among the major 20 non-national languages in the participating cities, 10 languages are of European origin and 10 languages stem from further afield. These findings clearly show that the traditional concept of language diversity in Europe should be reconsidered and extended. The outcomes of the local language surveys also demonstrate the high status of English among primary school pupils across Europe. Its intrusion in the children's homes is apparent from the position of English in the top five of languages referred to by the children in all of the cities. This outcome cannot be explained as an effect of migration and minorization only. The children's reference to English also derives from its status as the international language of power and prestige. English has invaded the repertoire of all of the national languages under consideration. Moreover, children have access to English through a variety of media, and English is commonly taught in particular grades at primary schools.

Children in all participating cities expressed a desire to learn a variety of languages that are not taught at school. The results of the local language surveys also show that children who took part in instruction in particular non-mainstream languages at school reported higher levels of literacy in these languages than children who did not. Both the reported reading proficiency and the reported writing proficiency benefited strongly from language instruction. The differences between participants and non-participants in language instruction were significant for both forms of literacy skills and for all the 20 language groups. In this domain in particular, the added value of language instruction for language maintenance and development is clear. Owing to the monolingual *habitus* (Gogolin, 1994) of primary schooling across Europe, there is an increasing mismatch between language practices at home and at school. The findings on multilingualism at home and those on language needs and language instruction reported by the children should be taken into account by both national and local educational authorities in any type of language policy.

6. Beyond the Multilingual Cities Project: Methodological Considerations

The MCP has led to a range of requests from across Europe to cooperate in similar follow-up studies. The rationale for carrying out studies of this kind in multicultural *cities* derives from at least the following considerations:

- As an effect of globalization, international migration concentrates in urban settings.
- The same holds for reciprocal processes of acculturation.
- Multilingualism is an inherent property of multicultural cities.
- Processes of intergenerational acculturation can clearly be observed in processes of language maintenance vs. language shift across different ethnocultural groups, depending on the degree to which the language of origin is a core value of culture in contexts of migration and minorization.

- Cities are the primary spaces where urban planners design policies on dealing with multiculturalism and multilingualism.
- Cities are also the primary spaces where urban planners reinforce national and international dynamics in dealing with diversity.

Responding to all requests for cooperation and support in this domain was beyond the scope of our project. In three cases, we agreed on cooperation, i.e. in Vilnius (in conjunction with Kaunas and Klaipeda in Lithuania), in Vienna and in Dublin. The rationale for focusing on these cities beyond the MCP was based on the following considerations.

The constellation of languages across the Baltic Republics has a unique history of migration which is widely different from the experiences in western Europe. In a comparative review of this constellation, Hogan-Brun (2008) goes into the effects of former Russification and recent accession to the European Union. As holds for other EU nation-states, Lithuania, Latvia and Estonia have to meet the new challenges posed by globalization while at the same time supporting minority rights. The focus of the MCP in Lithuania is on its multicultural capital, Vilnius, in conjunction with Kaunas and Klaipeda, two major cities nearby. For an overview of the outcomes of the project in these three cities, we refer the reader to Ramonienė and Extra (2011).

Seen from a historical perspective, Vienna has been the traditional meeting point between western and eastern Europe. The diversity of its multicultural population and the languages spoken at home is a reflection of this phenomenon. As a result, a home language survey in Vienna amongst primary school pupils will result in a stronger representation of eastern and south-eastern European languages than have been observed in the MCP in Göteborg, Hamburg, The Hague, Brussels, Lyon and Madrid, all of them being cities along a western European north-south axis. For an overview of the outcomes of the project in Vienna, we refer the reader to Briziç et al. (2015).

Dublin is a city where both indigenous and non-indigenous languages meet, apart from English. While Irish is the indigenous language with the highest symbolic value of Irish identity, it is not the language spoken most widely by primary school pupils at home. Apart from English and Irish, an increasing number of immigrant languages from across the world are becoming home languages in Dublin. Ireland has an institutionalized support structure for bilingual education in English and Irish at primary schools (Ó Murchú, 2001). There is, however, a wide gap between the top-down support of educational authorities for bilingual education in English and Irish, and the bottom-up support of parents keen to have bilingual education in English and immigrant languages.

In this final section, we will focus on methodological considerations for the latest home language survey in Dublin. For an overview of the outcomes of the initial pilot study in Dublin, we refer the reader to Carson and Extra (2010). The draft questionnaire to be formatted for automatic data processing was arranged in the following five 'boxes':

Box 1
(1) School code
(2) Pupil code
(3) How old are you?
(4) Are you a boy or a girl?

Box 2
(5) In which country were you born?
(6) In which country was your father born?
(7) In which country was your mother born?

Box 3
(8) To which ethnic group do you belong?
(9) Which language(s) is/are used in your home?
   (to be pre-coded: top-10 plus English for follow-up questions)
(10) Which language is used in your home most often?

Box 4
(11) Which of these language(s) can you understand/speak/read/write?
(12) Which language do you usually speak at home with your mother/father/younger siblings/older siblings/grandparents/best friends?
(13) Which language do you speak best?
(14) Which language do you like to speak most?

Box 5
(15) Which language(s) do you learn at this school?
(16) Which language(s) do you not learn at this school but would you like to learn at this school?
(17) In which language(s) do you take classes outside this school?
(18) In which language(s) do you watch TV or DVDs?

The design of the resulting questionnaire is presented in the Appendix to this text. Here, we discuss the list of 18 questions derived from the Appendix.

Q1 + 2   The school code and pupil code should be filled out by research assistants before the forms are distributed in the classroom in the main project phase. In the case of the pilot study, pupil codes were not used; schools and classes were assigned a simple alphanumeric code. The resulting database contains no data that can be traced back to individuals. No names of individual pupils were stored. The completed school codes make it possible to determine the number of participating pupils per school and school district and to determine the distribution of languages (types and tokens) per school.

Q3   The chosen age range is dependent on the chosen aim of the research project, in particular with respect to younger children, which requires additional time and money. The chosen age range makes it possible to carry out pseudolongitudinal analyses.

Q4   This question offers a wide range of possibilities to study gender effects.

Q5–10   Pre-specified categories are provided for the top ten countries, ethnic groups and home languages, estimated on the basis of the most recent national statistics about immigrant minority groups/children. There is room for additional handwritten information. The answers to these questions make it possible to compare the status of birth country data, home language data and ethnicity data as demographic criteria.

Q8   The ethnicity question is much less transparent than the home language question, in particular for children. The ethnicity question provides some additional hints about ethnic background. In analysing the data, however, the focus is on language groups, not on ethnic groups.

Q9   This question aims to offer maximum scope from two different perspectives, i.e. by the passive construction *are used* instead of *do you use*, and by asking about use instead of one of the four language skills.

Q11–18   In all cases, deliberately except for Q11, *do*-scales rather than *can*-scales are used.

Q11–14   The language profile, specified by questions 11–14, consists of four dimensions:
- *language proficiency*: the extent to which the pupil can understand/speak/read/write the home language;
- *language choice*: the extent to which the home language is commonly spoken with the mother and father, grandparents, younger and older siblings, and best friends;
- *language dominance*: the extent to which the home language is spoken best;
- *language preference*: the extent to which the home language is preferably spoken.

Q11 allows for studying reported oral skills vs. literacy, Q12 for studying patterns of intergenerational language maintenance vs. shift, and Q13/14 for studying divergent age-related patterns of language dominance vs. preference. Taken together, the four dimensions of language proficiency, choice, dominance and preference result in a language vitality index, the calculation of which is explained in Extra and Yağmur (2004: 125–128). This index will allow for cross-cultural and cross-linguistic analyses.

Q15 + 16   The answers to these questions allow for educational considerations, e.g. in terms of reported (mis)matches between the offer and demand of languages at school.

Q17 + 18   Are related to other types of language input.

References

Alterman, H. (1969) *Counting People. The Census in History*. New York: Harcourt.
Briziç, K., Hufnagl, L. and Extra, G. (2015) *Multilingualism in Vienna. Languages at Home and at School* (to appear).
Broeder, P. and Extra, G. (1995) *Minderheidsgroepen en Minderheidstalen [Minority Groups and Minority Languages]*. Den Haag: VNG Uitgeverij.
Broeder, P. and Extra, G. (1998) *Language, Ethnicity and Education. Case Studies on Immigrant Minority Groups and Immigrant Minority Languages*. Clevedon: Multilingual Matters.
Carson, L. and Extra, G. (2010) Multilingualism in Dublin. Home language use among primary school children. Report on a pilot study. Dublin/Tilburg: Trinity College/Tilburg University.
Clyne, M. (1991) *Community Languages: The Australian Experience*. Cambridge: Cambridge University Press.
Clyne, M. (2003) *Dynamics of Language Contact*. Cambridge: Cambridge University Press.
European Commission and EuroStat (2004) Documentation of the 2000 round of population and housing censuses in the EU, EFTA and candidate countries, Parts I–III and Annexes. Luxembourg: Office for Official Publications of the European Communities.
European Commission and EuroStat (2005) Population and housing censuses 2001. Results at national and regional level with documentation and detailed tables. Luxembourg: Office for Official Publications of the European Communities (CD-ROM).
Extra, G. and Gorter, D. (eds) (2001) *The Other Languages of Europe. Demographic, Sociolinguistic and Educational Perspectives*. Clevedon: Multilingual Matters.
Extra, G. and Gorter, D. (eds) (2008) *Multilingual Europe. Facts and Policies*. Berlin/New York: Mouton de Gruyter.
Extra, G. and Yağmur, K. (eds) (2004) *Urban Multilingualism in Europe: Immigrant Minority Languages at Home and School*. Clevedon: Multilingual Matters.
Extra, G., Aarts, R., van der Avoird, T., Broeder, P. and Yağmur, K. (2001) *Meertaligheid in Den Haag. De Status van Allochtone Talen Thuis en op School [Multilingualism in The Hague: The Status of Immigrant Languages at Home and at School]*. Amsterdam: European Cultural Foundation.
Extra, G., Aarts, R., van der Avoird, T., Broeder, P. and Yağmur, K. (2002) *De Andere Talen van Nederland [The Other Languages of the Netherlands]*. Muiderberg: Coutinho.
Gogolin, I. (1994) *Der Monolinguale Habitus der Multilingualen Schule [The Monolingual Habit of the Multilingual School]*. Münster: Waxmann.
Grimes, B. (ed.) (1996) *Ethnologue. Languages of the World* (13th edn). Dallas: Summer Institute of Linguistics. See www.sil.org/ethnologue.
Hogan-Brun, G. (2008) Language constellations across the Baltic Republics: A comparative review. In G. Extra and D. Gorter (eds) *Multilingual Europe: Facts and Policies* (pp. 135–154). Berlin/New York: Mouton de Gruyter.

Kertzer, D. and Arel, D. (2002) *Census and Identity. The Politics of Race, Ethnicity, and Language in National Censuses.* Cambridge: Cambridge University Press.

Nicholas, J. (1994) *Language Diversity Surveys as Agents of Change.* Clevedon: Multilingual Matters.

Ó Murchú, H. (2001) *The Irish Language in Education in the Republic of Ireland.* Mercator: Regional Dossiers Series. Ljouwert/Leeuwarden: Fryske Akademy.

Poulain, M. (2008) European migration statistics: Definitions, data and challenges. In M. Barni and G. Extra (eds) *Mapping Linguistic Diversity in Multicultural Contexts* (pp. 43–66). Berlin/New York: Mouton de Gruyter.

Ramonienė, M. and Extra, G. (2011) *Multilingualism in Lithuania: Languages at Home and at School in Vilnius, Kaunas and Klaipeda.* Klaipeda: University of Klaipeda.

Verlot, M., Delrue, K., Extra, G. and Yağmur, K. (2003) *Meertaligheid in Brussel. De Status van Allochtone Talen Thuis en op School* [*Multilingualism in Brussels: The Status of Immigrant Languages at Home and at School*]. Amsterdam: European Cultural Foundation.

Appendix: Design of the Follow-Up Home Language Survey in Dublin (2009)

Many children, many languages!

Trinity College Dublin — in cooperation with Tilburg University

Please fill out this form in black or blue ink.
Do not use a pencil!

1. School code:

2. Pupil code:

3. How old are you?
   - O 6
   - O 7
   - O 8
   - O 9
   - O 10
   - O 11
   - O 12
   - O 13

4. Are you a boy or a girl?
   - O Boy
   - O Girl

Please answer the questions below by colouring the circles. Countries not mentioned can be filled out in the boxes above the last columns.

	China	Germany	Ireland	Latvia	Lithuania	Nigeria	Poland	United Kingdom	USA			
5. In which country were you born?	O	O	O	O	O	O	O	O	O	O	O	O
6. In which country was your father born?	O	O	O	O	O	O	O	O	O	O	O	O
7. In which country was your mother born?	O	O	O	O	O	O	O	O	O	O	O	O

Many children, many languages!   *Continue with question 8 on the next page!*

Urban Diversities and Language Policies

Many children, many languages! *Continuation of questions 1-7*

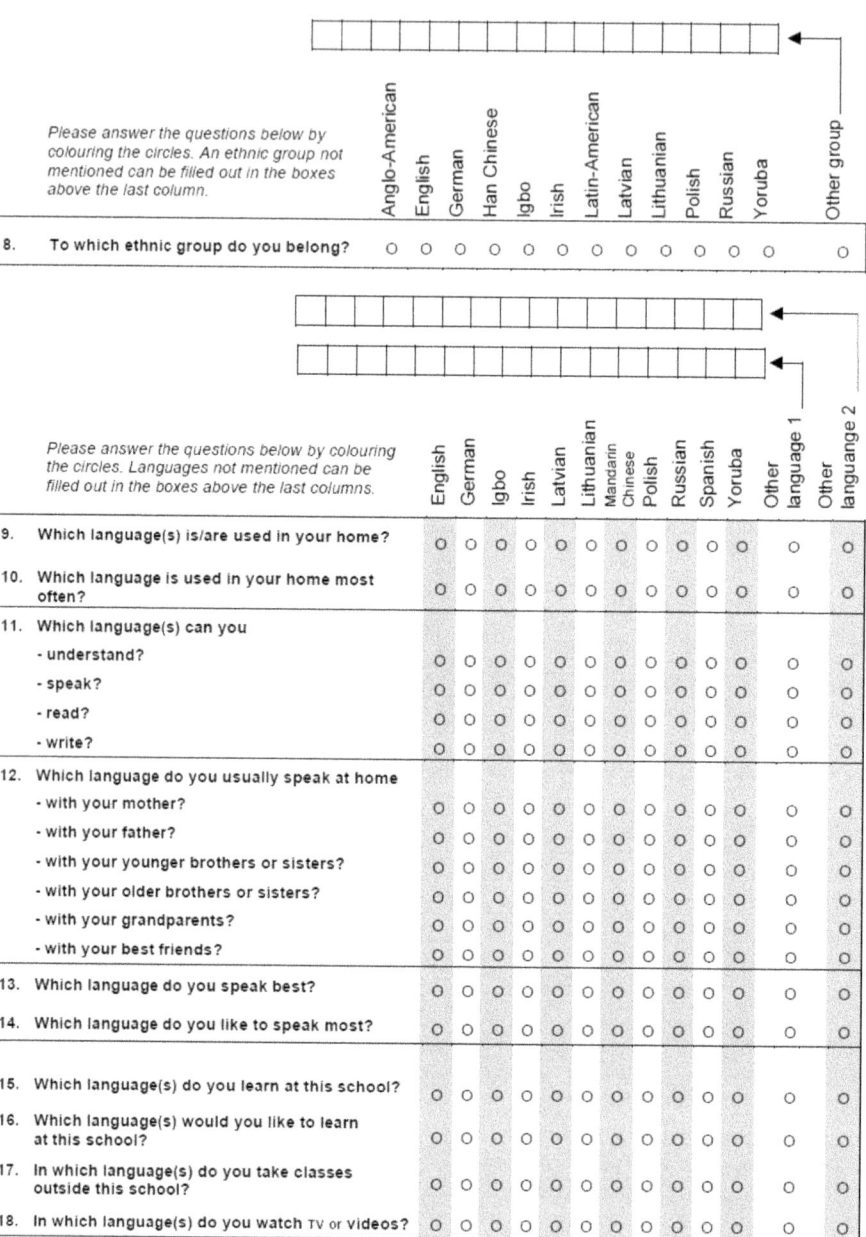

2 Competitive and Cooperative Orientations in Language Policies: A Critical Look at the Situation of Dutch in Brussels

Philippe Hambye

Summary

This chapter analyses the sociolinguistic situation of Dutch in Brussels and identifies the challenges faced by the Dutch-speaking community as a medium-sized language community in an urban context characterized by a high level of linguistic diversity and by the coexistence of three languages that play the role of lingua francas (Dutch, English and French). It also examines how Flemish authorities have tried to meet these challenges so far and points out a tension between two understandings of the political struggle that the Dutch community has to engage in – one that views it as competitive, the other as cooperative. These two understandings are themselves linked to different conceptions of the community and the language it is related to. The chapter shows that this tension can be analysed in terms of the opposition between 'anonymity' and 'authenticity', as formulated by Woolard (2008). It argues that while these two conceptions coexist in the ideology that underlies Dutch language policy in Brussels, the policy has now reached a point where it is more and more difficult to hold them together, and where they may lead to distinct ways of defining and assessing language policies.

1. Introduction

Since it is spoken by about 22 million speakers, mainly in two small countries with little economic and political power on the international scene, the Dutch language can clearly be considered a medium-sized language (see Boix-Fuster's introduction to this volume). Medium-sized language communities face specific challenges that differ from those faced by major linguistic communities and small linguistic minorities. Their challenge is not linked to survival or revitalization as it has been the case for many minority languages in recent decades. For Dutch in Belgium, survival used to be an issue, at least in Brussels: the number of native Dutch speakers has been declining in the city since the 19th century. Before the language laws of the sixties were passed, there was indeed a threat to the long-term survival of the language, which was clearly minoritized. However, language shifts toward French are now very unusual and, as I will show later, language maintenance is no longer an issue.

Unlike major linguistic communities, medium-sized language communities do not compete to maintain or reinforce their position in the international linguistic market in a way to increase the resources available to their members.[1] For medium-sized linguistic communities, the challenge is often simply to *maintain* the resources associated with mastery of their language in the face of pressure from more widely used or prestigious languages (see Boix-Fuster's introduction to this volume).

In this contribution, I will examine the situation of Dutch in Brussels in order to analyse what is really at stake for this medium-sized linguistic community. I will also consider the political responses to this situation and their consequences. I will start by presenting some facts concerning the linguistic situation in Brussels in order to highlight the strengths and weaknesses of the position of Dutch in Belgium's capital city and the particular challenges faced by the Dutch community. I will then describe the main orientations of language-related political action taken by Flemish authorities in Brussels. My aim is to analyse the underlying goals of this political action and highlight two understandings of the political struggle the Dutch-community has to engage in, which are grounded in the history of the relationships between the Flemish and francophone communities in Belgium. I will argue that these two visions of the objectives of language policies are in fact anchored in two conceptions of the community and of the link between its language and its identity. Finally, I will show that current language policies regarding Dutch in Brussels are marked by a tension between these two conceptions that creates some ambivalence in the way policies are defined and evaluated.

2. Official Language Policy

In a narrow sense, the city of Brussels is only one of the 19 municipalities gathered into the region of Brussels-Capital, one of three administrative regions in Belgium (along with Flanders and Wallonia), each of which has its own parliament and government. The territory of the political and administrative entity Brussels-Capital is also the only officially bilingual 'linguistic region' of Belgium; the others are monolingual and offer only some special rights to linguistic minorities, in the so-called *communes à facilités*.

Two features of official bilingualism in Brussels should be stressed. First, this bilingualism is not primarily the result of a shared commitment on the part of Dutch- and French-speaking *Bruxellois* to promote a bilingual and bicultural community, but it is the outcome of a political compromise reached at the federal level within the framework of institutional negotiations between the francophone and Flemish communities. Promoting bilingualism is thus not viewed and experienced as a choice and a political objective of public authorities in Brussels but rather as a constraint and a legal obligation to be dealt with, like it or not. In public institutions, for instance, the quota for the ratio of Dutch-speaking civil servants (about a third of the total) is sometimes a source of tension. These public employees are supposed to manage only the affairs of Dutch-speaking citizens, which often account for less than 10% of cases (see Section 3). They therefore have less work than their French-speaking colleagues, who also complain that these quotas represent an unfair roadblock for French-speaking employees.[2] In the same vein, the proportion of Dutch-speaking deputies in the Brussels Regional Parliament (about 20%) is often criticized by some francophone political parties as being anti-democratic as it over-represents the Dutch-speaking population of Brussels. As a result, authorities rarely choose to proudly highlight bilingualism; they simply apply the law strictly and seldom stress the valuable role bilingualism could play, though many inhabitants of Brussels now see it as one of the main positive features that distinguish their city (see Section 5.3).

Second, and in line with the first point, official bilingualism in Brussels is actually what Monica Heller calls a 'double monolingualism' (Heller, 2006: 83). What we find in Brussels is not a single network of bilingual institutions and services, but two parallel networks of monolingual institutions and services (cultural centres, universities, schools, day-care centres, media, etc.). This is particularly clear in the documents sent to citizens, which are either in French or in Dutch but never in both languages. In many cases the two languages do not appear *together* but side by side on separate signs, documents or posters. In other words, this form of official bilingualism allows the two communities to live alongside one another and thus reproduce, within the bilingual region, the principle of linguistic homogeneity (principle of territoriality) that constitutes the basis of Belgium's language policy and institutional organization.

3. The Demolinguistic Balance

Since there are no official statistics on language use in Belgium,[3] for many years estimates were based on electoral results (vote ratios for Flemish and francophone parties) or administrative data (language of registration for newborns, weddings, etc.). These data were not very reliable and tended to underestimate the Dutch-speaking population in Brussels, who often use French in dealing with civil servants. Fortunately, two recent surveys conducted by sociologist Rudi Janssens have filled this gap. In 1996 and 2005, Janssens collected data from two representative samples of 2500 inhabitants of Brussels (see Janssens, 2001, 2007, 2008). His results provide many insights into Brussels' sociolinguistic situation, but only the major trends he observed will be discussed in what follows.

3.1. French: Brussels' *lingua franca*

In the 2005 survey, more than 95% of respondents said they speak French well or perfectly. English was in second position at 35% and Dutch, third, at 28%. In the 1996 survey, 33% of respondents stated that they had a good or perfect mastery of Dutch (Janssens, 2008: 4). Apart from the three main languages, four languages stand at around 6% (Spanish, German, Italian and Arabic). The other (immigrant) languages (Turkish, Portuguese, Lingala, Greek, Russian, etc.) are at around 1% or below. With respect to the immigrant languages, we can observe that between 1996 and 2005 the percentage of Spanish and Italian speakers increased slightly, because these languages are gaining new speakers through language courses in schools or private institutions, while there has been a drop in the percentage of Arabic and Turkish speakers, probably due to a progressive decrease in family transmission.

These figures point to the gap between Brussels' official bilingualism and the actual predominance of one language in the city. The fact that only a third of Brussels' inhabitants can speak Dutch means it is not easy for Dutch-speaking *Bruxellois* to find all public and private services in Dutch and live out their lives in their own language. Needless to say, the difficulty of finding services in Dutch, especially in the health-care area, generates complaints within the Dutch-speaking community and gives rise to a problem that Flemish political authorities are trying to solve (see Section 5.1).

The predominance of French is highly visible in Brussels' linguistic landscape. Anyone paying attention to the use of language in signage in Belgium's capital can easily make the following observations:

- Apart from official signage put up by the city hall or the regional government of Brussels, *systematic* bilingualism in signs and billboards is more the exception than the rule. French, English and Dutch often coexist in the communication of a single shop, but French is almost always more present, and the use of Dutch is sometimes limited to essential information.[4]
- French monolingual signage is very common, while Dutch monolingual signage is extremely rare.

- English-only usage can be observed in some shops, either because they are tourist-oriented, or because they target relatively upper-class customers and use English to signify their prestige. More generally, English messages seem to denote a certain trendiness.

As for the labour market, Janssens (2008: 8) observes that French is the most important language, though he also notes that English is gaining ground. In interpersonal communication, French is almost always the default language when speakers do not share the same first language.

Another consequence of French's dominant position on the linguistic market is that in families of immigrant background language shifts are almost always towards French. As a result of this imbalance between the two official languages, Dutch has almost no chance to benefit from the constant arrival of newcomers in the city. In Janssens' survey, 95% of the respondents who spoke a language other than French or Dutch at home said they use French with the administration (Janssens, 2008: 6).

3.2. Brussels as a multilingual and multicultural city

The figures given below confirm the fact – often put forward by francophones in their political debates with the Flemish community – that French is by far Brussels' dominant language. However, Janssens' data show another fact that appears far less frequently in the public image projected by francophones: Brussels is not a francophone city, in the sense that it is not a city peopled almost exclusively by francophones, i.e. by individuals who speak mainly French and identify themselves as francophones (rather than Flemish or any other ethnolinguistic or ethnonational affiliation).

In terms of linguistic groups, defined by the language spoken at home, only 57% of Brussels' population is made up of monolingual francophones. About 7% of families in Brussels are monolingual Dutch-speaking and 9% use Dutch and French. Those who speak a language other than French or Dutch represent 16% of respondents, while 11% use a foreign language in combination with French (Janssens, 2008: 5). In these 'new bilingual' families, as Janssens calls them, French is the dominant language in 25–30% of cases.

Several observations can be drawn from these figures. The first is that Brussels' population is not composed of two monolingual linguistic communities (French and Dutch speakers), but rather of several monolingual and multilingual groups, among whom more than a quarter use (though not exclusively) a language that is not official in Brussels (see also Extra, Chapter 1, this volume). A second observation is that Brussels is far from being a microcosm of Belgium's demolinguistic balance. According to the 2005 Eurobarometer (EC, 2005), 56% of Belgians have Dutch as their mother tongue, for 38% it is French, and in 0.4% of cases it is German (Belgium's third official language). Five percent have another EU language as their first language, and 3% a non-EU language.

Compared to its status at the national level, the position of Dutch in Brussels is thus clearly weak. More generally, there is an obvious gap between the official status of Dutch in Brussels and its demolinguistic weight in the city.

Needless to say, this situation generates resentment in the Flemish community, since it is the result of the *verfransing* (Frenchification), from the end of the 19th century onwards, of a mainly Dutch-speaking city,[5] which remains the official capital of Flanders and which is situated on the Dutch side of the border that has divided Romance and Germanic languages in Belgium for centuries. The former socio-economic and symbolic domination of French and francophones in Belgium led many Dutch-speaking or bilingual families to teach their children French or send them to francophone schools, while French speakers who migrated to Brussels to find jobs were not in any way encouraged to learn Dutch. Rather, their immigration was another factor accelerating the assimilation of Dutch speakers to the dominant language (Francard, 1995). The linguistic evolution of Brussels is indeed a good illustration of the rule which states that in a situation of clear diglossia between two languages, a policy of official bilingualism that allows individuals to make 'free' linguistic choices leads to progressive assimilation to the dominant language. This is what Van Parijs (2010: 187–190) refers to as *Laponce's Law*:

> Languages can coexist for centuries when there is little or no contact at all between the parts of the population that speak it. As soon as people start talking, trading, working with each other, courting each other, having children together, the weaker of the two languages will be slowly but inexorably driven out by the other, by the one which people have a stronger incentive to learn because of its being more prestigious or more widely spread. (See Laponce, 1987, 2006; Van Parijs, 2010)

Consequently, at least at the linguistic level, Brussels does not fulfil its representative role as the capital of Belgium and Flanders in any obvious way, given that Dutch speakers represent such a tiny minority.

This relative weakness of Dutch in Brussels has to be qualified on two points. Though the figures cited above tend to indicate that one should expect to hear more English or Arabic than Dutch in Brussels, it is important not to overlook the fact that the value of Dutch in Belgium's capital is far from being directly linked to the number of Dutch-speaking families living in Brussels. Indeed, Brussels' linguistic environment changes five days a week, during working hours, when about 230,000 Flemish individuals (as opposed to 130,000 from Wallonia) come to work in Brussels (33% of the workforce of Brussels), thus doubling the number of Dutch speakers in the capital (IBSA, 2012: 13). More generally, Dutch is a very important language on the Brussels labour market because of its official status, but above all because of the political and economic weight of the Dutch-speaking community in the country. Consequently, Dutch is still more important than

English on the labour market; French–Dutch bilingualism is unanimously regarded as an asset to find a well-paid job (Janssens, 2008: 7–8) and can also entitle employees to a salary bonus in the public sector. More and more private services are provided in Dutch to meet the expectations of the numerous Dutch-speaking customers, who no longer accept that their language should be considered less important than French in Brussels. This is especially true in the restaurant sector. As a result, the respondents interviewed by Janssens think that services in Dutch are increasingly available and that one hears Dutch more and more frequently in the public sphere in Brussels (Janssens, 2008: 6).

Janssens also observes a decrease in the process of Frenchification. The improvement of Dutch's status and social value in recent decades is now impacting linguistic practices. Already in 2001, Janssens noted that there were almost no more French speakers in Brussels who were born from two Dutch-speaking parents (Janssens, 2001: 44). Janssens' more recent survey shows that French-Dutch bilinguals in Brussels tend to use Dutch with increasing frequency in situations where they used to speak French, notably in their contacts with the administration or with their francophone partner in mixed families (Janssens, 2008: 5).

4. Contextualizing the Challenges

Having presented the situation of Dutch in Brussels, we can now turn again to the challenges faced by the Dutch-speaking community in Belgium's capital. As I have already indicated, it is clear that language survival is not at stake in this case. With almost a third of its population able to speak Dutch, Brussels is not a place where the Dutch language is in any danger of disappearing or completely losing either its demographic base or its political, economic and symbolic status. Moreover, unlike Catalan, for instance, Dutch is the language of a very large majority of the population within the entire territory of a country (the Netherlands) and in the main region of Belgium (Flanders). In terms of linguistic minority rights, it should also be noted that Dutch speakers in Brussels already benefit from a very favourable legislation that ensures their right to use their language in dealings with the state and guarantees official recognition of the Dutch-speaking community in the Brussels Region.[6]

However, there are still social and political tensions and debates around the position of Dutch in Brussels, and Flemish political and social movements are still struggling to enhance the vitality of the Dutch-speaking community in the city and ensure its future. We will see below (see Section 5.2) that there are in fact two conflicting conceptions of the definition of this community, and hence an underlying tension between different understandings of what the ultimate goals of political action should be. Despite their divergences in relation to these main objectives, current policies stress the need to bolster the demographic weight of the Dutch-speaking community in Brussels and enhance the value of Dutch in general, i.e. two aspects of the sociolinguistic situation of Dutch in Brussels that are presently affected by two processes of particular significance for medium-sized languages: migration movements and the spread of English as a *lingua franca*.

The value of a given language is linked, among other factors, to the number of speakers of the language and the benefits one may derive from entering in contact with these speakers (Calvet, 2006; De Swaan, 2001). Within Brussels, it is undoubtedly useful to come into contact with Dutch speakers because of their political and economic position in the country. However, one can easily live in Brussels without having to speak a word of Dutch. Moreover, outside Belgium and the Netherlands, Dutch is not a very useful or widespread language. As a result, very few immigrants coming to Belgium have even a basic knowledge of Dutch or feel a pressing need to learn it once they have settled in Brussels. According to figures given by the national institute of statistics in 2008, 28% of Brussels inhabitants are not Belgian citizens (in comparison, this is only the case for 9% of the population of Belgium as a whole). If we consider nationality at birth, 46% of the population of Brussels was not of Belgian origin in 2001 (Deboosere et al., 2009: 8). As in many other places around the world, it is within this population of immigrant descent that the birth rate reaches its highest level (see Janssens, 2008: 8). According to Janssens, for 'foreign speakers, French is increasingly accepted as a second family language and Dutch does not come into the picture at all' (Janssens, 2008: 4). This means that incoming migration movements pose a specific challenge for Dutch in Brussels. Families with an immigrant background will probably have an increasing demographic weight in the future and could thus reinforce the dominant position of French. At the same time, internal migrations are also detrimental to the position of Dutch in Brussels: more families are moving from Brussels to Flanders than in the opposite direction, and more internal immigrants to Brussels come from Wallonia than from Flanders (IBSA, 2009).

The growing importance of English, especially in as international a city as the capital of Europe, could of course be of concern for the Dutch-speaking community. From the figures given above (see Section 3.1), one could think that English is progressively gaining ground at the expense of Dutch. But this interpretation would misread the fact that the status of English and its domains of usage are rather different from those of Dutch: English is a school language for the majority of its speakers and is mainly used in international institutions and in business communication, i.e. not in domains formerly dominated by Dutch, but in domains of activity where people have always used an international language in combination with local languages. In private communication, English usage is very unusual, and only 3% of Brussels inhabitants have English as their first language (Janssens, 2008: 5). In the professional sector, surveys show that English is expected by employers not instead of French-Dutch bilingualism but as a complementary competence (see Mettewie & Van Mensel, 2006).

Using English, however, is sometimes a way to bypass official bilingualism in advertising and public communication, since it reduces costs and is symbolically viewed as neutral. This is especially true in the private sector (and above all for services targeting international customers), but it is increasingly the case for official communication too. For instance, many messages related to the last Belgian presidency of the EU were issued only in English. However, one could argue that English competes mainly with French: it is in domains where one needs to use a *lingua franca* that Dutch speakers and speakers of non-official languages could progressively show a preference for English over French.

Nevertheless, it cannot be denied that increasing knowledge of English in Belgium (see O'Donnel & Toebosch, 2008; Van Parijs, 2007) is a factor that works against the learning of Dutch by francophones. Until recently, communication between members of the two linguistic communities was mainly managed in French, because proficiency in this language among Flemish people was far more common than proficiency in Dutch among francophones, especially in Brussels. For the younger generations, however, the situation is evolving. More and more Flemish young people are as competent in English as in French, if not more so. When a francophone wants to communicate with a Dutch speaker without disdainfully sticking to his or her own language, there is a strong temptation to switch to English, since francophones are often more proficient in this symbolically more neutral language than they are in Dutch, and this may soon be the case for Flemish speakers with respect to French. At a time when incentives for francophones to learn Dutch and reject an attitude of Franco-centrism are stronger than ever before (see Section 5.3), it would be somewhat paradoxical to see speakers drawing on English as a bridge language between two communities not able to speak each other's language.

The same tendency can be observed among the foreign population in Brussels. In their daily communication, temporary workers are relying more and more on English, the language most people have at least a basic knowledge of. Janssens has noted that in business communication foreign speakers address Dutch speakers more often in English than in French (Janssens, 2008: 7). Another factor that could increase the use of English in preference to French or Dutch is the diversification of the immigrant population. Immigration to Belgium used to take place mainly within the framework of agreements with emigration countries that were meeting the need for workers in Belgian industry (see Hambye & Lucchini, 2005). These emigration countries were Romance-speaking countries or former colonies where French was the official language. As a result, many immigrants felt more familiar with this language than with Dutch, or even had some knowledge of French, which was also a much more prestigious language. There was therefore no real question regarding the choice of French or Dutch as the language of integration. Now, the countries of origin of immigrants to Belgium are much more diverse (see Deboosere et al., 2009: 8), and many newcomers do not have any special connection to French. Consequently, they are now more likely to use English, and sometimes Dutch, as a vehicular language in a city like Brussels, where there is such notable linguistic diversity.

5. Political Responses to the Challenges Faced by Dutch in Brussels

Although the Dutch-speaking population in Brussels only accounts for 2.5% of citizens under the authority of the Flemish government, Flemish politicians decided some time ago not to 'leave' Brussels to the francophones (Witte, 2008). In particular, since 1989 and the establishment of the Flemish Community Commission[7] of Brussels (*Vlaamse Gemeenschap Comissie* – VGC), the Flemish government has introduced several measures to strengthen the presence of Dutch in Brussels and tackle the challenges identified above.

5.1. Three directions of political action

The political action of the Flemish government in Brussels can be surveyed by examining various sources: a scientific account of the action of the VGC since 1989 (Witte, 2008), the political orientations of the Flemish Minister for Brussels for the years 2009–2014 (Smet, 2009), and various documents promoting the action undertaken by several ministers within the framework of mass communication campaigns (De Troyer, 2004; Steenwinckel, 2006, 2010). These sources show that Flemish policy in Brussels took three main directions.

First, it fostered the development of Dutch-speaking institutions and, most importantly, a very competitive network of Dutch-speaking schools and day-care centres in Brussels, which have a reputation for high quality. More generally, the Flemish government worked on improving the presence of public services in Dutch in domains such as housing, health, sports and culture (Smet, 2009; Witte, 2008).[8]

Second, the general policy of Flemish authorities in Brussels for the last 15 years has been to open its cultural spaces to a non-Flemish audience, notably through cultural passports that are available to anyone living or working in Brussels, but also through the support of bicultural projects and cultural cooperation with the francophone counterpart of the VGC (Witte, 2008: 10). Flemish authorities also acted to facilitate learning of the Dutch language by non-Flemish people. The VGC developed promotional campaigns for elementary education and also set up the Dutch Language House (*Huis van het*

*Nederlands*⁹) in 2004. At this centre, anyone can find information on Dutch courses available in their neighbourhood, many of which are offered free of charge to Brussels residents (Witte, 2008: 9–10). The service is directed at both francophones and newcomers. Accordingly, the website of the Dutch Language House of Brussels provides information in eight different languages (Dutch, French, English, Spanish, Arabic, German, Russian and Turkish).

A third line of action focuses on improving the image of Flanders and Flemish in Brussels and of Brussels in Flanders. The VGC has stressed the need to affirm the Flemish nature of Brussels and underline the importance of the 'Flemish stamp' in Brussels' history and culture. It also promotes a discourse that emphasizes the Flemish community's openness to other cultural groups, especially those of immigrant background (Witte, 2008: 7). In 2006, for instance, (Steenwinckel, 2006), the Flemish authorities launched a communication campaign aimed at immigrant communities that stressed the idea of a partnership between *'Vlaamse Brusselaars'* (Flemish inhabitants of Brussels) and Brussels citizens with 'other cultural roots'.[10] This campaign and other similar communication actions were aimed at increasing the visibility of Flemish institutions in Brussels and invited inhabitants of the city to take advantage of the services offered by Flemish social and cultural institutions.

These communication efforts were also directed at the Flemish population outside Brussels. In Flanders, the image of Brussels is often affected by negative stereotypes (it is 'dirty', 'ugly', 'unsafe', and 'you can't go anywhere in Brussels with your Dutch'). As a result, Flemish authorities put a great deal of effort into communicating positive messages about Brussels and all the measures taken in favour of the Dutch-speaking community in the city. In 2004 and 2010, the Flemish Ministry for Brussels Affairs published a brochure (De Troyer, 2004; Steenwinckel, 2010) to promote Brussels and underline the 'major role' played by Flanders in the capital. The brochure seeks to dispel the four specific stereotypes mentioned above and highlights the importance and value of Brussels' multiculturalism and multilingualism, its rich cultural offering, the quality of education, and life and work opportunities in the city. Other very concrete measures have also been taken, including the launching of the 'large-scale promotional campaign *Living in Brussels,* which has to make the housing capacity of Brussels more attractive', the establishment of the *Monnaiehuis,* a centre in the heart of the capital that provides information on Brussels in Dutch, and the provision of an incentive for VGC employees who are willing to settle in Brussels (Witte, 2008: 4).[11]

5.2. Goals and normative principles underlying Flemish language policy in Brussels

The three sets of measures we have described above can be related to several political goals, which often remain implicit. One goal is to enhance the *autonomy* of the Dutch-speaking community and its capacity to protect its members from the assimilatory pressure of the dominant language. In this sense, the creation of specific institutions that serve and are run by the Dutch-speaking community in Brussels is a way to create a homogenous linguistic space where the interests of the minority group can be prioritized.

The second goal is to reverse the decline of Brussels' Dutch-speaking population, i.e. to maintain and even increase the *demographic weight* of this community in order to increase its political weight in the country's capital region and makes its institutions more sustainable. This is why it is essential to attract new Flemish families to Brussels by improving the quality of services offered in Dutch and creating homogenous linguistic spaces that allow them to live their day-to-day lives entirely in their own language. It is important to convince the Flemish population in general that it is possible to grow up in Dutch in Brussels. This is also viewed as a way of preventing an exodus of Flemish families seeking a genuine Dutch-speaking environment to the periphery of Brussels. In the same vein, many VGC initiatives play a political and symbolic role, seeking to legitimate the status of Dutch and of the Flemish community in Brussels: the city is the capital of Flanders, not a French-speaking city that could form a francophone federation with Wallonia if Belgium's two main communities were to split – a possibility evoked more and more frequently of late due to a political crisis in Belgium of unprecedented duration.[12]

However, since 1995 in particular (Witte, 2008), the policy has also been aimed at attracting *new members* to the Dutch-speaking community, especially individuals with an immigrant background. In order to enlarge the Dutch-speaking community, the *social value* of Dutch needs to be enhanced and an effort must be made to generate an interest in learning Dutch among outsiders in the hope that they will then contribute to the development of the community. The communication efforts of the Flemish government in Brussels are largely oriented toward this goal.

Thus, the political action of Flemish authorities may be understood as a policy aimed at increasing the resources of the *Flemish* community for the sake of its members and as a way to ensure the permanence of the community itself. However, this policy could also be interpreted in a rather different way. Increasing the attractiveness of Dutch and Dutch-speaking spaces could also be a way to make a claim for the value of the very existence of a Dutch-speaking community in Brussels, and thus to seek the *recognition* of this *value* by outsiders. In this sense, the aim would be not so much to reproduce and enlarge a *community* defined by its language and culture than to increase the number of people who are concerned about the presence of Dutch in the city and willing to recognize the right of Dutch-speakers to maintain and develop a public space in Dutch.

These two major understandings of the challenges faced by the Dutch-speaking community in Belgium are in fact historically intertwined. Indeed, it is through processes of social categorization (Heller, 2002) – by *symbolically constructing* members of the dominated group[13] as non-equals, as 'others', as second-class citizens – that dominant groups legitimate the fact that these others are not granted the same rights they have, and as a result do not have equal access to *power* and *resources*. During the first 50 years of the Belgian state's existence, for instance, those who did not speak French (because they spoke Dutch or Walloon) did not have effective access to the same rights and resources as those who did speak that language. Because it suffered historically from social, economic and political domination by the French-speaking elite (of both Flemish and Walloon descent), the Dutch-speaking bourgeoisie became clearly aware of the importance of gaining political power and fighting to defend its interests. The second half of the 19th century saw the emergence of a Flemish nationalist movement whose main demand was fair political representation of the Flemish majority and recognition of equal linguistic and cultural rights for Dutch and French speakers. Progressively, the Flemish movement demanded *political autonomy* in cultural and political matters, while the Walloon regionalist movement was interested in obtaining more autonomy in economic affairs at a time when Wallonia was still the most prosperous region in the country. The state reform that remodelled Belgium's political organization at the beginning of the sixties was the result of a compromise between these two demands (see Mabille, 2000; Witte & Van Velthoven, 2000).

These centrifugal movements were supported on both sides by discourses that legitimated a vision of two distinct communities with their own divergent interests. This led to a weakening of solidarity between the communities to the benefit of intra-group solidarity. The French-speaking elite had first developed a Belgian nationalist discourse that promoted a unified French-speaking Belgian identity which was a synthesis of Germanic and Romance cultures, while holding the popular Flemish and Walloon cultures and their 'dialects' in disdain. Meanwhile, the Flemish movement shaped a nationalist discourse aimed at reasserting the value of the 'Flemish nation', its popular culture, language and identity. The discourse of the Flemish movement was characterized by the common features of modern nationalist discourses on language and identity (see Heller, 2006). The Walloon movement soon adopted the same approach. As a result, public discourses in Flanders and Wallonia construct the neighbouring community as a distinct 'other', leading the two communities to view each other as *different, opposed* and *competing* social groups, defined by a congruence of distinctive features (with a relative overlap of linguistic, economic and religious boundaries; see Erk, 2005).

The equality of status that was not *recognized* in the dominant ideology was thus progressively gained though political struggle *against* the French-speaking community *in the name of the principle of equality between citizens*. However, because of the logic of nationalism itself (see Heller, 2006), the struggle has progressively been pursued for the sake of the Flemish community (in fact the Flemish *nation*) as such.

Therefore, one way to tackle the challenges faced by the Dutch-speaking community in Belgium in general and in Brussels in particular is to defend the community's specific interests, whatever the relative *fairness* of the current distribution of resources, within a *competitive* relationship with the French-speaking community, viewed as an *essentially* distinct group. This is why several policies carried out by the Flemish government in Brussels in the name of the Flemish community are aimed at increasing the resources available to *Dutch* speakers *as members of the Flemish community*, within the framework of a traditional nationalist ideology that equates nation, people, language and culture. In this sense, increasing the demographic weight of the Dutch-speaking community is important because it increases its political representation and creates a bigger public for the services offered in Dutch, which helps make these services financially sustainable.

If the linguistic problem is understood as a competition between two distinct communities for power and resources, the conflict could indeed be endless. One of the main developments in political debates in Flanders over recent few years is precisely that demands for the political and economic autonomy of the Flemish community are no longer legitimated by principles of equality and social justice, but rather by a determination to protect the Flemish people's own interests, regardless of the situation of the other community. Though a concern for issues of intergroup solidarity may still be expressed in discourse, it becomes clear, within the framework of this vision, that the main principle used to justify and evaluate a given language policy related to Dutch in Brussels is its capacity to improve the situation of the *Flemish* community.

However, I think one cannot understand the so-called 'linguistic conflict' in countries like Belgium, Canada or Spain merely as a competitive struggle for material resources. Indeed, I argue that the issue can also (and not exclusively) be understood in terms of the symbolic construction and *recognition* (Taylor, 1992) of the other group as an equal. In this sense, it seems that for many political actors and citizens, the linguistic issue in Brussels is linked to recognition of the value attributed to the bilingual and bicultural nature of the city. For instance, the reason why the lack of Dutch-language health services in Brussels matters is not because it actually makes access to health services difficult for Dutch speakers: the vast majority can speak French with ease. Rather, I believe it is perceived as a problem mainly because it appears to show that Dutch speakers are not recognized as equals, as citizens who deserve equal rights and respect.

Based on this understanding of the linguistic conflict, the issue is not only one of obtaining a formal right to use one's own language in particular domains; speakers need to feel that this right is *positively* granted and recognized. The perception that the presence of a minority-language community is seen as legitimate and valuable rather than simply being tolerated is also crucial. In other words, the minority community demands that its presence in the territory be deemed just as legitimate as that of the majority and, consequently, that it not be permanently subject to the assimilatory pressures of the majority simply because it claims to deserve *equal respect*.

With respect to Dutch speakers in Brussels, this demand for recognition may be all the more important as their situation is somewhat paradoxical: they live in a city that was once predominantly Dutch-speaking and which is the capital of a Dutch-speaking region and a country whose population is mainly Dutch-speaking, but they may feel that their position is not really recognized, much less valued, by the majority group in Brussels, because the bilingual status of the city is more often regarded as a constraint or a burden than as a blessing. In this sense, the challenge for the minority is not so much to increase its demographic weight as to ensure its visibility and the recognition of its legitimate position through the social valorization of bilingualism. While the struggle for power and resources is bound to be competitive, this quest for recognition intrinsically requires the *cooperation* of the 'other', who is asked to recognize the value of the minority.

5.3. Justifying and evaluating Flemish language policies in Brussels

These two visions of the struggle of linguistic minorities – one competitive, the other cooperative – are both present in the discourse used to justify policies put in place by the Flemish government, though they rely on two different conceptions of the 'community' that lead to different visions of the ultimate objectives of language policy. Up until now, these two conceptions have coexisted in the ideological discourse underlying Dutch language policy in Brussels. Now, I think the success of these language policies and their actual consequences have somehow highlighted the tension between these two conceptions, making it more difficult to cope with the ambivalence it creates.

The increasing population of Dutch-speaking schools, for instance, may be viewed as a problem or a success, depending on the underlying principles that shape the policy. These schools are in fact full of francophone and allophone students. The population of Brussels' Flemish schools was continuously shrinking in the seventies, but now 20% of children in Brussels are enrolled in a Dutch-speaking kindergarten (i.e. twice the estimated Flemish population of Brussels; see Section 3 above). In the cooperative conception defined above, the success of these schools could be viewed as a major achievement, since it indicates a clear change in the social value of Dutch and shows that francophones recognize the importance of bilingualism. Indeed, there has been a significant evolution in francophones' attitudes toward Dutch. Even though a large proportion of the French-speaking population is still reluctant to learn the language, a growing number of people in Wallonia and Brussels now consider proficiency in Dutch as an important asset, or even a necessity, to enter the labour market in Belgium (Hambye & Richards, 2012). Similarly, Janssens' results show that in Brussels attitudes toward Dutch are increasingly positive (see Janssens, 2001, 2008).

In contrast, from the perspective of the competitive vision, the presence of many French-speaking students may be viewed as a threat to the linguistically homogenous space these schools are supposed to represent: the proportion of students in Brussels' Flemish schools who have Dutch as their home language is estimated to range between 15% and 30%. Furthermore, the francophone students are unlikely to grow up to be Flemish citizens in Brussels; it is more likely that they will simply become bilingual adults – new competitors on the bilingual labour market. Indeed, French-speaking parents send their children to these institutions for various *instrumental* reasons, which do not generally include the *integrative* will to participate actively in the Flemish culture and community[14] and to use effectively the Dutch language outside the school – such a 'disconnection between competence and language' being also observed in other medium-sized language communities (see Nicolás Amorós & Hernández Dobonn, Chapter 6, this volume). Pupils are mainly from middle-class families, so these schools have a very good reputation. They are well-funded[15] and offer an opportunity to learn the first official language of the country. Based on a competitive vision of Flemish language policy, using public funding to offer education to these non-Flemish children may be seen as illegitimate and a waste of public money.

This is actually one of the reasons why the situation of Flemish schools has generated many tensions. New requirements for registering at these schools were established in 2010 in order to limit the access of middle-class francophone children while continuing to facilitate registration for students of immigrant descent,[16] who have more potential to ultimately 'count' as members of the Dutch-speaking community (in terms of their political choices, for instance).[17] Along the same lines, a recent decision (in early 2012) by authorities in charge of a Flemish school in Brussels to punish students for using French in the school playground has sparked harsh criticism from some French-speaking politicians, who see it as simply a measure of persecution to discourage francophones from registering at Flemish schools, rather than a legitimate educational practice. For those who believe it is essential to maintain an 'authentically' Dutch-speaking space in these schools (and thus to protect the community against external threats), measures of this kind could be seen as perfectly justified. On the other hand, this decision could be viewed as part of a strategy of 'linguistic protectionism' that would go against the principles of openness and solidarity.

The same tension between a competitive and a cooperative understanding of language policies underlies the efforts of the Flemish government to attract a broader public to its cultural and linguistic institutions. The non-Flemish people who use the facilities offered by the Flemish government do help make the Flemish institutions sustainable, but they still benefit from services which are mainly funded by Flemish public money. The beneficiaries in this case are the individual users rather than the Flemish community. As the director of the Dutch Language House says,

> two-thirds of [people who approach the Dutch Language House] do so to enhance their professional careers. They want to improve their prospects of finding a good job, perform better in their current job, and broaden their basic knowledge of Dutch. (Steenwinckel, 2010: 30)

In all these matters, the VGC has clearly chosen to privilege a cooperative approach, because 'locking yourself up in your own society is [...] resolutely discarded on ideological grounds by the [VGC]' (Witte, 2008: 8). In its communication, the VGC often stresses that multilingualism and multiculturalism are an 'asset' in Brussels and proudly states the large number of languages and nationalities one can find in the city (see Steenwinckel, 2006, 2010; Witte, 2008). The text of the brochure mentioned above, for instance, says that the *zinneke* (street dog) is 'the symbol of the Brussels identity' because it is 'a cross between Flemish, Walloon, Italian, Spanish, Arabic, English, German or any blood whatsoever' (Steenwinckel, 2010: 3). It also highlights that Flemish cultural institutions in Brussels serve as a 'bridge' between the majority French-speaking group and the many non-official minority communities. In other words, the promotion of linguistic diversity and 'interculturality' is a main thread of the campaigns launched by the Flemish authorities in Brussels,[18] which propose openness as 'an aspect of the Flemish identity' (Witte, 2008: 7).

This discourse is in line with the way bilingual *Bruxellois* view their identity. Indeed, since 2003 many civic and political associations have appeared in Brussels to call for recognition of the inherently bicultural and bilingual character of the city and even to insist on its increasingly multicultural and multilingual reality (see Nassaux, 2011). They want to escape the oppositional logic created by the political conflict between Wallonia and Flanders in order to recognize Brussels' identity as fundamentally hybrid and justify the existence of a specific policy designed by *Bruxellois* for *Bruxellois*. Yet the discourse of Flemish authorities in Brussels is clearly in tension with the nationalist discourse that is still popular in Flanders, which by necessity views the community as being defined by historically rooted and stable features and by its linguistic homogeneity.

This shows how the two political strategies regarding language policy that I have described above (competitive and cooperative) are rooted in two distinct conceptions of the community and of collective identities in general: one that views them as homogenous, bounded and stable; the other that sees them as plural, open and changing. While these two conceptions of the community are related to two distinct visions of relations between linguistic communities in a multilingual state, they are also related to two different conceptions of language, and hence to two ways of justifying the political importance of promoting the community's language. The opposition between these two conceptions of the community's language has been formulated by Woolard (2008) as an opposition between 'authenticity' and 'anonymity'.

Within the vision of the community as having a particular essence, its language has value because it is *authentic*, because it is the 'genuine expression' of the community, of its 'essential Self' (Woolard, 2008: 304). Within the vision of the community as an evolving gathering of heterogeneous individuals, the community's language is important because it is a bridge that allows communication between diverse people, because it is an *anonymous* 'public language' that 'can represent and be used equally by everyone precisely because [it] belong[s] to no-one-in-particular'; it is 'positioned as universally open and available to all in a society' (Woolard, 2008: 307). As Woolard shows, linguistic minorities usually base the importance of their language on a conception of authenticity. The problem with this conception is that the language can then only have value for those who are already members of the community, not for outsiders. How then does one convince these outsiders that they should take an interest in learning the language, which is what the Dutch-speaking community in Brussels needs to happen? In contrast, the other conception can be used to highlight why it is in the interest of outsiders to learn the language, which may enhance their communicative resources. In the case of Brussels, however, it is clear that French is better positioned to serve as a bridge language. Moreover, this type of justification does not recognize the specific value of the (co)existence of the minority language (in this case Dutch) and the community that identifies with it.

As stated above, a linguistic community which views itself as bounded and in conflict with another community will develop a competitive vision of its political struggle and a conception of language policies based on the principle of authenticity. But when the same community needs to open its symbolic boundaries (because of migration movements or to increase its demographic weight), it will also develop collaborative strategies and discourses on language anonymity. This is clearly the tension[19] we observe in the political action and discourse of the Flemish minority in Brussels. In line with the work of Soler Carbonell (2010 and Chapter 5, this volume) on Catalonia and Estonia, we can regard this as mainly due to its status as a medium-sized community and the specific challenges it faces (see Section 4 above). Unlike a small linguistic community, a medium-sized one is not condemned to concern itself only with authenticity: it can also aspire to welcome new speakers on the basis of anonymity. However, when it has faced the threat of assimilation, it cannot easily prioritize anonymity over authenticity; the struggle for language protection has almost always been undertaken on the basis of an essential relationship between the community as a bounded entity and its authentic language. In the case of Dutch in Brussels, this tension is the most evident in policies that target people of immigrant background. Drawing this group into the Dutch-speaking community is important to reinforce the presence of Dutch in Brussels. At the same time, it means privileging anonymity over authenticity, while in fact authenticity is historically the main justification for the struggle to protect and promote the Dutch language in Brussels.

In this sense, since Flemish schools are supposed to exist for the *Flemish* community, to control and preserve its interests, notably in terms of linguistic *and socioeconomic* homogeneity, children with an immigrant background could be regarded as unwelcome. On the other hand, they are a target group for educational policy aimed at increasing the number of Dutch speakers. As Witte (2008: 9) highlights:

> The [VGC] has been wanting to act on language activation of foreign language children for several years and decided to fully invest in such projects. Training teachers to deal with non-native children is also part of its policy. And because the active help of parents is of great importance in the learning and educational process, the [VGC] also wants to focus on non-native parents.

The way this kind of policy is justified by the VGC clearly reflects the two types of rationale I have referred to:

> The [VGC] also wants to avoid that the growing migrant population becomes fully Frenchified. The day that more Bruxellois have a command of Dutch, the application of the language laws will be much easier, it is claimed. Attracting foreign-language students in education is also a question of survival of the Dutch-speaking schools. Bilingualism is an asset for all the people of Brussels. Leading the Dutchification – and therefore the bilingualism process – is therefore one of the main goals of the VGC. (Witte, 2008: 8)

As this extract shows, helping immigrants learn Dutch is important because it contributes to the development of the Flemish community and its institutions, while also preventing them from swelling the ranks of the francophones. So the learning of Dutch by immigrants is justified because it serves the interest of the Flemish *Bruxellois,* since it is *their authentic* language. At the same time, because bilingualism is of value to immigrants, the learning of Dutch as an anonymous language is justified because it is clearly in their interest as outsiders.

In the official discourse of the Flemish authorities in Brussels, the anonymity principle has gradually become dominant, along with a vision of the community as open and evolving – a movement quite similar to the one observed in Barcelona (see Boix-Fuster, Chapter 7, this volume). Yet the tension between the two principles is still high. For instance, the way people of immigrant background use Dutch in Brussels is the subject of many negative attitudes. Their use of the language is seen as illegitimate, in contrast with authentic or 'proper' Dutch (Declercq, 2008). Similarly, Witte (2008: 9) highlights that the VGC 'pleads for a correct and proper use of Dutch in Brussels, i.e. no allotment Flemish'. The results of the policies targeting immigrant communities may also be seen as ambiguous: new Dutch speakers do not see themselves as part of the Flemish community, though the aim of the Flemish authorities is clearly that they should behave like Flemish (versus francophone) *Bruxellois*, particularly when it comes to their electoral behaviour. In this sense, the 2006 electoral campaign mentioned above was designed to prompt members of immigrant communities to vote for Flemish politicians (as opposed to their francophone counterparts) in the hope that they would be interested in helping, through this political choice, to ensure the development of the high-quality services offered by Flemish institutions and promoted in the campaign.[20]

While many parents of foreign origin are very motivated to help their children become bilingual and therefore eager to enrol them in Flemish schools (and they have no deep feeling of loyalty to French; see Hambye *et al.*, 2007), a large part of them is reluctant to move closer to the Dutch-speaking community.

In fact, effective incorporation of this population into the Flemish community is hindered by at least two factors. First, motivation and confidence in one's capacity to learn seems to play a major role. Because of the fear of academic failure, it is only those who already have a basic knowledge of Dutch or have contacts with Dutch speakers who express a desire to improve their skills in the language (see Janssens, 2008: 5–6). Second, Janssens' survey shows that for many non-Flemish *Bruxellois*, the Flemish community and the Dutch language are two dissociated categories, and that the learning of Dutch is therefore not linked to identification with the Flemish community, while those who still associate 'Dutch' with 'Flemish' may develop negative attitudes toward both categories:[21]

> [...] the identification with what is 'Flemish' is even more problematic. French speakers, foreign speakers and even a part of the Dutch speakers are least of all inclined to identify themselves with this Flemish side. This leads to a rather ambiguous situation whereby Dutch is becoming increasingly important and the need to learn this language is acknowledged by more and more people from Brussels, but where the term 'Flemish' seems to be driving the communities further apart. These tensions are not only expressed on a political level, also non-Dutch-speaking *Bruxellois* often associate 'Flemish' with Flemish extremism and intolerance. Even a major part of Dutch-speaking people in Brussels distance themselves from the adjective 'Flemish'. (Janssens, 2008: 12–13)

6. Conclusion

As a medium-sized community in an urban area, the Dutch-speaking community faces challenges linked to the fact that it is under pressure both from 'above' and 'below'. It is threatened by languages that are more widespread or useful (French and English), and at the same time has to protect its status from the pressure of other minority languages that increase linguistic diversity – and hence the need for a *lingua franca* – and that tend to put the Dutch-speaking group in the position of being one linguistic minority among others. Even if the status of the Dutch language is shored up by specific language laws, we can understand why it is important in this context for the Flemish authorities to highlight the particular symbolic value of the Dutch language (authenticity), and the fact that, like French or English, it can serve as a bridge language (anonymity).

However, these challenges differ depending on how we understand what is really at stake for Dutch speakers in Brussels, whether the focus is on protecting the interests of one community against others, or on calling for recognition of the value of this community, among others. If these two visions are in fact intertwined and not systematically exclusive, they are in tension as soon as the question of priorities arises. Should resources in general be used for the good of the *Flemish community* that is, very often, for the good of the dominant group having power position within the community – or for giving *Dutch speakers* an equal status, even if the latter choice is sometimes not *directly* in the interest of the Flemish community? This is indeed a fundamentally political question that no discourse on 'best practices' can help answer. I believe, nonetheless, that if a minority wants to escape the continuous feeling of tension and threat that the competitive option necessarily creates, one priority must be to struggle for cooperative symbolic recognition of its equal value and status. This does not mean that the main goal of language policies should be to obtain symbolic affirmation from the majority, a simple discourse underlining the importance of the Dutch language in Brussels with no practical consequences. The symbolic recognition of the fundamentally equal status of French and Dutch speakers leads to the affirmation of an equality of rights between the two communities that makes the principle of equality of both groups the horizon of language policies.

Because of the way francophones' attitudes toward Dutch have evolved, the possibility of such a political affirmation has never been so real. It presupposes a political will from both sides to adopt a collaborative logic that breaks with years of contentious relationships. It seems, however, to be the only way of ensuring an untroubled future for the Dutch language in Brussels. Considering the 'relatively limited number of children from monolingual Dutch-speaking families', Janssens (2008: 10) states that 'the future of Dutch in Brussels' lies increasingly in the hands of the individuals who will become bilingual or multilingual within the 'ideal school environment' he is calling for. Until now, the creation of such an 'ideal school environment' has been prevented by the difficulty Flemish and francophone authorities have working together to tackle the challenge of bilingualism. Even if both groups agree on the usefulness of collaboration, they are still hindered by the old competitive conception, under which education is viewed as a matter in which each community must have total autonomy. Only when the Dutch and French-speaking communities understand their common interest in promoting bilingualism will they be able to join forces in pursuit of a shared objective.

Notes

(1) A language that has an important international position gives its speakers access to many important resources, such as the opportunity to travel, share one's knowledge, attract material and human resources, etc.
(2) The Brussels fire department went on strike on 28 January 2009 because of problems related to the quota for Dutch-speaking employees, which was considered too high in relation to the proportion of matters the service had to deal with in Dutch.
(3) The official linguistic census was discontinued in 1961 after the 1947 census generated a great deal of political tension between the Flemish and francophone communities because of its alleged lack of reliability.
(4) There is no legal regulation of signage in the private sector: companies determine their own implicit or explicit language policy for external communication.
(5) In fact, before the creation of Belgium and the progressive spread of French in the capital, the main language spoken in Brussels was not properly spoken Dutch (as a standard language), but the local variant of the group of Flemish dialects.
(6) Notably through the guarantee of political representation in the Brussels Regional Parliament: at least 17 out of 89 deputies in the Parliament must come from Dutch-speaking electoral lists, even if their effective electoral weight is lower.
(7) The Commission, which has its francophone counterpart, is the official representative of the Flemish government in Brussels.
(8) Sometimes, this is achieved through dedicated language courses offered in sectors where there is a lack of Dutch-speaking employees (see Witte, 2008: 10).
(9) See http://www.huisnederlandsbrussel.be/ (accessed 26 November 2011).
(10) See http://brussel.vlaanderen.be/campagnes.html (accessed 26 November 2011).
(11) Along the same lines, in 2010 a Flemish political party (CD&V) proposed a bonus for Flemish schoolteachers willing to move to Brussels and settle there.
(12) From June 2010, Belgium was without a federal government for more than a year, because francophone and Flemish political parties could not reach agreement on the design of a new constitutional reform aimed at increasing the power and autonomy of federated entities.
(13) A group that is not necessarily a minority group, as the Belgian case illustrates.
(14) Some recent surveys carried out in Walloon schools that offer Dutch immersion programmes show that the majority of parents who decided to enrol their children in immersive sections were primarily interested in the quality of the school and the employment-related benefits immersion could bring (De Longueville, 2010: 54–58). The moral or civic dimension of bilingualism often highlighted in discourse is not one of their main motivations: only 4% of the parents interviewed chose immersion because they wanted their children to come in contact with the language and culture of the Flemish people. Janssens' data on media consumption also clearly show that

francophones' interest in Dutch is mainly instrumental: in Brussels, Dutch speakers read French- and Dutch-language newspapers, while French and foreign speakers get their information only from the French-speaking media (Janssens, 2008: 7).
(15) 'The Flemish community provides 22.7% more funding for a primary school pupil than the French-speaking community, and 18.1% more for a secondary school pupil' (Janssens et al., 2009: 2).
(16) In fact, children who speak Dutch at home and those with a low socio-economic profile are given priority in the registration process. In practice, this means that students from middle-class francophone families have very little chance of enrolling in Flemish schools, despite the fact that francophone parents are the most eager to provide their children with bilingual skills.
(17) 'In French-speaking families this choice of school does not affect the language use in the family, but this is different for foreign speakers, where Dutch is regularly spoken with friends, but also with brothers and sisters' (Janssens, 2008 : 4–5).
(18) This is explicitly stated on the website of the Flemish authorities in Brussels, in the section on information campaigns (see http://brussel.vlaanderen.be/campagnes.html; accessed 16 November 2011).
(19) A tension that can also be understood as an opposition between *pride* and *profit* (see Duchêne & Heller, 2012).
(20) The discourse is formulated as follows: The Flemish community has experienced strong growth for several years. This community is, of course, composed not only of Flemish *Bruxellois*, but also of numerous *Bruxellois* with other cultural backgrounds. Based on this reality, the Flemish network works together with other groups to create an intercultural city where the different communities respect and are interested in each other. In this folder, you will discover what the Flemish authority and Flemish deputies do for you. In order to strengthen all these initiatives, the Flemish community and municipal administrations in Brussels must invest continuously in this Flemish network. This will also be one of the issues in the upcoming election. Let the Flemish community be your partner in Brussels. You can contribute to this effort by voting for a Dutch-speaking candidate in Brussels on 8 October 2006. (Steenwinckel, 2006: 3; author's translation)
(21) In this sense, note that *'Flamand'* ('Flemish') is an insult for many French-speaking youngsters of immigrant descent in Brussels (see Declercq, 2008).

References

Calvet, L.-J. (2006) *Towards an Ecology of World Languages*. Cambridge: Polity Press.
Deboosere, P., Eggerickx, Th., Van Hecke, E. and Wayens, B. (2009) The population of Brussels: A demographic overview. *Brussels Studies, Citizens' Forum of Brussels*, Synopsis n°3. See http://www.brusselsstudies.be/ (accessed 10 November 2011).
Declercq, K. (2008) Une ethnographie sociolinguistique de deux classes multiculturelles à Bruxelles [A sociolinguistic ethnography of two multicultural classes in Brussels]. PhD thesis, Université catholique de Louvain.
De Longueville, E. (2010) L'immersion linguistique pour qui, pour quoi ? Enquête sur les attitudes et représentations linguistiques [Linguistic immersion, for whom, for what? A survey about attitudes and representations]. Master's thesis, Université catholique de Louvain.
De Swaan, A. (2001) *Words of the World: The Global Language System*. Cambridge: Polity Press.
De Troyer, A. (ed.) (2004) *Brussels, A Warm Welcome. Meet Flanders in its Capital City*. Brussels: Ministry of the Flemish Community.
Duchêne, A. and Heller, M. (eds) (2012) *Language in Late Capitalism: Pride and Profit*. London: Routledge.

Erk, J. (2005) Sub-state nationalism and the left–right divide: Critical junctures in the formation of nationalist labour movements in Belgium. *Nations and Nationalism* 11 (4), 551–570.
European Commission (EC) (2005) Europeans and their languages. *Special Eurobarometer 243.* See http://ec.europa.eu/public_opinion/archives/ebs/ebs_237.en.pdf (accessed 10 November 2011).
Francard, M. (1995) Nef des Fous ou radeau de la Méduse? Les conflits linguistiques en Belgique [*Ship of Fools or raft of the Medusa? Linguistic conflicts in Belgium*]. *Linx* 33, 31–46.
Hambye, Ph. and Lucchini, S. (2005) Sociolinguistic diversity and shared resources. A critical look at linguistic integration policies in Belgium. *Noves SL* 6. See http://www6.gencat.net/llengcat/noves/ (accessed 14 November 2011).
Hambye, Ph. and Richards, M. (2012) The paradoxical visions of multilingualism in education: The ideological dimension of discourses on bilingualism in Belgium and Canada. *International Journal of Multilingualism* 9 (2), 165–188.
Hambye, Ph., Lucchini, S., Delcourt, I. and Forlot, G. (2007) *Francophones et plurilingues. Le rapport à la langue française et au plurilinguisme des Belges issus de l'immigration* [*French-speaking and multilingual. The relationship towards French language and multilingualism among Belgian of foreign origin*]. Unpublished report, Service de la langue française du Ministère de la Culture de la Communauté française Wallonie-Bruxelles.
Heller, M. (2002) *Éléments d'une sociolinguistique critique* [*Pieces of a critical sociolinguistics*]. Paris: Didier.
Heller, M. (2006) *Linguistic Minorities and Modernity: A Sociolinguistic Ethnography* (2nd edn). London: Continuum.
Institut Bruxellois de Statistique et d'Analyse (IBSA) (2009) Mouvements de population [*Population movements*]. Ministère de la Région de Bruxelles-Capitale. See http://www.ibsa.irisnet.be/fr/themes/population/population (accessed 20 November 2011).
Institut Bruxellois de Statistique et d'Analyse (IBSA) (2012) *Mini-Bru 2012. La Région de Bruxelles-Capitale en chiffres* [*The Region of Brussels-Capital in figures*]. Bruxelles, Ministère de la Région de Bruxelles-Capitale. See http://www.ibsa.irisnet.be/fr/publications/publications-par-annee (accessed 20 November 2011).
Janssens, R. (2001) *Taalgebruik in Brussel: Taalverhoudingen, taalverschuivingen en taalidentiteit in een meertalige stad* [*Language use in Brussels: Language balance, language transfers and linguistic identity in a multilingual city*]. Brussels: VUB Press.
Janssens, R. (2007) *Van Brussel gesproken: Taalgebruik, taalverschuivingen en taalidentiteit in het Brussels Hoofdstedelijk Gewest* [*Talking about Brussels: Language use, language transfers and linguistic identity in the Region of Brussels-Capital*]. Brussels: VUB Press.
Janssens, R. (2008) Language use in Brussels and the position of Dutch. Some recent findings. *Brussels Studies* 13. See http://www.brusselsstudies.be/ (accessed 10 November 2011).
Janssens, R., Carlier, D. and Van de Craen, P. (2009) Education in Brussels. *Brussels Studies, Citizens' forum of Brussels*, Synopsis no. 5. See http://www.brusselsstudies.be/ (accessed 10 November 2011).
Laponce, J. (1987) *Languages and Their Territories*. Toronto: University of Toronto Press.
Laponce, J. (2006) *Loi de Babel et autres régularités des rapports entre langue et politique* [*Babel law and other regularities in the relations between language and politics*]. Québec: Presses de l'Université Laval.
Mabille, X. (2000) *Histoire politique de la Belgique. Facteurs et acteurs de changement* [*A political history of Belgium. Factors and actors of change*]. Bruxelles: CRISP.
Mettewie, L. and Van Mensel, L. (2006) *Entreprises bruxelloises et langues étrangères. Pratique et coût d'une main d'oeuvre ne maîtrisant pas les langues étrangères* [*Companies and foreign languages in Brussels. Practice and cost of a labor force not mastering foreign languages*]. Unpublished report. See www.briobrussel.be (accessed 10 November 2011).

Nassaux, J.-P. (2011) *Le nouveau mouvement bruxellois* [*The new social movement of Brussels*]. *Courrier hebdomadaire du CRISP* 2103–2104, 1–88.
O'Donnel, P. and Toebosch, A. (2008) Multilingualism in Brussels: 'I'd rather speak English'. *Journal of Multilingual and Multicultural Development* 29 (2), 154–169.
Smet, P. (2009) *Beleidsnota Brussel 2009–2014* [*Political note Brussels 2009–2014*]. Brussels: Vlaamse Ministerie van Onderwijs, Jeugd, Gelijke Kansen en Brussel.
Soler Carbonell, J. (2010) Llengües mitjanes i llengües internacionals en contacte a Catalunya i Estònia en l'era glocal. Una anàlisi sociolingüística comparada [Medium languages and international languages in contact in Catalonia and Estonia in the glocal era. A comparative sociolinguistic analysis]. PhD thesis, Universitat de Barcelona.
Steenwinckel, A. (ed.) (2006) *'U ook' Vlamingen, partners in Brussel* [*You too. Flemings, partners in Brussels*]. Brussels: Vlaamse overheid, Coördinatie Brussel.
Steenwinckel, A. (ed.) (2010) *Brussels for You: A Unique Introduction to the Capital City*. Brussels: Flemish Government, Coordination Brussels.
Taylor, Ch. (1992) The politics of recognition. In A. Gutmann (ed.) *Multiculturalism and 'The Politics of Recognition'* (pp. 25–73). Princeton: Princeton University Press.
Van Parijs, Ph. (2007) Brussels capital of Europe: The new linguistic challenges. *Brussels Studies* 6. See http://www.brusselsstudies.be/ (accessed 10 November 2011).
Van Parijs, Ph. (2010) Linguistic Justice and the territorial imperative. *Critical Review of International Social and Political Philosophy* 13 (1), 181–202.
Witte, E. (2008) Looking back on fifteen years of FCC policy (1989–2004) *Brussels Studies* 17. See http://www.brusselsstudies.be/ (accessed 10 November 2011).
Witte, E. and Van Velthoven, H. (2000) *Language and Politics. The Situation in Belgium in a Historical Perspective*. Brussels: VUB Press.
Woolard, K. A. (2008) Language and identity choice in Catalonia: The interplay of contrasting ideologies of linguistic authority. In K. Süselbeck, U. Mühlschlegel and P. Masson (eds) *Lengua, Nación e Identidad. La regulación del plurilingüismo en Espana y América Latina* (pp. 303–323). Frankfurt am Main, Madrid: Vervuert Verlag, Iberoamericana.

3 Language Diversity in Vigo: The Challenges of a Minoritized Language in a Highly Castilianized City

Iago González Pascual and Fernando Ramallo

Introduction

For a sociolinguist, the city is a fascinating subject of study. A simple journey by subway or bus between two points of a global city activates our 'linguistic radar' (Block, 2006: vii) to capture a scenario in which the diversity of languages is overwhelming. Multilingualism has become visible in the city, both in oral and literacy practices. Cities are multilingual, which means that multilingualism is already a defining feature of the current city (Extra & Yagmur, 2004; García & Fishman, 2002). This has encouraged the proliferation of a complex semiotization of linguistic landscape (Backhaus, 2007; Ben Rafael & Barni, 2010; Gorter, 2006; Gorter *et al.*, 2012; Jaworski & Thurlow, 2010; Shohamy & Gorter, 2009).

Social monolingualism has become obsolete and now it is the marked term (Aronin & Singleton, 2012; Blackledge & Creese, 2010; Ellis, 2008). All this is having very important consequences for coexistence and social harmony in societies which, to the traditional conflicts of class or gender, are now added those arising from the presence of new actors emerging with globalization and defying the hegemonic construction of nation states (Moyer & Martin Rojo, 2007). These actors, immigrants from diverse backgrounds, deserve a responsible answer to their demands in terms of education, language rights, social welfare, etc. that any real democracy should meet.

Nowadays, each city is a metaphor of the world. Their most notable feature of identity is a very complex diversity. The coexistence in a same territory of a relevant number of distinct ethnic groups, some with many members and others with very few, with very diverse geographic and socioeconomic origins, constitutes the most outstanding feature of much of today's cities. This 'superdiversity' (Vertovec, 2007) is also a challenge for the social sciences. They need to rethink many of the concepts and theories used to describe urban areas in the preceding decades, and Sociolinguistics is no exception.

Since language plays a central role in the processes of social change and development, a new theoretical scenario that helps to describe these processes is necessary. In his epistemological proposal for a 'sociolinguistics of globalization', Blommaert (2010: 1) noted the need for 'a new vocabulary to describe events, phenomena and processes, new metaphors for representing them, new arguments to explain them'. Actually, this is a paradigm shift with unpredictable consequences for the ways to address a sociolinguistic analysis. It is the transformation from a 'sociolinguistics of distribution' typical of the variationist paradigm to one 'sociolinguistics of mobility' more in line with the new forms of dynamism in contemporary societies (Blommaert, 2001: 5). For Coupland (2011: 8), the answer to globalization requires a 'sociology of language that can model relationships among languages on a global scale'.

In this chapter, we present a description of multilingualism in the city of Vigo (Galicia), as an example of a medium-sized city. First, we address the demographic and sociolinguistic characterization of the city; then, we present the main results of an ongoing investigation into the linguistic landscape of the city. The chapter ends with a brief conclusion.

Demographic Characterization

Vigo is a medium-sized city located in Galicia, northwest Spain and a few kilometres from Portugal. It is the most populous city in Galicia and, after Vilanova de Gaia (Portugal) the second of the Galicia-North Portugal Euroregion. The city is the capital of a municipal district, which extends across the province of Pontevedra with 14 municipalities. Its demographic impact regarding the above areas is captured in Table 3.1 below.

Table 3.1 Demographics of Vigo and its areas of influence

Territorial scope	Inhabitants
Vigo	294,997 (2014)
Metropolitan area	423,842 (2014)
Galicia	2,748,695 (2014)
Euroregion (Galicia–North Portugal)	6,538,745 (2011)

Source: Spanish Statistical Office (2014) and Borobio Sanchiz and Vázquez Mao (2011).

The city has been shaped by migration, mostly endogenous. Over 30% of the current population was not born in the city. Among them, most come from other parts of Galicia. In 2014 registered immigrants totalled 14,561 people, which turns Vigo into the Galician city with the greater presence of residents born abroad (Spanish Statistical Office, 2014). In spite of being far from the migratory flows of other Castilian cities of similar size, since the beginning of this century the city has significantly increased its immigrant population. While in 2000 the percentage of immigrants was 1.2%, in 2014 they represented 5.6% of the total municipal population. This is higher than the average of Galicia (3.9%) but very much below the Castilian average (12.2%). Most immigrants come from America (45%) and the European Union (39%). The population of African origin represents 9% and Asians represent 4%.

Vigo is a city that has undergone a significant demographic change in the last century. Note that around 1900 the city had 23,000 inhabitants, which means that the population has multiplied by 13 in 100 years. The main demographic indicators of the city are the following: the population density is 2649 inhabitants per square kilometre; the average age of its inhabitants is 43 years, with a percentage of under-16s of 14% and over-65s of 19%. Consequently, the aging index, i.e. the ratio of the population higher than 64 years old and the under-16s is considered low. For each 100 young people in Vigo there are 109 who are 65 or older, while in the total of Galicia this number rises to 145.

Although in terms of economy the tertiary sector is dominant with 78% of the employment in this sector, the city and its surroundings make up the more industrial area of Galicia, contributing to 31% of the GDP of the region. The most important industries are the automobile industry, with a major factory of Citroën Hispania, shipyards, canneries, fisheries and textiles. In fact, the port of Vigo is recognized as one of the world's most important ports in the fishing industry. Moreover, in recent decades the city and its surroundings have increased their staffing in services, making it an attractive point of reference in culinary, cultural and green tourism.

Sociolinguistic Context

From a structural perspective, the sociolinguistic situation in Vigo is determined by the historical presence of two Romance languages, Galician and Castilian, with very different sociodemographic profiles. During the last century, the sociolinguistic order has been altered by various processes in three different directions.

First, the fact that the city has become the area of greater economic dynamism in Galicia has contributed to a very substantial increase of Galician language population from nearby areas. At first glance, this endogenous migratory process could have implied a greater social visibility for Galician. However, the outcome was different from that, due to different causes. Note that the most relevant part of this shift from the countryside to the city occurs in the late years of the Franco regime (1960s–1970s). At that time the ideological transformation designed by the dictatorial regime against Galician language had already consolidated, a fact which contributed to strengthen the language minoritization process (Freitas Juvino, 2008). The Galician language was detached from the referents of modernity and was relegated to the domain of traditions and emotions (Williams, 2005). Many families from rural areas, the vast majority of them traditional Galician speakers, came into contact with urban culture and in an effort to integrate themselves as quickly as possible, they accommodated to the system of references typical of the city, among which the Castilian language was one more element of modernity they wished to adopt. Thus, these speakers add Castilian to their communicative repertoire, not just in the more formal registers but also, and crucially, in the informal ones, including in the intergenerational transmission of the language. The most immediate consequence of this process was the gradual increase of bilingualism, especially in the generation of those who today are between 30 and 50 years old.

Second, and as a result of the officially bilingual regime that Galicia has since 1981, the formal consolidation and the functional expansion of the standard variety of Galician in domains reserved until recent decades to Castilian (such as the educational system, the public media and the regional administration) is favoured. Although in terms of the social revitalization of the language, the consequences of this functional expansion are far from being optimal, at least it has encouraged the emergence of a new profile of urban speakers of the language, known generically as *neofalantes* (O'Rourke & Ramallo, 2011, 2013).

Third, the migratory dynamics in the city has enriched its linguistic landscape. As in many medium-sized European cities, immigration does not imply a significant contribution in quantitative terms as it does in terms of diversity. In the city, among others, the following languages are spoken: Portuguese, Arabic, Wolof, Quechua, Igbo, Mandarin, Ewe, Guaraní, Urhobo, Hindi, Punjabi, Japanese, Yoruba, Fante, Edo, Russian, Ukrainian, Romanian, Bengali, Farsi, Italian, English, French and German (Ramallo, 2012).

Galician-Castilian Contact

Vigo is a very Castilianized city. Although bilingualism is consolidated from the standpoint of the law, in practice Castilian is the predominant language in most informal communicative interactions. Overall, Galician is in a regressive sociolinguistic situation, with little social dynamism, especially among the youth.

The Galician-Castilian contact situation has had as a main consequence the social displacement of the first language and the consolidation of Castilian as the urban language, at least in the downtown. In contrast, in the suburbs traditional Galician still maintains a relative vitality (Vaamonde Liste, 2003).

Mother tongue

Castilian monolingualism is present in most families. One in four people learned to speak in Galician, almost half in Castilian and the other quarter is considered bilingual as far as mother tongue is concerned. In addition, 3% learned to speak in other languages. Differences by age groups show an intergenerational progressive decrease of Galician as the mother tongue. Almost half of the population over the age of 65 learned to speak in Galician, while in those under the age of 25 the percentage barely exceeds 5%. Between the two extremes a change went underway in the language transmission, increasing the preference for Castilian as mother tongue and the consolidation of early bilingualism in 29% of Vigo's younger population (see Table 3.2 below).

The table also shows the changes in intergenerational transmission between 2003 and 2013. In 10 years, an important decrease in Galician monolingualism is confirmed, from 28 to 16%. These tendency is present in all age groups. If we observe the increase in the rate of bilingualism in the same period, from 19 to 27%, it can be understood that the process of language shift towards Castilian is at an intermediate stage, especially considering that early monolingualism in this language remains almost the same in this 10-year period.

Table 3.2 Mother tongue in Vigo by age from 2003 to 2013 (in percentages)

	Galician		Castilian		Galician and Castilian		Other(s)	
	2003	2013	2003	2013	2003	2013	2003	2013
5–14 years	9	1	72	70	19	27	0	2
15–29 years	15	4	57	68	26	26	2	3
30–49 years	24	9	54	55	20	32	2	4
50–64 years	41	18	41	56	16	24	2	3
Over 65 years	50	38	39	35	10	26	1	2
TOTAL	28	16	51	54	19	27	2	3

Source: Prepared by authors based on data from Instituto Galego de Estatística (2003, 2013).

Language use

In terms of language use, three distinct linguistic groups coexist in Vigo: monolinguals, either in Galician or in Castilian, and bilinguals. It is easy to realize that these are not symmetric groups in terms of quantity. Half of the population speaks only Castilian. Only 8% is monolingual in Galician, while those who use both languages represent 42% (Table 3.3). In addition, one in every 100 people speaks a language other than Galician or Castilian. Galician monolingualism has fallen by half in 10 years (15 to 8%).

Regarding age, we can observe a downslide in Galician-speaking generations and the option, increasingly common, to use only Castilian. Half of those under the age of 50 speak only Castilian, reaching 76% in the youngest population. The exclusive use of Galician in these age groups is residual, although this is a population group with a good formal command of the language, as a result of their learning in the education system. Even among the older population, many of them with Galician as their mother tongue, the exclusive use of Galician does not reach 20%.

Individual language retention, defined as the regular use of the mother tongue, is more consistent among those who learned to speak Castilian, while it is very low among the population that had Galician as their mother tongue (Table 3.4). Most Galician native speakers are bilingual in their practices and 33% use only their mother tongue. Meanwhile, 72% of those who declare Castilian as their mother tongue use only this language daily. On the other hand, people who grew up in a bilingual family use more Castilian than Galician.

The linguistic repertoire of the city is dominated by popular varieties of local Castilian in oral uses and standard Castilian in the written ones. Apart from them, different varieties of Galician survive. On the one hand, varieties of southern traditional Galician are used in the neighbourhoods which in

Table 3.3 Language use in Vigo by age from 2003 to 2013 (in percentages)

	Only Galician		Only Castilian		Galician and Castilian	
	2003	2013	2003	2013	2003	2013
5–14 years	5	1	55	76	40	24
15–29 years	8	2	42	59	50	40
30–49 years	12	5	37	53	51	42
50–64 years	22	8	27	48	51	43
Over 65 years	30	18	33	35	37	47
TOTAL	15	8	38	50	47	42

Source: Prepared by authors based on data from Instituto Galego de Estatística (2003, 2013).

Table 3.4 Language retention in Vigo (in percentages)

		LANGUAGE USE				
		Speak only Galician	Speak only Castilian	Speak Galician (and Castilian)	Speak Castilian (and Galician)	TOTAL
MOTHER TONGUE	Galician	33	7	37	23	100
	Castilian	2	72	2	24	100
	Galician and Castilian	5	31	17	47	100

Source: Prepared by authors based on data from Instituto Galego de Estatística (2013).

part still maintain a primary economy (Beade, Valadares, Zamáns, Teis). On the other hand, there are different varieties of urban Galician, mainly among young new-speakers. These varieties, heavily influenced by the standard, are dominant in the written uses.

Language attitudes

In general, linguistic attitudes towards Galician amongst the population of Vigo as well as in the rest of Galicia are positive, even in Castilian-speaking groups (Observatorio da Cultura Galega, 2012). This is partly a consequence of the bilingual education model implemented in Galicia during the last three decades. Even though this system has not been able to increase the use of the minority language, it has contributed to improve the social representation of Galician. Crucially, the presence of old prejudices towards the language, which had been strongly prevalent during the last two centuries, has been minimized. The symbolic value of the language has increased despite its low functional relevance. However, some attitudinal indicators could still improve. Table 3.5 shows several statements regarding the Galician language. A, B and C are negative statements concerning the language whilst statements D, E and F are positive. The data show that in general people do not agree with negative statements. Nonetheless, favourable attitudes towards the language are more nuanced in positive statements (column 'Agree').

Linguistic Landscape in Vigo

The linguistic landscape of a given territory is made up of the distribution of languages used in commercial billboards (which cover the whole private domain), in public signs (street and road names, buildings, etc.), and in

Table 3.5 Linguistic attitudes in Vigo (in percentages)

Statement	Don't agree	Agree	Indifferent
A. I wouldn't be concerned if no one spoke Galician anymore	84	9	7
B. Children have more difficulties at school when they learn both languages at the same time	81	13	6
C. The language of Galicians is only Castilian	65	25	10
D. The language of schooling should be Galician	47	41	13
E. I would like films to be dubbed in Galician	36	32	32
F. It isn't appropriate that someone answers me in Castilian if I speak to them in Galician	27	33	40

Source: González González (2011).

other types of texts written on the supports of the town (for instance, graffiti). Our aim in this section is to analyse the linguistic situation in Vigo by visualizing its linguistic kaleidoscope. This will account for the degree of linguistic diversity present in the town.

Linguistic landscape has been given several different definitions over the years, yet some consensus has been reached since the seminal work by Landry and Bourhis (1997). They define the term as:

> The language of public road signs, advertising billboards, street names, commercial shop signs, and public signs on government buildings combines to form the linguistic landscape of a given territory, region, or urban agglomeration. (Landry & Bourhis, 1997: 25)

Therefore, when dealing with linguistic landscape, we refer specifically to written language as used in public space. This means that the use of spoken language, important as it is to describe the sociolinguistic situation of a given territory, is not the main area of concern in research on linguistic landscape. We believe that written language use in the public arena can serve as a heuristic tool to determine to what extent the official language policies in a given social milieu are actually enforced and to measure the relative vitality of the different languages present in that society.

From this perspective, we set out to develop an approach to the urban linguistic objects which are particularly salient in those areas where speakers live together. These objects contain messages originating in both public and private institutions: signs, billboards, street names, big and small businesses, texts in spaces for leisure, for work, etc. Thus by means of the linguistic images of the city, we can obtain information about the vitality and status of the languages spoken in Vigo as well as the identity of the linguistic groups towards which the images are directed.

The first thing we think when dealing with linguistic landscape is that the dominant spoken language in a given territory will be the most widely used language in the linguistic landscape of that territory, but is this really the case? Is it the case in all contexts? In this sense, it is interesting to account for the differences between official and private texts. Official texts are issued by public institutions and that is the reason why they reflect (or not) the official language policy. This could be confirmed in street names, public buildings, signs for directions, text on urban furniture, and so on. Private texts offer either commercial or non-profit information that does not depend on official policy. In this domain, we can find shops, offices, banks, markets, bars, restaurants, posters, graffiti, etc.

So far there are only a handful of studies that have dealt with the linguistic landscape in Galicia. Dunlevy (2010) compared the linguistic landscape of an urban area (A Coruña) and a rural one (Cee), López Docampo (2011) analysed the linguistic landscape of several streets in the city of Pontevedra. Likewise, Kakihara (2013) and Wellings (2013) focused their work on the linguistic landscape of Santiago de Compostela and Mosquera Castro and Wellings (2014) have studied the spread of linguistic strategies typical of social networks to the linguistic landscape of Galicia.

Despite the fact that many studies on linguistic landscape around the world have been carried out, this kind of research is still in its infancy, and that shows clearly when methodological issues need to be addressed. There is not a strictly defined set of methodological procedures yet, but several different ways of gathering data and defining the key concepts (such as what counts as an 'item' for the purpose of sampling) exist at the moment.

When dealing with the linguistic landscape of a city like Vigo, there is a key categorization that we deem very relevant to make sense of the use of languages in public signs (mainly Galician and Castilian, but also foreign languages), and that is the distinction between 'top-down' and 'bottom-up' signs. 'Top-down' signs are those placed by official institutions such as the government or other public bodies, while 'bottom-up' signs are those placed by private organizations or individuals. This distinction is especially important in polities where there is more than one official language because differences might be perceived in the use of language by public institutions on the one hand, which are supposed to obey more closely the principles of official language policy, and private companies and individuals on the other, which may tend to use language following criteria different from those of the official language policy.

Methodology

In order to analyse the linguistic landscape in Vigo two different types of observation were made, one of a quantitative type and the other of a qualitative type. The quantitative study was carried out in one of the main commercial streets of the city, the Rúa do Príncipe. We consider it as one of the most representative streets of the town to study its linguistic landscape because of its important commercial activity and also because it is one of the busiest streets in the city centre. For our study we took more than 1000 pictures that captured exhaustively all the signs that contained any written message. The pictures were taken between the months of December 2011 and January 2012. A first selection was made to rule out those pictures that only contained signs with commercial brands, due to the difficulty of assigning a specific language to most of them. After having ruled out those pictures, 400 were randomly chosen among all the units of analysis of the remaining sample. These 400 pictures make up our final sample for this study. The criterion followed in order to delimit the units of analysis was to consider as a unit every sign that had a clear-cut physical boundary.

In addition to this, we carried out the qualitative study by choosing several buildings of public institutions that we deem representative of the type of linguistic landscape referred to as 'top-down', in contrast to the 'bottom-up' landscape predominantly found in the Rúa do Príncipe. In these buildings we took a lower number of pictures, focusing primarily on some of the most visible signs. These signs allow us to determine which kind of language policy is followed by each institution.

Analysis of the quantitative observation

Out of the 400 items in our sample, 369 are monolingual, 22 are bilingual and 9 are multilingual. Regarding monolinguals (see Table 3.6) the absolute superiority of Castilian language signs must be highlighted (283 items, 77% of monolingual signs), while there are 34 written in Galician (9%). See Figure 3.1 for an example in each language.

Considering that Galician and Castilian are very similar formally, some signs with few words or short sentences are ambiguous and make it impossible to determine in which of the two languages the message is written (see Figure 3.2). The number of monolingual ambiguous signs is 43 (12% of monolingual items). The rest of the monolingual signs are in English (9 items, 2%).

Table 3.6 Distribution of monolingual items according to language

Language of monolingual items	No. of items	%
Castilian	283	77
Ambiguous (Gal./Cast.)	43	12
Galician	34	9
English	9	2
Total	369	100

60 Urban Diversities and Language Policies

Figure 3.1 Monolingual signs in Castilian (left) and Galician (right)

Even though Galicia is an officially bilingual region, it is quite uncommon to see this fact reflected in the linguistic landscape, as can be deduced when one observes that only 5.5% of the signs in the sample are bilingual. Even more striking in this case is the fact that in half of those bilingual signs, the language pair present is Castilian-English, without necessarily being the

Figure 3.2 Ambiguous monolingual sign (Galician or Castilian)

Figure 3.3 Bilingual sign in English and Castilian with the languages in complementary distribution

text in one language the translation of the text in the other language. On the contrary, the languages often appear in complementary distribution, as shown in Figure 3.3.

It is important to note the presence of signs that express their message in more than two languages (the so called 'multilingual signs', see Figure 3.4). Despite their low numbers, some are particularly flashy because of the large number of languages in which the message is displayed.

Another noteworthy aspect of the linguistic landscape in an officially bilingual town as Vigo is the distribution of languages depending on the source of the sign (see Table 3.7). Since the Rúa do Príncipe is a predominantly commercial street, 97% of signs of our sample are of the 'bottom-up' type, of which 73% use Spanish as the only language of the message. In fact, all monolingual signs in Spanish in our sample are 'bottom-up'. However, in the remaining 3% that can be described as 'top-down' (mainly signs placed by the city council), 75% are exclusively in Galician. In this case, the signs reflect the official language policy followed by the municipal government, in which Galician takes precedence over Spanish or other languages.

Analysis of the qualitative observation

In order to carry out the analysis of the linguistic landscape displayed in the buildings of official institutions, hence of the 'top-down' type, we chose the central office of some institutions that operate at national level (National Police, Post Office, tax office, courts of law and the port authority), and

Figure 3.4 Multilingual sign in seven languages (from top to bottom: Italian, French, Castilian, Portuguese, Catalan, Basque and Galician)

Table 3.7 Distribution of languages according to item typology

	Top-down	Bottom-up
Castilian	0	283 (73%)
Ambiguous (Gal./Cast.)	2 (17%)	41 (11%)
Galician	9 (75%)	25 (6%)
Bilingual/Multilingual	1 (8%)	30 (8%)
English	0	9 (2%)
Total	12 (3%)	388 (97%)

others that operate at a regional and local level (regional, provincial and municipal governments).

Following the observation of the signs found in these institutions we have elaborated a model that describes the four types of language management adopted by these institutions:

- Predominantly Galician: Although with exceptions, this is the most common type in the institutions that operate at regional (i.e. Galician)

level. Both the regional government (Xunta de Galicia) and the municipal government use Galician in public signs almost exclusively. The observation of the local council is consistent with the data obtained in the qualitative study in the Rúa do Príncipe.
- Bilingual: The systematicity in the display of bilingual signs is only present in institutions that operate at national level, although not in all of them. This is the model used mainly by the post office and the tax office.
- Asystematicity: With this term we refer to the sometimes chaotic use of the two official languages, without being able to ascertain which linguistic model is followed by these institutions. It is the case of the provincial government and the courts of law.
- Predominantly Castilian: It is found exclusively in national-level institutions such as the National Police or the port authority.

In order to interpret the data and to assess what are the sociolinguistic causes and consequences of the distribution of languages in the linguistic landscape in Vigo, or in any other urban space for that matter, we need to ask the following question: what is the meaning and value of the linguistic landscape in a particular area for the recovery of a minority language? The answer can be two-fold: on the one hand, the increased visibility of a minority language is a sign of a new empowerment for its speakers, as well as a more or less explicit recognition of the symbolic value it has in its particular society. On the other hand, though, there exists the risk of creating a gap between the visual presence of the language in public spaces and its purported spoken use, which may lead to a perceived ritualization in the use of language and thus to a sense of 'unnaturalness' or 'artificiality'. This is exactly what has happened in Galician urban areas in the last decades. The presence of the language in its written form in public spaces has not gone hand in hand with its vitality as a spoken language.

In any case, this can be said of all languages present in any linguistic landscape. The relative distribution of languages in the LL does not necessarily match their spoken use for reasons that have to do with the different functions that spoken and written language have in society. Policymakers should be well aware of this when designing language policies in favour of minority languages: an increase in the visual written presence of a minority language does not necessarily go parallel to an increase in its spoken use because of the different symbolic value of a written language and that of its spoken counterpart.

In the last decades, the linguistic landscape of Vigo has changed. While at the end of the 1970s the visibility of written Galician was very sparse, at present it has strengthened its position, at least in the regional and local institutions. In contrast with other European cities of comparable size, the impact of immigration in the linguistic landscape is still relatively low.

Conclusions

Globalization transforms everything; from politics to the environment, from economy to culture, from *global* issues to local ones. And of course, it transforms (and is transformed by) discourse. Amongst its many implications for communicative practices, language and discourse, globalization has contributed to the rapid change of the sociolinguistic, demographic and cultural order in most countries, particularly in the cities. Thus, in the last few years, many things have changed in urban areas around the world as a consequence of globalization's current stage of development, as the hegemonic form of capitalism. In just a few decades, transformations have been dramatic. In sociolinguistic, demographic and cultural terms, the cities at the beginning of the 21st century do not have much in common with those in the middle of the 20th century.

Over the years, the revitalization of Galician has been associated with a set of different social values ranging from a specific political and national allegiance to a commitment to linguistic and cultural diversity, as well as a sense of cultural closeness in times of globalization. We can also observe how Galician has been progressively commodified by taking advantage of the aforementioned values and putting them to the service of consumerism and capitalism.

However, the commodification of language does not only apply to the written mode. Spoken language takes part in the same processes as written language, and thus it could be argued that one of the ways (but of course not the only one) to revitalize a minoritized language is to increase its economic value, considering the importance of this process of commodification of languages in late capitalism.

Even if Galicia can be considered a peripheral area, not only in geographic but also in socioeconomic terms, it is not alien to these globalizing processes, particularly in an urban environment such as Vigo. The growing visibility of multilingualism, including those languages deemed as 'foreign' as well as Galician, bears witness to that. Not only the big European or other immigrant languages are products of this increase in global interrelationships, but also the increase of the prestige and visibility of the Galician language can be considered as the *local* result of a *global* process of revitalization of minority languages.

Note

(1) Data come from the specific module on language contained in the *Enquisa de Condicións de Vida das Familias* conducted by the Galician Statistics Institute (IGE) in 2003 and 2008. This is a periodic survey carried out every five years. The number of respondents in 2008 totalled 27,542 (IGE 2008), of which 2263 lived in Vigo. Technical details of the methodology and sample design can be found at: http://www.ige.eu/estatico/pdfs/s3/metodoloxias/met_ecv_2009_ga.pdf. The questionnaire is available

at: http://www.ige.eu/estatico/pdfs/s3/cuestionarios/Cuestionario_galego_2008.pdf. The only sociolinguistic survey exclusively designed for the population of Vigo was conducted a decade ago (Vaamonde Liste, 2003). Given its methodological differences, in this description we will not use the results of that research. However, we recommend reviewing the detailed analysis of the different districts of the city.

References

Aronin, L. and Singleton, D. (2012) *Multilingualism*. Amsterdam: John Benjamins.
Backhaus, P. (2007) *Linguistic Landscapes. A Comparative Study of Urban Multilingualism in Tokyo*. Clevedon: Multilingual Matters.
Blackledge, A. and Creese, A. (2010) *Multilingualism: A Critical Perspective*. London: Continuum.
Block, D. (2006) *Multilingual Identities in a Global City. London Stories*. Basingstoke: Palgrave Macmillan.
Blommaert, J. (2010) *The Sociolinguistics of Globalization*. Cambridge: Cambridge University Press.
Borobio Sanchiz, M. and Vázquez Mao, X.F. (eds) (2011) *Sustentabilidade da Eurorrexión Galicia-Norte de Portugal 2011* [Sustainability of the Galicia-North Portugal Euroregion 2011]. Santiago de Compostela: Eixo Atlántico.
Coupland, N. (ed.) (2011) *The Handbook of Language and Globalization*. Malden, MA and Oxford: Wiley-Blackwell.
Dunlevy, D.A. (2010) A sign of the times: Language contact in the Galician linguistic landscape. M. Phil. Thesis, Trinity College Dublin.
Ellis, E.M. (2008) Defining and investigating monolingualism. *Sociolinguistic Studies* 2 (3), 311–330.
Extra, G. and Yagmur, K. (eds) (2004) *Urban Multilingualism in Europe: Immigrant Minority Language at Home and School*. Clevedon: Multilingual Matters.
Freitas Juvino, M.P. (2008) *A represión lingüística em Galiza no século XX*. [Linguistic repression in Galicia in the 20th century]. Vigo: Xerais.
García, O. and Fishman, J.A. (eds) (2002) *The Multilingual Apple. Languages in New York* (2nd edn). Berlin: Mouton de Gruyter.
González González, M. (dir) (2011) *Mapa sociolingüístico de Galicia 2004. Volume III. Actitudes lingüísticas en Galicia*. [Sociolinguistic map of Galicia 2004. Volume III. Language Attitudes in Galicia]. A Coruña: Real Academia Galega.
Gorter, D. (ed.) (2006) *Linguistic Landscape. A New Approach to Multilingualism*. Clevedon: Multilingual Matters.
Gorter, D., Marten, H.F. and van Mensel, L. (eds) (2012) *Minority Languages in the Linguistic Landscape*. Basingstoke: Palgrave Macmillan.
Instituto Galego de Estatística (2003) *Enquisa de condicións de vida das familias. Módulo de Lingua galega*. [Survey on living conditions of families. Galician language module]. Santiago: Instituto Galego de Estatística.
Instituto Galego de Estatística (2013) *Enquisa de condicións de vida das familias. Módulo de Lingua galega*. [Survey on living conditions of families. Galician language module]. Santiago: Instituto Galego de Estatística.
Jaworski, A. and Thurlow, C. (eds) (2010) *Semiotic Landscapes*. London: Continuum.
Kakihara, T. (2013) O uso lingüístico no ámbito comercial reflectido na paisaxe lingüística no centro de Santiago de Compostela. [Language use in business reflected in the linguistic landscape in the centre of Santiago de Compostela]. *Cadernos de Lingua* 35, 39–65.
Landry, R. and Bourhis, R.Y. (1997) Linguistic landscape and ethnolinguistic vitality: An empirical study. *Journal of Language and Social Psychology* 16 (1), 23–49.

López Docampo, M. (2011) A paisaxe lingüística: unha análise dun espazo público galego. [Linguistic landscape: An analysis of a Galician public space]. *Cadernos de Lingua* 33, 5–35.
Mosquera Castro, E. and Wellings, M.P. (2014) Os códigos lingüísticos da rede e a paisaxe lingüística galega. [Online linguistic codes and the Galician linguistic landscape]. *Estudos de Lingüística Galega*, 6, 173–197.
Moyer, M.G. and Martín Rojo, L. (2007) Language migration and citizenship: New challenges in the regulation of bilingualism. In M. Heller (ed.) *Bilingualism: Social Approaches* (pp. 137–160). New York: Palgrave Macmillan.
Observatorio da Cultura Galega (2012) *A(s) lingua(s) a debate. Inquérito sobre opinións, actitudes e expectativas da sociedade galega*. [*Debating language(s). Survey on opinions, attitudes and expectations of Galician society*]. Santiago de Compostela: Consello da Cultura Galega.
O'Rourke, B. and Ramallo, F. (2011) The native-non-native dichotomy in minority language contexts: Comparisons between Irish and Galician. *Language Problems and Language Planning* 35 (2), 139–159.
O'Rourke, B. and Ramallo, F. (2013) Competing ideologies of linguistic authority amongst *new speakers* in contemporary Galicia. *Language in Society* 42 (3), 287–305.
Ramallo, F. (2012) *Vigo cidade Babel. O Verbum da diversidade lingüística* (DVD). [*Vigo Babel City. The verbum of language diversity*]. Vigo: Concello de Vigo.
Shohamy, E. and Gorter, D. (eds) (2009) *Linguistic Landscape. Expanding the Scenery*. New York: Routledge.
Shohamy, E., Ben-Rafael, E. and Barni, M. (eds) (2010) *Linguistic Landscape in the City*. Bristol: Multilingual Matters.
Spanish Statistical Office (2014) *Municipal Register*. Madrid: Spanish Statistical Office.
Vaamonde Liste, A. (coord.) (2003) *Estudio sociolingüístico sobre o uso da lingua galega no Concello de Vigo 2002*. [Sociolinguistic study on the use of Galician in the city of Vigo 2002]. Vigo: Concello de Vigo.
Vertovec, S. (2007) Super-diversity and its implications. *Ethnic and Racial Studies* 29 (6), 1024–1054.
Wellings, M. (2013) Un estudo da paisaxe lingüística en Santiago de Compostela. [A study on the linguistic landscape of Santiago de Compostela]. *Cadernos de Lingua* 35, 5–37.
Williams, G. (2005) *Sustaining Language Diversity in Europe. Evidence from the Euromosaic Project*. Basingstoke: Palgrave Macmillan.

4 Helsinki as a Multilingual City

Pirkko Nuolijärvi

Summary

During the past decades Helsinki, officially the bilingual capital city of Finland, has been steadily turning multilingual. Around 12% of the inhabitants living in the city had mother tongues other than Finnish or Swedish in 2013. As a background, this chapter gives a brief overview of the language legislation in Finland and the country as a linguistic environment. The main part of the chapter concerns the linguistic repertoire in Helsinki, the multilingual image and public services, language education at schools and in universities and the use of languages in the private sector. In addition, this chapter discusses what activities will be necessary to protect the official and minority languages in order to support multilingualism and language skills in the future.

1. Introduction

Helsinki is situated on the southern coast of Finland (Figure 4.1). It was founded by decree of King Gustav Vasa of Sweden in 1550. For a long time, Helsinki was a small Swedish-speaking town but, gradually, it grew and became more and more bilingual with Finnish and Swedish speakers, especially in the 19th century.

Helsinki has been Finland's capital since 1812, three years after Finland became an autonomous Grand Duchy of the Russian Empire. Today, Helsinki is the centre of the Helsinki Region, a functional urban region of about 1.3 million inhabitants and 738,000 jobs, and the centre of the Metropolitan Area, including the nearby cities, Espoo, Vantaa, and Kauniainen (Figure 4.2). The cities, with their many differences and similarities, work in close cooperation.

This chapter concentrates on the capital Helsinki as a multilingual city. The official bilingualism in Helsinki and other bilingual municipalities in Finland can only be understood by considering key events in Finland's history.

68 Urban Diversities and Language Policies

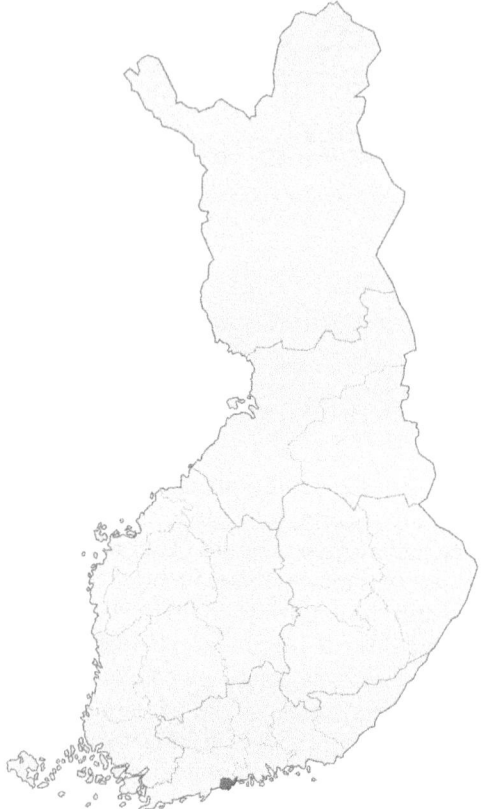

Figure 4.1 Helsinki situated on the southern coast of Finland

Therefore, this chapter briefly touches upon the history and use of Finnish and Swedish over the centuries, as well as on the language legislation and language diversity found in Finland today. Then, it moves on to describe Helsinki as a linguistic environment, presenting its linguistic repertoire, examining the linguistic reality that characterizes education, research, and higher education contexts, business, as well as the public image and services.

2. Finland as a Linguistic Environment

There are three main stages in Finland's political history: a period of Scandinavian hegemony and union with Sweden prior to 1809, a period of partial autonomy under Tsarist Russian rule from 1809 to 1917, and a period of independence since 1917 (McRae, 1999). A fourth period began in 1995, when the country became a member state of the European Union.

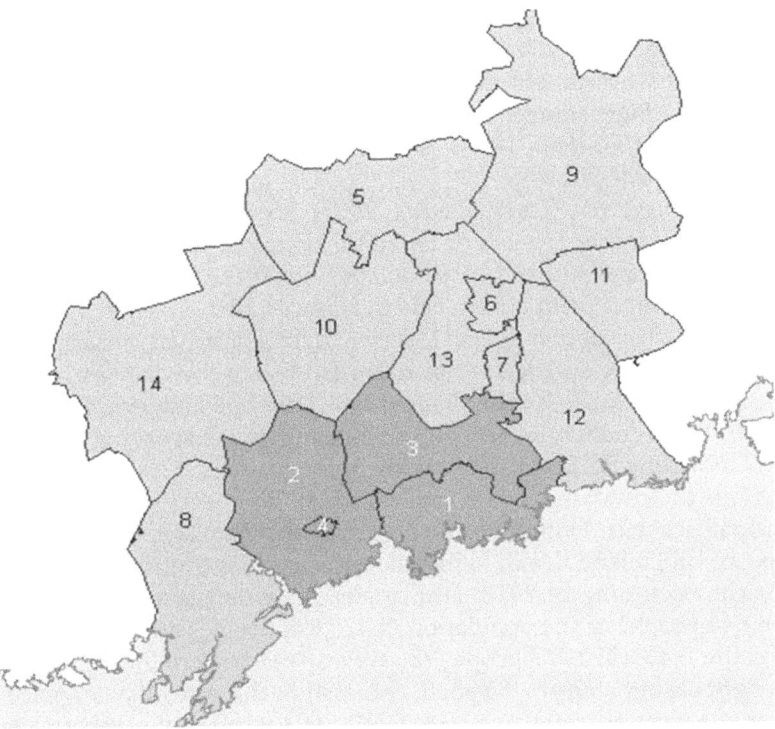

Figure 4.2 The Helsinki Region (light grey) and the Helsinki Metropolitan Area (dark grey, 1 = Helsinki) on the southern coast of Finland

In the Middle Ages, the areas of today's Finland were gradually absorbed by the Swedish realm, and the south-west coast was populated by Swedes, while Finns (i.e. people speaking a Finno-Ugrian language) were spread across the rest of country. As the Swedish State became more centralized during the 1500s, Swedish increasingly became the leading language for official use and the language of the educated élite. Conversely, Finnish was used by the Church (Vikør, 2000) and was the first language of the majority of people.

After the 1808–1809 war between Sweden and Russia, Sweden lost the area of Finland to Russia. The first emperors of Russia were relatively liberal, allowing Finns a high degree of autonomy, and they did not change the linguistic situation. Thus, Swedish remained the official standard language of the country and its status was strong. However, in 1863, Finnish was officially put on an equal footing with Swedish, and as a result it expanded steadily (Vikør, 2000). When Finland became independent in 1917, Finnish also acquired the status of a standard language.

Finland today is one of the five Nordic countries and a member state of the European Union. Finland is officially recognized as a bilingual country with two national languages, Finnish and Swedish. Finnish and Swedish are official languages not only in Finland, but also in the EU (European Union, 2014), and the Government must provide for the cultural and social needs of the country's Finnish and Swedish-speaking population on equal terms (Constitution of Finland, 1999). As a result, Swedish remains a co-official language alongside Finnish.

The Language Act (Language Act, 2003) states that a Finnish citizen is entitled to use either Finnish or Swedish in courts of law and in dealings with other national authorities. In practice, what the law requires concerning language will depend on local circumstances, that is, whether a municipality is monolingual or bilingual (Section 5). In a bilingual municipality like Helsinki, people are entitled to use either Finnish or Swedish with the local authorities, whereas in a monolingual one, only one language can be used. As of 2014, the country has 287 monolingual Finnish-speaking municipalities, 19 monolingual Swedish-speaking municipalities, 12 bilingual municipalities with Swedish as the predominant language, and 18 bilingual municipalities with Finnish as the predominant language. Overall, 1.5 million people in Finland live in bilingual municipalities (Kuntaliitto, 2014).

At the beginning of 2013, Finnish-speaking people account for 89.7% (4,866,848 people) of the population (5,426,674 people), and Swedish speakers account 5.4% (290,977 people) (Statistical Yearbook of Finland, 2013). In the neighbouring country Sweden, Swedish is the majority language and Finnish the minority language (specifically, in a number of northern, central and western municipalities). The rest of the people in Finland (4.9%) speak languages other than Finnish or Swedish as their first language (Statistical Yearbook of Finland, 2013: 112).

As regards the linguistic situation in Helsinki and in Finland as a whole, it is important to stress that neither the majority language, Finnish nor Swedish is a worldwide language. This is an important factor that also influences everyday life in Helsinki, especially in higher education, research and business. Thus, in addition to the national languages, English, particularly, is an essential language for many working people. The Government and companies have to take into account the need not only for English but also for other languages that are widely used both in Helsinki and throughout the country. Moreover, although Helsinki is officially bilingual it is, in practice, multilingual and 12.2% (2013) of the city's inhabitants have a language other than Finnish or Swedish as their mother tongue (cf. Table 4.2).

Today, the majority of Finns (over 60%) live in the south-western urbanized areas of Finland and in other large cities. The speakers of Swedish live along the southern and western coasts, and in Åland. As mentioned above, it is especially the southern coastal area, including Helsinki and other nearby cities, which is largely bilingual, with Finnish as the predominant language.

Traditionally, the languages in Finland besides Finnish and Swedish have been three Sámi languages, Finnish Romani, and the Finnish and Swedish Sign Languages. Especially since the 19th century there have also been speakers of Russian and Tatar, notably in Helsinki, as well as other languages, including Estonian and German (for the traditional Finnish minorities, see, for example, Myntti & Nuolijärvi, 2006). During the past two decades in particular, members of language groups not previously represented in Finland, especially from Africa and Asia, have been moving to Finland. These groups are, however, small when compared, for example, with those found in the other Nordic countries.

It should be clear from the above that the linguistic map of Finland has undergone a number of interesting changes over the past few decades. Steadily the number of speakers of different languages has increased, and according to official statistics as many as 150 languages are now spoken in Finland. Figures for 1 January 2013 show that the ten most widely used first languages (according to the number of speakers) were Finnish, Swedish, Russian, Estonian, Somali, English, Arabic, Kurdish, Chinese and Albanian (Table 4.1).

In Finland's Population Register a person can only report one language. Many bilingual families, as well as many linguists, have asked whether it would be possible to report two first languages, e.g. languages used at home, but such a change has not yet been introduced. At present, many bilingual families with Finnish and Swedish register their children as having Swedish as their first language. A further point is that there are more and more people who are fluent from an early age in two languages, and who also have a good command of either the majority language Finnish, or the second national language Swedish. In Helsinki in particular, this is very common. Thus, the statistics only offer a partial view of what a multilingual environment is. As Extra points out in Chapter 1 in this volume, Finland only registers mother tongue and religion, but not ethnicity or variation in language use.

3. Linguistic Repertoire of Helsinki

As mentioned in the introduction, Helsinki has been the capital of Finland since 1812, during which time it has developed from a small Swedish-speaking town into a bilingual capital city in which both Finnish and Swedish are used officially. In addition, Helsinki is today the most multilingual environment in Finland. This shift is a result both of Helsinki becoming the centre of power in Finland and the subsequent urbanization of what is now the metropolitan area (Nordberg, 1994; Paunonen, 1994).

In 2013, the City of Helsinki had a population of 603,968 people, and up to 1.3 million when the whole metropolitan area was taken into account (figures for 1 January 2013, Table 4.2). Finnish was the first language for the

Table 4.1 The 25 largest language groups in Finland, as of 1 January 2013

Language	n	%
Finnish	4,866,848	89.7
Swedish	290,977	5.4
Russian	62,554	1.2
Estonian	38,364	0.7
Somali	14,769	0.3
English	14,666	0.3
Arabic	12,042	0.2
Kurdish	9280	0.2
Chinese	8820	0.2
Albanian	7760	0.1
Thai	6926	0.1
Vietnamese	6549	0.1
Persian	6422	0.1
Turkish	6097	0.1
German	5792	0.1
Spanish	5470	0.1
Polish	3598	0.1
French	3333	0.1
Hungarian	2316	0.04
Romanian	2233	0.04
Bengali	2195	0.04
Italian	1961	0.04
Portuguese	1921	0.04
Bosnian	1895	0.04
Tagalog	1871	0.04
Other languages	40,115	0.7
Total	**5,426,674**	**100.0**

Source: Statistical Yearbook of Finland (2013).

majority of people (81.9%), whereas Swedish native speakers represented 5.9%, and people having other first languages 12.2% (Statistical Yearbook of Helsinki, 2013: 38). Ever since 2007, Helsinki has had a larger international than national (from the rest of Finland outside the Helsinki Region) net migration gain, whereas the gain from the rest of Finland has remained fairly stable over these past few years (Helsinki by District, 2013: 19). Helsinki resembles the capital cities Copenhagen and Brussels that also house more than 10% of their respective national populations (City Mayors Statistics, 2013).

Table 4.2 The 20 largest language groups in Helsinki 1 January 2013

Language	n	%
Finnish	494,627	81.9
Swedish	35,674	5.9
Russian	15,341	2.5
Estonian	10,207	1.7
Somali	7193	1.2
English	4879	0.8
Arabic	3446	0.6
Chinese	2691	0.5
Kurdish	2264	0.4
Spanish	2073	0.4
German	1665	0.3
French	1462	0.2
Persian	1457	0.2
Vietnamese	1416	0.2
Turkish	1408	0.2
Thai	1123	0.2
Albanian	1005	0.2
Bengali	939	0.2
Nepali	768	0.1
Italian	746	0.1
Other languages	13,584	2.2
Total	**603,968**	**100.0**

Source: Statistical Yearbook of Helsinki (2013: 38).

As a result of immigration, the language landscape in Helsinki and across its metropolitan area has changed. Over the past 30 years the number of people speaking languages other than Finnish or Swedish has increased in the region as a whole, although this change has been most evident in Helsinki. The number of foreign residents in Helsinki has also grown rapidly since the early 1990s for a number of reasons. At that point, the largest group consisted of citizens of the former Soviet Union, mostly Ingrians (Finnish-speaking Russian citizens who lived near St. Petersburg) who, in 1990, had been granted the status of returning emigrants and who subsequently moved to Finland in their thousands. Around the same time, however, considerable numbers of refugees also arrived from Somalia, and in 1993 and 1994 many people from the former Yugoslavia found refuge in Finland.

The growing number of foreigners in Finland is also a consequence of internationalization, accelerated by Finland's EU membership in 1995. After the rapid growth in the early 1990s, the number of foreigners arriving in

Helsinki, its urban region and in Finland generally, has decreased. This slowdown can partly be explained by an increase in the number of foreigners receiving Finnish citizenship (Nyholm & Selander, 2009) and by an increase of foreigners in other towns. The number of foreign citizens is still rather low in Helsinki, about 50,600 (8.4%), as compared with other urban regions of Europe.

Around 18,400 citizens from EU countries lived in Helsinki in 2013, and more than a half of them (9700) were Estonians. During the past years the number of British, Spanish and German citizens has increased, and the numbers of Latvian, Bulgarian, Romanian and Hungarian citizens have increased even faster. The share of Russian citizens and citizens of African and Asian countries has increased all the time (*Helsingin tila ja kehitys – The state and development of Helsinki,* 2013: 28).

As mentioned above, more than 12%, around 73,000 people, of Helsinki's entire population have a mother tongue other than Finnish or Swedish (Table 4.2). The most widely spoken first language (after Finnish and Swedish) is Russian, with 15,341 native speakers. The next two largest groups are Estonian and Somali. These three groups account for around 44% of native speakers of other languages than Finnish or Swedish in Helsinki. Although immigrant groups are not concentrated in one part of the city, there are more immigrants and their families in eastern than in western Helsinki.

It should be clear from the above that Helsinki and the whole metropolitan area is becoming increasingly multilingual and that it is also more multilingual than the many other cities or areas in Finland. This means that using more than one language every day is a way of life for a number of children in Helsinki, Espoo and Vantaa, in the cities of the metropolitan area, just as in many other larger European cities (cf. Extra, Chapter 1 in this volume). At the end of 2013, in Helsinki 12.8% of the inhabitants had other mother tongues than Finnish or Swedish, in the second largest city Espoo the share was 12.3%. In Vantaa, 13.2% of the inhabitants had other mother tongues than Finnish or Swedish (Statistics Finland, 2014). Hence, the linguistic landscape in the Helsinki metropolitan area changes rapidly.

4. Multilingual Image and Services in the Public Domain of Helsinki

During the past century, the proportion of Swedish-speaking people in Helsinki has decreased from 50% to 5.9%, due to the rapidly increasing migration of Finnish-speaking people from other parts of Finland to Helsinki (Reuter, 2006). Hence, the urbanization of Finland has changed the environment of Swedish-speaking people in Helsinki, even though the absolute number of Swedish-speaking people has not decreased. However, as a minority in Helsinki, Swedish-speaking people are worried about losing the option of obtaining services in their own language. Yet, the Swedish environment is still lively, with schools, theatres and other cultural activities, literature, newspapers, etc.

The authorities of the State and bilingual municipalities are obliged by law to offer their services in both Finnish and Swedish. According to the Government, the application of language legislation and the competence of the authorities to implement linguistic rights should be clarified as part of existing monitoring tools, such as the evaluation of basic municipal services, as well as by means of other clarifications (Ministry of Justice, 2013).

Many municipalities evaluate their own operations. In particular, during the past few years larger bilingual municipalities have been monitoring and evaluating the practical implementation of language legislation at different handling stages of service chains. The metropolitan area (the officially bilingual cities Helsinki, Espoo, Vantaa and Kauniainen) has, *inter alia,* special self-evaluation guidelines relating to services in Swedish. For example, the functionality of certain social welfare and healthcare services has been evaluated. Over the past four years, the management and minority language board of the Hospital District of Helsinki and Uusimaa (HUS) has actively promoted the availability of services in both national languages. The minority language board has promoted cooperation to improve Swedish-speaking activities and has received complaints about linguistic service (Ministry of Justice, 2013).

The legislation does not, however, mean that all employees must master both languages. In practice, the authorities can act in the way they consider most appropriate with regard to their own duties. If, for instance, there are several service points, then different points can provide a service in different languages. This model has been used in Helsinki in relation to healthcare services. Another possibility is to organize work shifts and work distribution in such a way that employees mastering both languages are always available. Whichever the case, the service in Finnish and Swedish is usually offered at the same service point, although this will obviously depend on the models available.

The City of Helsinki offers information on its websites in Finnish, Swedish, English, German, French, Russian and Easy to Read. In addition, the Info Bank online service supports immigrant integration by providing information on Finnish society and its services in 15 languages. The Info Bank gathers basic information about permits, education and work, housing and social services, society, culture and leisure, and other issues (Infopankki, 2014). Virka Info is a public information service for Helsinki residents. The centre serves as a Citizens' Office and offers general information and advice on living and working in the Helsinki area, as well as special advice and guidance on immigration issues. Information is provided in Finnish, Swedish, English, French, German, Russian, Bulgarian, Arabic, Turkish, Kurdish and Somali.

The bilingual city of Helsinki offers a rich supply of art and culture. There are Finnish and Swedish theatres and small theatre groups, the National Opera, dance theatres, orchestras and museums. Cultural institutions publish their material in Finnish and Swedish, and also in English. The City Government publishes an online English version of its Annual Report, and the message from the Mayor is also given in German, French and Russian (City of Helsinki, 2013). Thus, rather than just two languages, there are three languages used in practice. And, of course, there are also brochures and leaflets available in many other languages, including German, French and Russian. Occasionally, some catalogues and brochures have been published in Finnish and English but not in Swedish. As a result, Swedish-speaking people in Helsinki sometimes have to ask for texts in their own language. This means that the reality of bilingual life is not always as well-organized as it could be.

Public transport has a positive image in Helsinki, and passengers on buses, trams and the metro are likely to hear the two national and other languages every day. Audio-visual displays are generally multilingual: you can hear many languages and see the street signs and other signs and instructions in Finnish and Swedish. As Finnish is the majority language in bilingual Helsinki, the Finnish signs always come before the Swedish ones, as follows:

Fabianinkatu
Fabiansgatan   ('Fabian Street')

Mannerheimintie
Mannerheimvägen   ('Mannerheim Street')

Kaupunginteatteri
Stadsteatern   ('The City Theatre')

Public libraries are the most popular cultural service in Finland, and the use and loaning of collections is free of charge. The largest collections in the Helsinki City Library are in Finnish and Swedish, but there are also good collections in worldwide languages, as well as in the minority languages used in Finland. Libraries have become more of a living room for visitors, especially when computers and wireless internet are available. Alongside the traditional library services and materials, libraries offer electronic material and web services which enable the remote use of libraries. Thus, the library is both a physical and a virtual space. In addition, libraries have become a meeting point for people from various cultural backgrounds living in the city. A good example is the Somali Book Fair, *Bandhigga Buugta Soomaaliyeed*, which has been held in Helsinki City Library since 2005.

Today, it is typical that new novels by Swedish authors are simultaneously published in Finnish. In fact, many authors are bilingual, a good example being Kjell Westö, who has written a number of novels about the history of Helsinki and its contemporary life. He is very popular among both the Finnish and Swedish-speaking population. There is a large number of novels about Helsinki, and the main library has a large collection of Helsinki books from various periods in many languages.

5. Language Education in Helsinki

5.1 Language landscape in Helsinki comprehensive schools

There are two main lines in the Finnish school system: Finnish municipalities offer schools for Finnish-speaking children and separate schools for Swedish-speaking children. For supporting the bilingualism in these languages, there are also several language immersion classes in Swedish in Helsinki. Immersion is offered at kindergarten level (ages 3–5), at preschool (age 6) and at primary levels (grades 1–9). The Finnish-speaking families are very interested in immersion programmes, and the demand for language immersion instruction is bigger than the city can offer. There are also language immersion day-care groups in English and Northern Sámi and classes in English in Helsinki.

Multiculturalism and multilingualism are a part of everyday life at schools in Helsinki. Schools support children of immigrant origin, helping them to integrate into both school and society. About 4000 children of immigrant origin study at comprehensive schools in Helsinki. The largest language groups at schools are Russian, Somali, Estonian, Arabic and Vietnamese. The number of native languages taught is about 40 (City of Helsinki, Education Department, 2014).

Many bilingual children study their mother tongue and literature, covering Finnish or Swedish as a second language. The objective of instruction is for pupils to be able to study efficiently in the Finnish language and to function in a Finnish linguistic community. Each school is responsible for assessing its pupils' needs for instruction in Finnish as a second language.

Basic education and learning materials are provided free of charge at all schools maintained by the City, at private contracting schools and at state-owned schools. Private special schools may charge enrolment and tuition fees (City of Helsinki, Education Department, 2014).

Upon completion of basic education, all young people have the opportunity to apply for further study. The task of the general upper secondary education is to provide extensive all-round learning and to continue the educational task of basic education. The objective is to offer sufficient skills and knowledge with a view to further study.

Every pupil has to learn, besides the mother tongue, at least two other languages in the comprehensive school in Finland. Mostly, these languages

78 Urban Diversities and Language Policies

are English and Swedish or Finnish (the two last mentioned ones are obligatory). The opportunities to learn several foreign languages are better in the capital region than in many smaller towns and villages. However, there is a lively ongoing debate on how to offer other languages than English earlier at school (cf. Suomen kielen tulevaisuus, 2009: 76–82).

There are more resources for language learning in the upper secondary school. All upper secondary school students follow their own personal study plans. The upper secondary school syllabus can be completed in 2–4 years. Towards the end of their studies, students may take the national matriculation examination. In addition, many young people study in vocational schools.

Certain schools and classes in Helsinki use English, Estonian, Chinese, German, French, Russian or Spanish as their language of instruction. These offer a choice of study programmes and international examinations for students of Finnish or foreign background. The foreign language schools in Helsinki are either privately run or maintained by or the State. In addition, some comprehensive schools maintained by the City of Helsinki offer special classes where the teaching is either bilingual or entirely in a foreign language. Students at schools using a foreign language of instruction can take an international school leaving examination in addition to or instead of the Finnish matriculation examination. The schools also offer a variety of separate language examinations (City of Helsinki, Education Department, 2014).

5.2 Higher education and research in Helsinki

In the Helsinki region the proportion of people with a higher education degree is higher than elsewhere in the country. The level of education is high: 68% of all inhabitants aged 15 and over have attained post-comprehensive level educational qualifications. In the Helsinki metropolitan area, 37% of all inhabitants aged 15 and over have tertiary level education. Helsinki also ranks high in the comparison between urban regions of Europe, and is second only to Oslo (39% of all inhabitants in Oslo have tertiary level education). Amsterdam and the Nordic urban regions, as well as Tallinn, Estonia and Vilnius, Lithuania, also have highly educated population (Statistics and Information Service, 2009).

Helsinki is a city of universities and research institutes. Indeed, the city and its environment provide a rich source of higher education. In 2014, there are five universities in the metropolitan area: Aalto University (including the three former independent universities: University of Art and Design Helsinki, Helsinki School of Economics and Helsinki University of Technology), Finnish National Defence University, Hanken School of Economics, University of Helsinki, and University of the Arts Helsinki (including former independent universities: The Finnish Academy of Fine Arts, Sibelius Academy and Theatre Academy Helsinki). Both the University of Helsinki and Aalto University are bilingual Finnish and Swedish institutions, while the Hanken School of Economics is a Swedish university.

There are also five polytechnics in Helsinki: the Arcada Polytechnic, the Haaga-Helia University of Applied Sciences, the HUMAK University of Applied Sciences, Laurea University of Applied Sciences and Metropolia University of Applied Sciences. Arcada is a Swedish polytechnic.

The Finnish universities, including the country's largest institution, the University of Helsinki, have published their language principles. According to the University of Helsinki Language Policy (Helsingin yliopiston kieliperiaatteet, 2007) the university maintains, encourages and supports an active bilingual environment. Because the University of Helsinki is the academic flagship of an officially bilingual society, bilingualism within the university community must be both omnipresent and functional, and teaching and learning must meet the requirements set by Finland's bilingual society and by legislation. The internationalization of teaching and research requires ongoing activity in foreign languages. According to the Language Policy, arranging teaching in English supports the educational targets set by the university without undermining the position of Finland's national languages.

Currently, and in spite of bilingual principles and language policy programmes, English is used in the universities and polytechnics very widely, both in tuition and, especially, in research. There are presently a number of Master's programmes in English at all the universities. In the natural sciences the whole course programme may be solely in English from the outset, even for Finnish and Swedish-speaking students. Thus, many students and teachers ask whether they still have the right to study and teach in their own language, and to develop scientific research in both Finnish and Swedish in Finland. In addition, foreign students are interested in learning Finnish in the Finnish environment.

The language policy in the University of Helsinki is not unique in the Nordic countries. According to Moring *et al.* (2013: 316–317), a similar policy can be found at the University of Tromsø in Norway, which is bilingual in Norwegian and Sámi, with English included as one of the main languages. Instead, the universities analysed in Sweden, Mälardalen University and Södertörn University, are more limited with only Swedish and English.

Most of the research institutes financed by the Finnish Government are located in Helsinki or the metropolitan area. These institutes cover a number of research areas, including health and welfare, the environment, forestry, technology and engineering, economics, consumption, judicial policy and languages. One of these institutes is the Institute for the Languages of Finland, located in the City Centre Campus of the University of Helsinki. The Institute's tasks include language planning and guidance, dictionary work as well as research into Finnish and Swedish. As a State organization, the Institute for the Languages of Finland is bilingual.

In many research areas the results are published solely in English, although researchers in the social sciences and arts publish in the national languages and in other languages. These researchers can be regarded as multilingual. Unfortunately, the scientific work and publications of many researchers in diverse areas suggest that they are presently monolingual in English. Hence, in recent decades, Helsinki, as a city of science and higher education, has become more English than ever before, as academic experts use English as their working language in research groups and give lectures only in English. This means that the role of Swedish has declined in research institutes and universities, and even the majority language, Finnish has lost some ground within the academic life. Therefore, as Moring *et al.* (2013: 319) point out, more attention should be paid to the continuous monitoring of higher education institutions and their members' capacity, opportunity and desire regarding the use of languages in the universities.

6. Private Sector: The Use of Finnish, Swedish and Other Languages in Business Communication in the Helsinki Region

Numerous Finnish multinational companies having their main offices in Helsinki metropolitan area, including Nokia, Kone and UPM, have adopted English as their corporate language or common working language. Although no actual language policy has been stated other than with an announcement of a general nature concerning the corporate language, the practice is to write all official texts in English and to provide all spoken information to owners and the international public in English. English is used increasingly at the headquarters of multinational companies located in Finland for official records, memoranda, internal reporting and other internal communication (Piekkari, 2007).

The use of English ensures that basic information concerning the company is available throughout the company, in all parts of the world, with the same content and at the same time. Documents of significance solely to Finnish employees and the Finnish markets are mainly written in Finnish. On the other hand, spoken communication is still often in Finnish: among Finnish employees and in meetings in units in Finland, Finnish (or Swedish) remains the primary language. If there are many employees with different language backgrounds from other countries at the workplace, English is used as the common language (see Nuolijärvi, 2010 and the literature cited in the article).

Although English is part of everyday life in companies that are international or are undergoing the process of internationalization, all companies need adequate proficiency in written and spoken Finnish and even other languages. The aim ought to be bilingual or multilingual speakers who maintain their national identity and who have the skills needed to communicate with non-natives (Virkkula, 2008). Thus, corporate internationalization obviously requires more than the use of English; it also requires spoken and written proficiency in either Finnish or Swedish, preferably in both. The more proficient in languages a company's employees are, the better and more reliably they will run the operations and attain success.

7. Discussion

In Finland the national languages Finnish and Swedish still have a strong status, although they have lost ground in the higher education and science contexts. The use of English has become more common in higher education and in universities and, as mentioned above, many researchers publish in English only. This is typical in environments like Helsinki.

People in Finland have always understood that it is necessary to use other languages in addition to their own mother tongues, and it is quite possible to live with two languages side by side, as people in bilingual environments have always done (for the Finnish situation, see Nuolijärvi, 2007). Today, the problem in academic settings like the Finnish universities, or in the Helsinki region as a whole, is not the use of English per se but, rather, the absence of people's own languages. This is especially true in the context of the natural sciences. Of course, these developments in Finland are not unique, and similar changes have occurred in universities in many other European countries.

In the light of the above there is a need for language strategies and good practices that can enable creative solutions in each environment. It is also necessary to analyse specifically how languages can be supported in multilingual circumstances, for example, Swedish in Helsinki or Finnish in the wider context of science and enterprise, as well as the minority languages at school or in other environments. This is not merely of symbolic importance, for it has to do with people's right to use their own national language in every domain. This issue is currently the subject of much discussion in Finland, especially in the academic world.

Another important aspect in a bilingual city and in its cultural institutions concerns the availability of material in two languages. In countries like Finland and in cities like Helsinki it is necessary to publish material in other languages, but without forgetting the native languages. It is nonetheless important to be sensitive to other languages and to support other language groups in the use and development of their own languages and culture.

In Finland today Finnish and Swedish have equal status officially. In practice, however, Swedish-speaking people often find it difficult to use their own language in every situation, even in Helsinki, because many people working in the service sector do not have a good command of Swedish.

Therefore, one might ask how the balance – if balance is the right word – could be maintained in the future. My own view, based on the situation in 2014, is that Finland is clearly not ready to become an officially monolingual country in the near future. Finnish society has been officially bilingual for a long time, and a shift towards monolingualism could be too great a leap. Furthermore, politicians and the majority of Finnish-speaking people are in favour of bilingualism, even if there are many people in Finland who never use Swedish. Hence, the wish to preserve bilingualism in Finland is not limited to the Swedish-speaking people but is shared by most of the Finnish-speaking majority. In fact, there are many historical, political and psychological reasons why Finnish society has been and will remain bilingual, even if the statistics suggest an imbalance.

The City of Helsinki and the whole region around the capital are not merely bilingual but multilingual. This poses many challenges to Finnish society both today and in the future. One of these challenges is how to enable immigrants to use and develop their own language and culture within the Finnish context. Fostering children's first language is essential for their learning and future. Therefore, it seems insufficient that children with other languages can only study their first language for two hours per week at school. Immigrants are by and large bilingual, but Finnish society has yet to find a way of maximizing this competence. Finnish or Swedish tuition is needed for adult immigrants, too, so that they can both adapt and maintain their own identity and, of course, get a job in Finland. In fact, therefore, the main challenges do not concern the situation of Swedish-speaking people or the extent to which Finnish has lost ground in academic life, but rather the emerging situation of minority groups. Even though Finnish society is pragmatic and forward thinking, and can organize many things very well, much remains to be done in relation to the multilingual life in Helsinki and across the country as a whole.

References

City Mayors Statistics (2013) A comparison of UK and European cities. Research by City Mayors, Eurostat and the UK Office for National Statistics. See http://www.citymayors.com/statistics/uk-european-cities.html (accessed 24 July 2014).

City of Helsinki (2013) Annual Report 2013. See http://www.hel.fi/wps/wcm (accessed 20 June 2014).

City of Helsinki, Education Department (2014) See http://www.hel.fi/hki/Opev/en/ (accessed 20 June 2014).

Constitution of Finland (1999) *Suomen perustuslaki/Finlands grundlag 731/1999*. See http://www.finlex.fi/en/laki/kaannokset/1999/en19990731.pdf (accessed 28 June 2014).

European Union (2014) *European Union Member Countries*. See http://europa.eu/about-eu/countries/member-countries/index_en (accessed 28 June 2014).

Helsingin tila ja kehitys (2013) [*The state and development of Helsinki 2013*]. City of Helsinki Urban Facts. See http://www.hel.fi/hel2/tietokeskus/julkaisut (accessed 28 June 2014).

Helsingin yliopiston kieliperiaatteet – Språkprinciper för Helsingfors universitet – University of Helsinki Language Policy (2007) Helsingin yliopisto. See http://www.helsinki.fi/strategia/index.html (accessed 20 June 2014).
Helsinki alueittain – Helsingfors områdesvis – Helsinki by District (2013) Helsingin kaupunki. Tietokeskus – Helsingfors stads faktacentral – City of Helsinki Urban Facts. See http://www.hel.fi/hel2/tietokeskus/julkaisut (accessed 30 June 2014).
Infopankki [Information Bank] (2014) See http://www.infopankki.fi/en/frontpage (accessed 28 June 2014).
Kuntaliitto [Local Finland] (2014) See http://www.kunnat.net/fi/kunnat (accessed 28 June 2014).
Language Act (2003) Kielilaki/Språklag 423/2003. See http://www.finlex.fi/en/laki/ kaannokset/2003/en (accessed 28 June 2014).
McRae, K.D. (1999) *Conflict and Compromise in Multilingual Societies. Finland.* Suomalaisen tiedeakatemian toimituksia, Annales Academiæ Scientiarum Fennicæ, Humaniora 306. Waterloo, Ontario: The Finnish Academy of Science and Letters and Wilfrid Laurier University Press.
Ministry of Justice (2013) Report of the Government on the application of language legislation 2013. See http://www.om.fi/en/Etusivu/Perussaannoksia/Kielilaki (accessed 20 June 2014).
Moring, T., Godenhjelm, S., Haapamäki, S., Lindström, J., Östman, J-O., Saari, M. and Sylvin, J. (2013) Language policies in universities and their outcomes. The University of Helsinki in an Northern European context. In A-C. Berthoud, F. Grin and G. Lüdi (eds) *Exploring the Dynamics of Multilingualism. The DYLAN Project.* Amsterdam: John Benjamins Publishing Company.
Myntti, K. and Nuolijärvi, P. (2006) The case of Finland. In S. Spiliopoulou Åkermark (ed.) *International Obligations and National Debates: Minorities around the Baltic Sea* (pp. 171–225). Mariehamn: The Åland Islands Peace Institute.
Nordberg, B. (1994) Introduction. In B. Nordberg (ed.) *The Sociolinguistics of Urbanization: The Case of the Nordic Countries* (pp. 1–15). Berlin & New York: Walter de Gruyter.
Nuolijärvi, P. (2007) Språken bredvid varandra – Kielet rinnakkain [Languages side by side]. In M. Nordman, S. Björklund, Chr. Laurén, K. Mård-Miettinen and N. Pilke (eds) *Förhandlingar vid Tjugonionde sammankomsten för svenskans beskrivning* [Negotiations at the Twenty-ninth meeting of the Swedish language description] (pp. 28–29). Vasa den 4 och 5 maj 2007. Skrifter utgivna av Svensk-Österbottniska samfundet 70. Vasa: Svensk-Österbottniska samfundet.
Nuolijärvi, P. (2010) Language in business and commerce in Finland. In G. Stickel (ed.) *Language Use in Business and Commerce in Europe.* Contribution to the Annual Conference 2008 of EFNIL in Lisbon. Duisburger-arbeiten zur Sprach- und Kulturwissenschaft. Duisburg Papers on Research in Language and Culture. Herausgegeben von Ulrich Ammon, René Dirven und Martin Pütz. Band 78. Peter Lang, Frankfurt am Main 2010, 91–104.
Nyholm, A.S. and Selander, P. (eds) (2009) *Foreigners in Helsinki 2009.* Statistics 2/2010. Helsinki: City of Helsinki Urban Facts.
Paunonen, H. (1994) The Finnish language in Helsinki. In B. Nordberg (ed.) *The Sociolinguistics of Urbanization: The Case of the Nordic Countries* (pp. 223–245). Berlin & New York: Walter de Gruyter.
Piekkari, R. (2007) Yhteisestä bisneskielestä voi olla niin hyötyä kuin haittaakin [A common business language can be both an advantage and a disadvantage]. *Helsingin Sanomat* 23.8.2007.
Reuter, M. (2006) Svenskan i Finland på 1900-talet [Swedish in Finland in the 20th century]. In A-M. Ivars, M. Reuter, P. Westerberg and U. Ådahl-Sundgren (eds) *Vårt bästa arv* [Our best inheritance] (pp. 29–45). Skrifter utgivna vid Svenska handelshögskolan Nr 165, Helsingfors: Svenska handelshögskolan.

Statistics and Information Service (2009) The State of Helsinki Region 2009 – European Comparisons. City of Helsinki Urban Facts. See http://www.hel2.fi/tietokeskus/eng/index.html (accessed 28 June 2014).
Statistics Finland (2014) See http://pxweb2.stat.fi/database/StatFin/vrm/vaerak/vaerak_fi.asp (accessed 30 June 2014).
Statistical Yearbook of Finland (2013) Helsinki: Statistics Finland.
Statistical Yearbook of Helsinki (2013) City of Helsinki Urban Facts. See http://www.hel.fi/hki/helsinki/en/news/statistical (accessed 28 June 2014).
Suomen kielen tulevaisuus. Kielipoliittinen toimintaohjelma [The future of Finnish language. Language policy programme] (2009) Kirjoittajat: A. Hakulinen, J. Kalliokoski, S. Kankaanpää, A. Kanner, K. Koskenniemi, L. Laitinen, S. Maamies and P. Nuolijärvi. Kotimaisten kielten tutkimuskeskuksen verkkojulkaisuja 7. See http://scripta.kotus.fi/www/verkkojulkaisut/julk7/ (accessed 28 June 2014).
Vikør, L.D. (2000) Northern Europe: Languages as prime markers of ethnic and national identity. In S. Barbour and C. Carmichael (eds) *Language and Nationalism in Europe* (pp. 105–129). Oxford: Oxford University Press.
Virkkula, T. (2008) Työntekijän kokemuksia englannista yritysmaailman yhteisenä kielenä [Experiences of an employee on English as a common language in the business world]. In S. Leppänen, T. Nikula and L. Kääntä (eds) *Kolmas kotimainen. Lähikuvia englannin käytöstä Suomessa* [*The third domestic language. A close-up view of the use of English in Finland*]. Tietolipas 224, 382–420. Helsinki: Suomalaisen Kirjallisuuden Seura.

5 Tallinn, a Multilingual City in the Era of Globalization: The Challenges Facing Estonian as a Medium-Sized Language

Josep Soler-Carbonell

Summary

This chapter[1] deals with the greatest challenges currently facing the Estonian language in Tallinn in this era of globalization. It starts by reviewing the macro-sociolinguistic figures that most clearly illustrate these challenges and then presents data gathered from in-depth interviews and focus group discussions with native speakers conducted at a language school in the city centre in 2008–2009. It examines these data through the prism of the language ideologies framework (Woolard, 1998), and, in particular, the conceptual divide between the ideological constructs 'authenticity' and 'anonymity' (Gal & Woolard, 2001; Woolard, 2008), arguing that these can help us understand the main challenges facing Estonian today.

In line with other contributions to this volume, this chapter also argues that these challenges are felt not only by speakers of the language under discussion here but by speakers of many of the so-called 'medium-sized' languages of independent nation-states. As one of these languages, Estonian enjoys some self-assurance and protection but its small number of speakers regularly needs to use another language to communicate in broader contexts and today that language tends to be English. The shift in Estonia from the one-time hegemony of Russian to the present, when English has become the language for international purposes, highlights one of the most common dilemmas faced by medium-sized languages. In Estonia, this is accentuated by the undeniable presence of a community whose L1 is Russian.

1. Introduction

This chapter argues that globalization is setting new challenges for Estonian as a medium-sized language and that these are particularly notable in the country's capital city, Tallinn. Throughout the chapter and as suggested by Blommaert (2010), the notion of 'language' will be considered in terms of 'linguistic resources' to help us understand the complexity of the current sociolinguistic climate, where Estonian has gained such 'currency' in the last two decades but where, at the same time, Russian continues to be spoken and is also increasingly valued not only by its L1 speakers but by others for whom it is not L1. In other words, the chapter will demonstrate that the 'renewed economic capital' (Bourdieu, 1991) of both Estonian and Russian is a consequence of the new economic, legal, social and ultimately sociolinguistic order that has increasingly dominated the country since its reattainment of independence in 1991. Another important sociolinguistic consideration in this chapter will be the growing role and impact of English as an inter-ethnic language and a challenge to the Estonian language community. It will be argued that, even though the presence of English might be construed as a challenge to the Estonians' ideological construct of 'authenticity' (Woolard, 2008), it is essentially consistent with that construct and may eventually help reinforce and maintain ethnolinguistic boundaries. All in all, the challenges encountered by Estonian in Tallinn as one of the so-called 'medium-sized languages' are very much locally grounded and case-specific and for these reasons the conclusions drawn at the end of the chapter are nothing if not tentative. Nevertheless, an effort will be made to extrapolate from the case at hand and consider what circumstances other examples of medium-sized language communities might share with speakers of Estonian, thus producing overarching observations on the challenges faced by such language communities.

Since 2009, a research group at the University of Barcelona's *Centre Universitari de Sociolingüística i Comunicació* (CUSC-UB) has studied medium-sized language communities of the post-industrial European continent, taking as its subject communities comprising between half a million or one million and 25 million speakers. The research suggests that a significant number of communities face the same challenges, which include their speakers' need to attain a relatively high degree of polyglotism and a balance between using their language and using other (dominant) languages employed to communicate in broader contexts and key domains. The CUSC-UB research has brought together experts on different language groups and compares their views on such subjects as language communities' legal and education systems and their use of the media (for details on the group's project and activities, see www.ub.edu/cusc/llenguesmitjanes; see also Vila i Moreno, 2012).

Since 1991, the discussion of language issues in Tallinn and Estonia has become increasingly accompanied by heated debate on such delicate issues as personal identity and belonging; and yet as local experts have noted (Verschik, 2005a, 2005b), there remain few written studies on this subject, especially from a micro-sociological point of view. In the last 20 years, political scientists, historians and sociologists have devoted ample attention to the key questions of citizenship and integration (Budryte, 2005; Chinn & Kaiser, 1996; Hallik *et al.*, 2006; Heidmets & Lauristin, 2002; Järve, 2002; Kolstoe, 1995; Kymlicka, 2000; Laitin, 1996, 1998, 2003; Pettai, V. 1998; Pettai, I. 2002; Poleshchuk, 2009a, 2009b; Shafir, 1995; Vetik, 2000, 2003; Vihalemm, 2009). The sociolinguists, however, have tended to lag behind: although a growing number of papers have been published in the same period, most do not focus on Tallinn and instead adopt a more general frame of reference; and very few use micro-sociolinguistic methodology (see, nevertheless, Verschik, 2007). There are, however, thorough accounts of the current sociolinguistic situation in the Baltic in general and Estonia in particular (e.g. Hogan-Brun *et al.*, 2007) and Rannut (2004) focuses on Estonia's language policy and planning. Moreover, we now know more about the Estonian people's language skills and attitudes and how these have changed since 1991; and we know that the number of people who claim to have no proficiency in Estonian has decreased and that, consequently, the number of those who now say they have greater knowledge of the language has increased (Lauristin *et al.*, 2011; Masso & Vihalemm, 2005). Finally, we also know that people's immediate language environment has considerable influence on their readiness to use one language or another: in those parts of the Estonia where there is a higher percentage of L1 speakers of Russian, Estonian is far less widely spoken; and where there is a higher percentage of L1 speakers of Estonian, the degree of incorporation of Russian is far lower (Ü. Rannut, 2003). Verschik (2007) observes that in the multilingual setting of Tallinn, L1 Russian speakers no longer aspire to monolingual communication in Russian; instead, a growing number attempt to use Estonian as their L2, inserting lexical items and pragmatic markers into their L1 speech and otherwise adopting features of Estonian in a manner which is 'unambiguously at odds with the Russian (monolingual) grammar' (Verschik, 2007: 90). In the last two decades, Estonian appears to have progressed as the language of choice in the public domain (Skerrett, 2012), especially in Tallinn. This trend is corroborated by the data presented below in Section 6 and the intentions of the chapter are therefore to engage with and build on the sociolinguistic research being undertaken.

2. Demographic Data

The report *Estonia's Population and Housing Census for 2011* (hereafter, PHC 2011) records that in 2011 there was a total of 1,294,236 permanent residents in Estonia comprising 192 ethnic nationalities. In that year, most of the population (889,770 or 68.74%) was Estonian, and the largest minority group (321,198 or 24.81%) was Russian. The remaining ethnic groups or nationalities were far less broadly represented (in descending order there were 22,302 Ukrainians, 12,149 Belarusians and 7423 Finns). The population of Tallinn on 1 January 2012 was 401,072, of which 222,814 people declared that they were Estonians and 145,149 declared that they were Russians.

Most of Estonia's inhabitants have Estonian citizenship and PHC 2011 recorded a total of 1,101,761 Estonian citizens living in the country (85.1%). However, there are two other main groups in the country: foreign citizens, who in PHC 2011 represented 8.1% of Estonia's permanent residents, and stateless persons, who accounted for 6.5%. Of those foreign-born residents, 89,913 had Russian citizenship (the majority), while far behind these came those with Ukrainian and Latvian citizenship (4707 and 1739 people respectively). Moreover, most foreign-born citizens were recorded as living in the urban areas of Harju County (where Tallinn is situated) and in Ida Viru County (on Estonia's northeastern border with Russia, in mainly Russophone cities such as Narva, Sillamäe and Kohtla-Järve). On the other hand, those who had Estonian citizenship mostly lived in rural areas and in Tartu County, with the city of Tartu as their centre (note that even if Tartu is only Estonia's second largest city, it is located in what remains a highly Estonianized language environment).

Finally, demographic data can also illustrate the relationship between people's citizenship and their place of birth. As the *Census for 2000* shows (and in the absence, for the time being, of similar figures for the current year), in 2000 most of the country's Estonian-born inhabitants held Estonian citizenship, while those who were Russian-born or had been born elsewhere were Russian citizens or stateless persons. Approximately 78% of those born abroad were citizens of the Russian Federation (of which 65% had been born in Russia itself). But interestingly enough, most of Estonia's stateless persons were born in Estonia and only one third were born in Russia. Finally, the *Census* showed, those born abroad who were Russian citizens or stateless persons also tended to live in urban areas.

3. Data from the Labour Market

Article 29 of the Estonian Constitution states that all Estonian citizens shall freely choose their profession and that foreign-born citizens and stateless persons shall have this right equally, unless otherwise provided by law. Note, however, that only Estonian and EU citizens can occupy certain professional positions (bailiff, patent agent, sea captain of a vessel flying the Estonian flag, harbourmaster, certified translator, and notary) and that data on the country's unemployment rate indicate that people whose ethnic origin is not Estonian are over-represented in all the age groups surveyed (Table 5.1).

Moreover, it would appear that neither mastery of the Estonian language nor possession of Estonian citizenship reduces these differences. Table 5.2 on

Table 5.1 Unemployment rates depending on age and ethnic origin, 1997–2007, %

Ethnic origin/Age group	1997	2001	2003	2004	2005	2006	2007
Estonians							
15–24		11.2	21.8	17.6	17.0	9.5	9.6	8.5
15–74		7.8	10.4	7.3	6.4	5.3	4.0	3.6
Non-Estonians							
15–24		21.2	22.9	26.0	30.9	29.4	18.5	13.7
15–74		13.2	16.8	15.2	15.6	12.9	9.7	6.9

Source: Estonian Labour Force Surveys (in Poleshchuk, 2009b: 97).

unemployment rates in the city of Tallinn illustrates the significant disparity between ethnic Estonians and non-Estonians in the period 2001–2006.

Citizens whose ethnic origin is not Estonian are also over-represented among those in the low-quality work force, especially in Tallinn (Table 5.3).

In the *Estonian Human Development Report 2008*, Lindemann and Saar's conclusions are consistent with the data presented above where they examine the possibilities for non-Estonians to occupy higher-ranking professional positions:

> It appears that non-Estonians have a much smaller probability of working on top positions than Estonians even if they have equal human capital, be this in the narrower or broader sense. [...] However, non-Estonians are only able to be competitive if the Estonians have lower levels of education. (Lindemann & Saar, 2009: 96)

The same authors are also critical of the 'human capital' variable, arguing that although poor knowledge of the country's official language and not

Table 5.2 Unemployment rate in Tallinn for people aged 15–74 depending on ethnic origin and other traits, 2001–2006, %

	2001–2003	2004–2006
Ethnic Estonians	7.0	3.5
Ethnic non-Estonians	14.8	11.7
...including ethnically non-Estonian Estonians citizens	11.4	8.2
...including ethnic non-Estonians with a good level of command of Estonian*	8.9	7.1

Source: Estonian Labour Force Surveys.
*Non-Estonians with a good level of command of Estonian are those who said they could write and speak it, plus those who communicated in Estonian at home (Poleshchuk, 2009b: 98).

Table 5.3 The share of those belonging to the low-quality work force among ethnic Estonians and non-Estonians aged 15–74 depending on place of residence, 2001–2006, %

	2001	2002	2003	2004	2005	2006
Tallinn						
Ethnic Estonians	6.5	7.4	7.9	6.8	6.0	5.3
Ethnic non-Estonians	14.5	14.5	14.7	17.0	13.7	11.7
Estonia						
Ethnic Estonians	10.0	10.0	10.3	10.3	9.4	8.6
Ethnic non-Estonians	15.5	14.7	13.9	15.4	13.9	13.3

Source: Estonian Labour Force Surveys (Poleshchuk, 2009b: 98).

having Estonian citizenship may marginalize job seekers, language competence and citizenship do not in themselves improve a person's chances of getting work; that in order to be more readily considered for employment than their ethnic Estonian counterparts, non-Estonians with language competence in Estonian or Estonian citizenship also need to have a higher level of education. The question becomes more individually centred, then, than it would first appear. Other earlier studies already pointed to the fact that language competence and ethnicity alone could not explain the disparity in employment rates (Kulu & Tammaru, 2004; Aasland, 2002).

Poleshchuk (2009b) stresses that acquisition of Estonian citizenship and language competence puts the members of a minority group in a more competitive position than those in their group who have not acquired either, but that this alone cannot make them as competitive as most ethnic Estonians. According to this author, the situation in Tallinn is even worse (Poleshchuk, 2009b: 102).

Finally, if we look at income rates, Poleshchuk (2009b: 103) offers further data to illustrate the disadvantageous position of the Russophone population (Table 5.4).

Several other authors in the *Report* suggest that the feeling of alienation experienced by the Russophone community and particularly by younger Russophones may be increasing. Because they were born in what was already independent Estonia, Lauristin and Vihalemm observe, this younger cohort expects to be treated on an equal footing with their autochthonous Estonian contemporaries and so their labour market expectations surpass the opportunities actually available to them. This makes the challenge they face to integrate even higher:

> Therefore, it can be said that in Estonia there is sufficiently fertile ground for interethnic tensions and conflicts in the form of general dissatisfaction.

Table 5.4 The distribution of ethnic Estonians and non-Estonians over income quintiles for ages 16 and up, 2006, %

	Estonia		Tallinn	
	Ethnic Estonians	Ethnic non-Estonians	Ethnic Estonians	Ethnic non-Estonians
Lower 20%	19	21	10	16
2nd quintile	20	21	14	17
3rd quintile	18	23	12	20
4th quintile	21	19	25	25
Upper 20%	22	16	39	22
Total	100	100	100	100

Source: 2006 Estonian Social Study (Poleshchuk, 2009b: 103).

> On the imaginary 'map' of European majority-minority relations, Estonia is quite a tense area, and the change in generations will not significantly ease the situation. (Lauristin & Vihalemm, 2009b: 101)

And as these authors conclude, 'Therefore it is naïve to think that the situation will improve by itself' (Lauristin & Vihalemm, 2009: 102).

One instance of the inter-ethnic tension these writers refer to was the Bronze Soldier crisis in Tallinn in April 2007 (for a thorough account of the crisis and its sociological consequences, see Ehala, 2009; Lauristin *et al.*, 2007; and Poleshchuk, 2009a). In the aftermath of such events, Lauristin and Vihalemm have these difficult but important questions to ask:

> Are young people who have been socialised during the two transition decades into the 'new Estonian society' more satisfied and integrated than their parents and grandparents? Or are new problems developing for the younger generation that was born and has grown up in the Republic of Estonia upon entering the Estonian labor market and public sphere? Can a 'third-generation problem' similar to the Western European countries develop in Estonia, which could culminate in protests by Russian young people? (Lauristin & Vihalemm, 2009: 81)

4. Sociolinguistic Data

PHC 2011 records that in the year 2011 a total of 157 languages were spoken in Estonia (in the *Census for 2000*, the total was 109). The majority language was Estonian (886,859 speakers or 68.5% of the total population) and this was followed by Russian (383,062 speakers or 29.6%) and Ukrainian

(8012 speakers or 0.6%). In total, 25 of the 157 languages were spoken by more than 100 people.

4.1. Language skills and attitudes in Estonia

The prevailing linguistic pattern in Estonia can be described as follows. With regard to speakers of Estonian, the younger generations (meaning those who received their school education during the last years of the Soviet occupation or during the transition and who are now in their twenties or thirties) tend to have a limited knowledge of Russian and invest more effort in learning English and then other foreign languages. Meanwhile, the older generations (meaning middle-aged or elderly citizens educated and socialized in 'Soviet times') usually have at least a working knowledge of Russian, which they speak with greater or lesser competence as their professional or personal needs dictate. With regard to speakers of Russian, the opposite occurs: the older generations generally do not speak Estonian because they did not learn it when they first migrated to the country, unless they settled in rural areas or smaller towns where the presence of Estonian was so overwhelming that they could not live there without it (Ü. Rannut, 2003), while the younger generations speak Estonian better than their parents or grandparents and often add to that second language a third, most commonly English. However, the socialization of these younger Russophones is a determinant factor in the shaping of their language skills and those who were born and socialized in parts of the country where Russian is most dominant do not acquire Estonian language skills. This, for example, is the case with younger Estonians in the northeastern border county of Ida-Viru (Narva, Kohtla-Järve, Jõhvi and Sillamäe) or in certain districts of the capital Tallinn (Lasnamäe, Mustamäe and Kopli) or towns nearby (such as Maardu or Paldiski).

As documented by Masso and Vihalemm (2005), the overall pattern described above was already present in Estonia at the end of the first decade after the country had reattained its independence. Even though their data are based on self-reported answers by speakers and different grading scales are employed for different polls (three levels for 1987 and four for 2003), these authors show that the adult Estonian-speaking population's English skills had increased considerably (from 61% not fluent in 1987 to 3% not fluent in 2003) but that their Russian language skills had decreased (from 23% fluent in 1987 to 19% fluent in 2003), while the adult Russian-speaking population's language skills had increased in both Estonian (from 58% not fluent in 1987 to 12% not fluent in 2003) and in English (from 80% not fluent in 1987 to 49% not fluent in 2003).

More recent data from the report *Estonian Integration Monitoring 2011* (Lauristin *et al.*, 2011: 31) indicate that this trend is growing. From 2002 to 2010, an improvement in the Estonian-speaking population's English language skill was recorded in all the age groups but was most notable in the two youngest (an increase from 69% to 82% in the adolescent group, aged 15–19, and an increase from 53% to 70% in the young adult group, aged 20–29). A similar improvement in English language skill was recorded for the Russophones, of whom the young adult group scored particularly high (from 15% to 40%) and the adolescent group also showed an improvement (from 53% to 56%). At the same time, Russian-speaking adolescents' and young adults' Estonian language skill also improved but not as notably (from 53% to 58% and from 35% to 44% respectively). Finally, the Estonian-speaking population's Russian language skill appears to have significantly decreased inter-generationally: while the older age groups show a high level of skill, in the young adult group the level has fallen from 43% to 12% and, in the adolescent group, from 26% to 10%. And while to a certain degree younger generations of the Estonian-speaking population may regard Russian as 'an advantage in the labour market' (Siiner & Vihalemm, 2011: 136), this renewed interest in Russian is still too slight to yield significant data.

To sum up, younger generations of speakers of Estonian tend to be more fluent in English than in Russian, while the older age groups are generally more fluent in Russian. On the other hand, younger generations of Russophones are more likely to speak Estonian and English, while the older age groups tend to be monolingual. Note that in the two studies cited (Lauristin *et al.*, 2011; Masso & Vihalemm, 2005) the youngest age group of the Russian-speaking population self-estimated that it had the same level of language skill in English as in Estonian. The picture this gives us of Estonia in general and of Tallinn in particular is of a society that is becoming plurilingual but that plays out its plurilingualism in different directions: the Estonian-speaking population tends to be bilingual in Estonian and English, while the Russophones tend to be fluent in Russian, Estonian and English (probably in that order), depending very much on their age group, place of residence and educational level.

In other words, Russophones have gained greater knowledge of Estonian in recent years, particularly when compared with the period immediately following Estonia's reattainment of independence. The data from *Estonia's Eighth and Ninth Periodic Report on Implementation of the Convention on the Elimination of All Forms of Racial Discrimination* (2009) indicates that the number of people declaring that they had no proficiency in Estonian decreased over the years (from 23% to 19%), while the number of those who chose the categories 'Active' and 'Fully proficient' increased (from 15% to 17% and from 12% to 15% respectively).

The *Periodic Report* also observes that the older Russophone population regards Estonian pragmatically, as a language of instrumental value rather than a marker of identity or integration. In other words, this community values Estonian because it needs the language to apply for citizenship, it can be a very good lever for promotion in the labour market and it generally broadens the scope of their opportunities and prospects. However, among the younger generation of Russophones who are in the process of acquiring higher education, Estonian is also valued as a means to achieve integration. For those people, the report says, 'Estonian language proficiency is a precondition for integration and the level of language proficiency determines the extent to which a person feels integrated in society' (Poleshchuk, 2009b: 60). Finally, the report comments on the particular plurilingualism which younger Russophones are starting to display and which may put them in a more advantageous position when they compete with their Estonian peers, who tend to be fluent in Estonian and English but not in Russian. Järve (2002) has already noted that proficient bilingual speakers in Tallinn would be better positioned for certain jobs. And Verschik (2007: 100) observes that L1 speakers of Estonian who are also speakers of Russian as L2 (i.e. R2 speakers) 'rely on the fact that now many Russian speakers have at least a minimal understanding of Estonian, and do not hesitate to introduce Estonian lexical items and convergent forms into their R2.' As a result and at the basic level of everyday communication, it seems that a more heterogeneous and varied use of the different languages in contact is gaining ground.

4.2. The pressure of English and the ideological construct of 'authenticity'

Some sociolinguistic studies have focused on younger Estonians' language attitudes (Ehala & Niglas, 2006; Kirss, 2008) and the growing influence and impact of English on the younger generations of the Estonian-speaking public. In their study, Ehala and Niglas (2006) suggest that younger speakers think English has greater prestige than Estonian and they conclude that these generations are 'divided between reason and emotion' (i.e. while reason tells them to value English, emotion prompts them to value Estonian). What worries the authors is that Estonian is undervalued in education and training, where once again English is more positively rewarded. In more general terms, they also observe that the globalizing tendencies of our times may be having a serious effect on less widely spoken languages.

In the same vein (and as discussed below), Kirss (2008) has presented data collated from focus group discussions in Tallinn, Narva and Tartu to illustrate that English may often be used in inter-ethnic contact instead of Estonian or Russian:

> English could also be sometimes used in majority Estonian regions when training partners include Russians. A male student in Tallinn had Russians in his training group and when necessary they talked in English as the Estonians cannot speak Russian and the particular Russians were bad at Estonian. A female participant in Tartu also brought out that

sometimes she has to use English to communicate with one of her Russian practice partners. (Kirss, 2008: 6)

The question is whether these are isolated cases or indicate that English may eventually become a sort of inter-ethnic language, as David Laitin (1996) first suggested. Several authors (Hogan-Brun *et al.*, 2007; Verschik, 2005b; Vihalemm, 2009) have argued that this has still not become a perceivable trend. However, Estonian society has undergone a major transformation in the last two decades. And in the light of Woolard's definition of 'language ideology' as 'representations, whether explicit or implicit, that construe the intersection of language and human beings in a social world' (Woolard, 1998: 3), Estonian society's perception of English could be described as ambivalent. We need to emphasize the importance of language ideologies because people's ideas about language play a crucial role in shaping their development: in the words of Monica Heller, 'Our ideas about language(s) are, in other words, not neutral; we believe what we believe for reasons which have to do with the many other ways in which we make sense of our world and make our way in it.' (Heller, 2008: 518).

On the one hand, the English language has been hailed as the means by which the Estonians might achieve their longed-for 'return to the West' (Fonzari, 1999); on the other, that language is also perceived as a serious threat to Estonian, a homogenizing force that comes with our globalizing world and is therefore also a 'killer language'. Moreover, younger generations of the Estonian-speaking population appear to value English in terms of the status and leverage it offers them but still hold Estonian close to their hearts as a marker of identity and as means to express solidarity with one another (Ehala & Niglas, 2004). And it may also be true that these generations do not value Estonian in instrumental terms simply because they have already mastered that language and see no need to make the extra effort with it that they make with English.

English thus conflicts with the value of authenticity[2] (Woolard, 2008) that speakers of Estonian so firmly attach to their language. Very briefly put, the ideological construct of authenticity identifies the value of a language as its 'core' or 'authentic' features and observes how these help to fashion a particular kind of identity or character, supporting those features that most genuinely portray a particular community. Traditionally, this value has given minority or minoritized languages their authority (Woolard, 2008). This perception of the Estonian language is institutionally affirmed (see the Estonian Minister of Education's foreword to the report *Development Strategy of the Estonian Language 2004–2010*), cited by many commentators (the opinions collated by Liiv & Laasi, 2006) and commented upon by people in general when they discuss the threat to Estonian posed by the English language.

5. Aims, Scope and Methodology of the Study

Over a ten-month period during the academic year 2008/2009, I conducted a study at a language school in Tallinn's city centre as part of my fieldwork for a larger-scale research project. I used ethnographic tools (in-depth interviews, focus group discussion and participant observation) to collate data on speakers' language ideologies, meaning how they valued the language(s) they spoke and also their immediate sociolinguistic environment. My intention was to determine (a) the value attributed to Estonian by those who speak it as their L1, their L2 or as a foreign language and (b) the value attributed to Russian, again by those who speak it as their L1, their L2 or as a foreign language. The initial stage of the fieldwork consisted in participant observation. At the language school in question, I taught Spanish as a foreign language to several groups of students of different ages and I was able to observe these students and also other SFL teachers. During this period, I asked students to participate in a group discussion about language issues and this led to two focus group discussions, one with L1 Estonian speakers and the other with L1 Russian speakers. In-depth interviews were implemented with informants gathered by means of the snowball technique. In total, the number of participants in the study was $N = 26$, with ages ranging between 20 and 40 and participants sharing a well-educated, middle-class background (most were either studying a university degree or already held one).

6. Results

First, this section considers the results of the participant observations conducted in the classrooms at the language school. In one of the groups, which was highly heterogeneous in that there were equal numbers of L1 Estonian and L1 Russian speakers (a total of four L1 speakers of each language), the students tended to 'naturally' group according to language or ethnicity, making the observation process more difficult. But when the classroom setting was adjusted or when an L1 Estonian speaker and a Russophone happened to sit together, I observed that Estonian most frequently became the language of interaction.[3] And when two younger learners could not understand each other in Estonian, it was English that most frequently gained the upper hand. As argued above, this could have happened because the language repertoires of the two groups had developed differently and, also importantly, because the two languages in contact here were so very dissimilar. As a result, however, that playful use of the two languages together (in theory the most commonly used form of inter-ethnic communication and, according to Vihalemm (2008), the mixture of the two languages that is most commonly chosen) demands that each speaker should already have some knowledge of the other's language. In other words, in this particular context the often-cited notion of 'passive bilingualism' proves to be somewhat less than passive. It is only natural, one might argue, that when two speakers cannot understand each other in either of their first languages then they resort to an external code. And what happens nowadays is that this code will almost always be English. This also happened in my observations, especially when the participants were members of the youngest age groups; and even if this choice never became the norm, I recorded several instances when two younger speakers talked to each other in English. The observation that English could be used in inter-ethnic contact situations was also made during the focus group discussions and in-depth interview sessions.

At the same time, Estonians contradict themselves by using English as an inter-ethnic language even while they value the authenticity that Estonian offers them as their L1 and a marker of identity. On the one hand, such speakers are quite ready to use English as a foreign language, especially if they can choose it over Russian; on the other, they perceive English as a threat to their language and identity. So it is that in the first transcript below[4] the speaker believes that it is positive for Estonians to preserve their language in a world where everything is 'in English' (but note, by comparing this translation with the original Estonian text in the appendix to this chapter, that although most of his contribution was made in Estonian, he actually says the two words 'in English' *in* English). But as I argue below in Section 7, the use of English in inter-ethnic contact is essentially consistent with the ideological construct of authenticity since it may help maintain and reinforce ethnic boundaries.

Transcript 1: An exotic, difficult language faced with a world globalized by English

1. **JA2ML1EST:** Another is that it's like you're one member of this small group of people – well, let's say this group of a little more than a million people – that speak what we could call a difficult language and that somehow they teach this language, an exotic language in the globalized world today where
5. everything is *in English* [my italics – see note above], isn't it? This, for me, is especially interesting; what I'm saying is, it's about my language.

Note that the conversation transcribed above was immediately preceded by the intervention of another participant whose words (Transcript 2) highlight the importance of the authenticity of Estonian for its speakers (see lines 4–6 in particular).

98 Urban Diversities and Language Policies

Transcript 2: 'We identify with this language because it's not anonymous'

1. **JA2FL1EST:** Let's say that we identify with this language; like it's ours, a part of our identity. And not just that but it's like part of the world, isn't it? Our small language and our identity, they're different from the other big European languages or world languages. [...] That's it: it's about identity, isn't it? That in
5. our world nowadays everything is so much like... like there's a lot of indifference, isn't there? [...] But our small language, our culture, our society, it's *not anonymous*, is it?

Estonians do value their own language in terms of its authenticity, as the discussion in the following transcript shows. To make an even stronger case for how important they think this is (and to further illustrate what is meant by the term itself), additional data from the group discussion with L1 Estonian speakers can be considered here: when the students discussed the features of Estonian that they preferred, they all agreed that it was the way the language sounded (line 4 of Transcript 3). Moreover, the particular words they chose to illustrate this contain some of the sounds which most clearly distinguish Estonian from other languages and which, perhaps not simply by chance, are absent from Russian (lines 2 and 7 of Transcript 3).

Transcript 3: Estonian 'sounds good'

1. **JSC:** Okay, so what do you like about the Estonian language?
    JI2FL1EST: *Jäääär* [a word which means 'the edge of the ice' and which carries particular weight in Estonian because of the predominance of the vowel sound /æ/ in the character ä].
5. **JA1FL1EST:** That it sounds good.
    JSC: It sounds good, does it?
    JÕ3FL1EST: *Jüriöö ülestõus* [more words containing typically Estonian sounds including the French-sounding /u/ in the character 'ü', /œ/ in 'ö', and the close-mid back unrounded vowel /ɤ/ in 'õ'].
    JSC: What kind of bonus do you feel that gives you?
    JR1FL1EST: The fatherland.

In other words, it is not only the sound of the language that makes its speakers feel good but what those sounds stand for: the language's aural or physical force and its symbolic features are both important. The question of accent also reinforces Estonian speakers' feelings of their language's authenticity and, as Korts observes (2009: 134–135), those L1 Russian speakers who can speak Estonian without a Russian accent are clearly approved of by native Estonian speakers (while those who speak the language with a Russian accent do not fare as well).

With regard to Russophones' feelings about the social side of their immediate language environment, those who participated in the study declared their preferred language of interaction with Estonians to be Estonian. The data that they provided and that are cited here may indeed be significantly biased: the informants' age is one factor that might contribute to this; and as members of younger generations, they would already have acquired some knowledge of Estonian and would accept the fact that if they wanted to go on living in Estonia (especially in such a heterogeneous language environment as Tallinn), they would not go very far without Estonian. Part of the data gathered from the in-depth interviews with young Russophones point clearly to this, as the transcript below illustrates.

Transcript 4: It's important to know Estonian in Estonia

1. **JSC:** Do you think it's important to speak good Estonian?
   JE1ML1RUS: In Estonia? Yes, I think it is. It's difficult to find a good job without it; but if you don't speak the majority language that's just the way it's always been. I know from experience that if you speak good Estonian you have
5. more chances of getting ahead. You'll have more chances in more places, and there'll be a lot more points in your favour.

In fact, this same informant considered that it was much easier to start a conversation in Estonian than in Russian, particularly in Tallinn, and that by speaking Estonian from the start, the conversation was more likely to succeed.

Transcript 5: Starting a conversation in Estonian, a language in which 'everyone will understand you'

1. **JSC:** What language do you use to start a conversation?
   JE1ML1RUS: Estonian. Many, many people speak Estonian in Estonia. The Russians also know a little Estonian but the Estonians usually don't know any Russian. So if you speak in Estonian then everyone will understand. Once you
5. get started, you might decide that it makes more sense to switch to Russian, but usually you can tell from the beginning who's Russian and who's Estonian anyway.

The data from another interview with two Russophones and one bilingual speaker (of an Estonian mother and a Russian father) suggest that Estonian is steadily gaining ground, especially in Tallinn, and that it is becoming the country's most commonly used language: the language people use by default. The following transcript reinforces this idea, where the speakers observe that even when two Russian speakers who have initiated a conversation in Estonian realize that the other person is of Russian origin, they may continue to speak in Estonian for practical reasons. This is especially common if the language environment is a public space: for example, those whose professional positions involve attending the general public understand that speaking just Estonian can help protect their jobs or even facilitate promotion (see lines 7–8).

Transcript 6: Not shifting languages is more comfortable and convenient

1. **JE1FL1RUS:** You always start in Estonian and then you see: if the person attending you is Russian you might switch to Russian, though often that doesn't actually change things and you just continue in Estonian.

   JSC: Really?

5. **JA1FL1RUS:** Even if the other person is Russian, it doesn't matter: you speak in Estonian.

   JSC: You mean that even if they realise you're Russian, you stick to Estonian?

   JA1FL1RUS: Yes, it doesn't make any difference.

   JE1FL1RUS: For many people it's become a principle. People who work in
10. good companies want to hold onto their positions and so they make an effort to keep speaking in Estonian to their clients.

   JM1FL1BILING: Also it's not that comfortable to have to keep switching languages all the time.

The transcript above illustrates how far the demands of the job market can act as a variable that affects people's language skills and attitudes. Younger Russophones are well aware that sooner or later they will need Estonian to progress socially and economically; and they also know that if they learn it well, this may be to their advantage in professional terms (also observed by Järve, 2002). In Transcript 7, the same speakers discuss exactly this (lines 1–4).

Transcript 7: Knowing Russian: An advantage in the job market

1. **JE1FL1RUS:** Me, for example, I used to work in a hotel. When they saw I spoke Russian, they hired me at once. A lot of people come from Russia, a lot of tourists. Intelligent people understand that it's a language you need. It proves that it's necessary for business, for objectives.

5. **JSC:** Is this something that many Estonians still don't believe? That Russian is a necessary language?

   JA1FL1RUS: We hope that more and more people will think this way.

   JM1FBILING: In fact I think they do; I think younger people already understand it this way.

The advantage of being a bilingual Russian and Estonian speaker is also appreciated by L1 speakers of Estonian. When members of the Estonian-speaking group were being interviewed, one informant observed this when she was describing a job interview.

Transcript 8: The need to know Russian to compete in the job market

1. **JK2FL1EST:** I went for a job interview and they asked me to speak Russian and I was like 'argh' [the informants laugh].

    JSC: What kind of job was the interview for?

    JK2FL1EST: For [the informant names a bank], a year ago. You need to know
5. Russian to work here in Tartu. In Valga it's easier, there are a lot of people who think Valga's full of Russians but there aren't actually that many and they usually speak Estonian – with a strong accent, but they speak it. I have some Russian friends who speak Estonian very well.

In the transcript above, apart from the reference to the 'strong accent' (which recalls the question of authenticity), note the informant's proposal that 'you need to know Russian to work here in Tartu' (lines 4–5). Of course, she may have formed this opinion simply from her experience of that one interview, but it does suggest that for certain relatively desirable jobs the ability to speak Russian might be considered an advantage. Note, moreover, that the informant is talking about Tartu (lines 4–5), which, as observed further above, is a much more Estonianized language environment than Tallinn. And given the transnational mobility that globalization entails (Blommaert, 2010), both Russophones and L1 Estonian speakers are aware of Russian's market value and 'economic capital' (Bourdieu, 1991), maybe increasingly so. In Tallinn the situation is also complicated by the fact that Russian has become 'glocal' (i.e. simultaneously global and local) and therefore carries with it all such languages' attendant contradictions, particularly in questions of identity and culture (Castells, 2003).

On a daily basis, therefore, those who find themselves in the trilingual language environment of present-day Tallinn need to negotiate an intricate web of linguistic and symbolic resources. More recently, other authors have also observed that Russian may be regaining its attraction, noting that it is still the most commonly known foreign language in Estonia and Latvia, and that its growing influence in global politics and economics will sustain its importance and the attraction to it. As Siiner and Vihalemm observe, 'many young Estonians who graduate from secondary school with a rather poor command of Russian regret this later on, as they discover that a good command of Russian is an advantage in the labour market' (Siiner & Vihalemm, 2011: 136).

7. Discussion and Conclusions

Today, Tallinn is clearly a thriving, multilingual city. Its varied repertoire of languages is predominated by Estonian and Russian, and English is also taking on an increasingly important role in the city's daily life. The events of the last few decades have significantly transformed Tallinn's linguistic landscape (Gorter, 2006), not only the public language of its street signage but also its citizens' language repertoires, ideologies and attitudes. And although until the early nineties, the future of Estonian still looked uncertain because it was not employed to effect social and economic change, today that situation has changed. Today, Estonian is necessary for anyone seeking qualified employment. For those who are not L1 Estonian speakers, the language has become a kind of social ladder. Finally, L1 Russian speakers manoeuvring for better positions in the job market need a certain level of Estonian as well as some form of secondary or even higher education.

On the other hand and as we have seen, other challenges also face the citizens of Tallinn: the relatively recent phenomenon of globalization has brought with it a series of changes, such as the renewed interest in the Russian language and the impact that English may be starting to have in inter-ethnic contact. This final section addresses these changes, especially the impact of English, and draws some general conclusions about how the challenges English sets Estonian are the same challenges faced by all medium-sized languages in our globalized environment.

First, while English has not yet established itself as Estonia's *lingua franca*[5] (at least along the lines suggested by Laitin, 1996), Siiner and Dabašinskiene (2011: 138) argue that it may eventually become such a language, overtaking Russian in inter-ethnic conversation. The data presented here suggest that in the country's ideological sphere the conditions could arise for this takeover, especially when combined with the fact that Estonian and Russian (the two languages in contact here) are so typologically dissimilar. Also, the differences in the historical development of the language repertoires of L1 Estonian and L1 Russian speakers are ideologically grounded: it is for ideological reasons that Estonians have switched from Russian to English when choosing a second or foreign language, and it is because of ideology – albeit pragmatically-oriented – that the Russian-speaking population has started to incorporate Estonian into its language repertoire. And it is within these ideologically grounded spheres that the everyday contact between speakers of different languages is negotiated and assured.

In these negotiations, using the homogenizing and global language that is English might initially be perceived as contradictory to Estonian speakers' ideological construct of authenticity. In short, it might be perceived as a threat to Estonian. But I would argue that the Estonians' use of English is actually consistent with their value of Estonian authenticity, since English may help maintain and reinforce the ethnic boundaries between the two language groups, the L1 Estonian and L1 Russian speakers, particularly from Estonian side of the equation. It is more than understandable that, when circumstances require, Estonians and Russophones should make use of a common resource to facilitate and enhance communication with one another. And even though the presence of English might suggest that Estonia is being faced with that 'return to the West' (i.e. the pressure of English as the language of globalization), I would argue that the readiness to use the English language is in fact prompted by and so consistent with the ideological construct of authenticity at the core of Estonian identity.

It could be argued, finally, that Estonian is still an ethnic language, meaning a language spoken only between its L1 speakers (rather as Woolard concluded with regard to Catalan after her first period of fieldwork in Catalonia [Woolard, 1989]). And although further data will be needed to determine whether this is truly so (particularly ethnographic data), the results of my research and the time I spent in Estonia lead me to conclude that the L1 Estonian- and L1 Russian-speaking communities are still fairly impervious to one another, at least linguistically speaking. On the other hand, the younger generations are displaying a more positive attitude towards interaction and the not-for profit youth organization KoosVmeste[6] is a very good example. In their website, they explain what they do in one short but illustrative paragraph (my italics):

> Each month, mainly for the youngsters who speak Estonian or Russian at home, we organise *group activities that are fun and teach important social values*. Even though the topics are always different, the objective of these activities is always the same: *to learn to do something TOGETHER.*[7]

This kind of initiative is wholly positive, I believe, and should be further examined and analysed. Returning to the Catalan case, we might note how matters have also progressed in Catalonia since the time of Woolard's first fieldwork studies. Ethnographic research conducted in the 1990s (Boix, 1993; Pujolar, 1997) and more recent papers (Pujolar et al., 2010; Soler-Carbonell, 2012; Woolard, 2009, 2011) have described Catalan's ongoing process of 'de-authentication', by which the language is losing its group-marker connotations of earlier decades. The entire process cannot be described here, but the research shows that because Catalan has been adopted by so many different 'voices' (particularly as a result of the immigration to Catalonia in recent years) having an 'authentic' Catalan accent is no longer considered to be as important or is as highly valued as simply using the language is. A more recent longitudinal study by Woolard (2011) also points to another very interesting trend: that adolescents who spoke no Catalan at all during their upper secondary school education and even showed a certain degree of animosity to the language are now beginning to use it at a later stage in their lives. From the point of view of language policy and planning, Branchadell (2011) has observed that Estonia and Catalonia respond differently to the treatment of their internal multilingualism, proving that whenever controversy has arisen with regard to Estonia's language policy instruments and its compliance with international standards (e.g. the Framework Convention for the Protection of National Minorities), the solution it was advised to adopt with its Russian-speaking community was already present in Catalonia's language policy documents for its own relationship with a parallel language community, in this case not Russophones but the Spanish-speaking population.

Therefore, at the basic level of everyday communication, we might wonder whether Estonian may eventually follow Catalan as a language appropriated by speakers from different backgrounds and with different accents, particularly by those Russian speakers who have already put this process in motion. Of course, in many respects the case for Estonia and Catalonia is very different: first, Estonia is a sovereign state with everything this means for its citizens' collective mindset, while Catalonia is not; second, Catalan and Spanish are very closely related languages, unlike Estonian and Russian; third, the demographics also differ because the Catalan-speaking population occupies a minority position (it generally resides within Catalonia), unlike the position occupied by Estonian-speakers in Estonia; and finally and most importantly, the presence of English is not as strongly felt in the Catalan-speaking territories as it is in Estonia, with the result (as considered above) that the impact of that language on Tallinn's ecolinguistic environment will inevitably be much greater than any such effect experienced in Catalonia. To conclude, however, the comparable nature of the two cases does illustrate one important fact and that is the way in which medium-sized language communities face many of the same challenges in this era of globalization. One of these is how the new speakers in these communities are to gain the legitimacy they need to become veteran speakers. And as this chapter has sought to illustrate, the linguistic and ideological features that characterize them become crucial as they travel this path.

Notes

(1) The fieldwork for this chapter was conducted while I was Catalan Visiting Lecturer at the University of Tartu, sponsored by the Ramon Llull Institute. I also benefited from the studentship Segimon Serrallonga 2008, awarded by the city council of Torelló, and from the studentship Estophilus 2009, awarded by the Estonian Institute. Later on, I worked with these data at the Linguistic Anthropology Laboratory of the University of California, San Diego, thanks to a

fellowship program from the 'La Caixa' Foundation. I am deeply indebted to all these institutions, for their economic support. (I should add, however, that none of the views expressed in the paper represent the opinions of these institutions.) I am also very grateful to the participants in the study, the students who offered me their free time and allowed me to record their conversations on language matters in Estonia. Aina and Ahti Saares and Maria Kall and Merilin Kotta were most helpful with the Estonian transcriptions, and Maria Kall and Merilin Kotta also checked my translations to Catalan and English. Mona Lellsaar, Mall Orlova and Anna Samokhvalova performed the same task for the Russian-language data. All their help was most appreciated. These data were also presented at different conferences and symposia during 2009 and 2010 and I thank the participants there for useful comments, as well as those colleagues of mine who have dedicated their valuable time to my work, among them Albert Bastardas-Boada and Kathryn Woolard. Finally, thanks must also go to my colleagues and friends at the Linguistic Anthropology Laboratory at UCSD, who were very helpful and supportive throughout the time I spent there. Any errors or shortcomings that still dog the text are my own.

(2) Unless otherwise stated, the data presented in this section have been retrieved from *Statistics Estonia*, the database that is available online at www.stat.ee/en (accessed 20 October 2012).

(3) Woolard (2008: 304) defines the ideological construct of authenticity thus:
The ideology of *Authenticity* locates the value of a language in its relationship to a particular community. That which is authentic is viewed as the genuine expression of such a community, or of an essential Self. Within the logic of authenticity, a speech variety must be perceived as deeply rooted in social and geographic territory in order to have value. [...] When authenticity is the legitimating ideology of a language, the linguistically marked form is celebrated, and accent matters.

(4) I chose to observe the beginner or elementary level Spanish language learners because their language level was too low for them to use Spanish as a language of interaction to solve certain kinds of problems in the classroom activities. Note that they may have had some experience of learning Spanish but would have used English as the language of instruction, a common practice in Estonia (especially when the teacher has a Spanish-speaking background and is not fluent in either Estonian or Russian). This may have had an effect on the observed data and so it must be acknowledged that, in the future, data gathered from more 'naturalistic' contexts or situations will be very valuable for the ongoing examination of this chapter's proposals.

(5) Note that in these translations of the original Estonian or Russian texts recorded in the appendix, the code names used to identify the speakers describe three speaker features: first, his or her age (where the number 1 placed after the first two letters of the name identifies a speaker of 30 or less than 30 years old, 2 identifies a speaker of between 31 and 50 years old, and 3 indicates that the speaker is older than 51), then the speaker's sex (ML for male and FL for female) and finally the speaker's L1 (1EST for Estonian and 1RUS for Russian).

(6) The concept of *lingua franca* is itself problematic, as we know, and it is not my intention to discuss the subject in any detail here.

(7) The pairing of these two words is already an indication of that good will, given that the Estonian 'koos' and the Russian 'vmeste' both translate as 'together'.

(8) *Korraldame iga kuu peamiselt eesti ja vene kodukeelega noortele õpetlikke ning lõbusaid ühissündmusi ühiskondlikult olulistel teemadel. Ehkki teemad on meil alati erinevad, on sündmuste mõte alati üks – õppida ja teha midagi KOOS.*

Acknowledgement

This chapter has been supported by the Project research FFI2012-35502 'Globalization and social family multilingualism in European medium sized linguistic communities' (Spanish Ministry of Economy and Competitivity). GLOBLINMED

References

Aasland, A. (2002) Citizenship status and social exclusion in Estonia and Latvia. *Journal of Baltic Studies* 33 (1), 57–77.
Blommaert, J. (2010) *The Sociolinguistics of Globalization*. Cambridge: Cambridge University Press.
Boix, E. (1993) *Triar no és trair: identitat i llengua en els joves de Barcelona* [To choose is not to betray: Identity and language among youth in Barcelona]. Barcelona: Edicions 62.
Bourdieu, P. (1991) *Language and Symbolic Power*. Cambridge: Harvard University Press.
Branchadell, A. (2011) Assessing language policy. The treatment of Russian in Estonia and Spanish in Catalonia. *Revista de Llengua i Dret* 55, 123–150.
Budryte, D. (2005) *Taming Nationalism? Political Community Building in the Post-Soviet Baltic States*. Aldershot, Hampshire: Ashgate Publishing Limited.
Castells, M. (2003) *Globalització i identitat*. Barcelona: Tribuna Mediterrània.
Chinn, J. and Kaiser, R. (1996) *Russians as the New Minority. Ethnicity and Nationalism in the Soviet Successor States*. Boulder, CO: Westview Press.
Committee on the Elimination of Racial Discrimination (2009) *Estonia's Eighth and Ninth Periodic Report on Implementing the Convention on the Elimination of all forms of Racial Discrimination*. United Nations Human Rights Web Site. See http://www.un.org/en/rights/index.shtml (accessed September 2010).
Ehala, M. (2009) The Bronze Soldier: Identity threat and maintenance in Estonia. *Journal of Baltic Studies* 40 (1), 139–158.
Ehala, M. and Niglas, K. (2006) Language attitudes of Estonian secondary school students. *Journal of Language, Identity & Education* 5 (3), 209–227.
Fonzari, L. (1999) English in the Estonian multicultural society. *World Englishes* 18 (1), 39–48.
Gal, S. and Woolard, K.A. (2001) Constructing languages and publics: Authority and representation. In S. Gal and K.A. Woolard (eds) *Languages and Publics: the Making of Authority* (pp. 1–5.) Manchester: St. Jerome Publishing.
Gorter, D. (ed.) (2006) *Linguistic Landscape: A New Approach to Multilingualism*. Clevedon: Multilingual Matters.
Hallik, K., Poleshchuk, V., Saar, A. and Semjonov, A. (2006) *Estonia: Interethnic Relations and the Issue of Discrimination*. Tallinn: Legal Information Center for Human Rights.
Heller, M. (2008) Language and the nation-state: Challenges to sociolinguistic theory and practice. *Journal of Sociolinguistics* 12 (4), 504–524.
Heidmets, M. and Lauristin, M. (2002) Learning from the Estonian case. In M. Lauristin and M. Heidmets (eds) *The Challenge of the Russian Minority. Emerging Multicultural Democracy in Estonia* (pp. 319–332). Tartu: Tartu University Press.
Hogan-Brun, G., Ozolins, U., Ramonienė, M. and Rannut, M. (2007) Language politics and practices in the Baltic states. *Current Issues in Language Planning* 8 (4), 469–630.
Järve, P. (2002) Two waves of language laws in the Baltic states: Changes of rationale? *Journal of Baltic Studies* 33 (1), 78–110.
Kirss, L. (2008) NPLD Youth Project 08: Priorities for promoting language diversity among young people. NPLD Local Youth Report: Estonia/Estonian. NPLD Network

to Promote Linguistic Diversity. See http://npld.eu/Pages/default.aspx (accessed September 2010).
Kolstoe, P. (1995) *Russians in the Former Soviet Republics*. London: Hurst & Co.
Korts, K. (2009) Inter-ethnic attitudes and contacts between ethnic groups in Estonia. *Journal of Baltic Studies* 40 (1), 121–137.
Kulu, H. and Tammaru, T. (2004) Diverging views on integration in Estonia: Determinants of Estonian language skills among ethnic minorities. *Journal of Baltic Studies* 35 (4), 378–401.
Kymlicka, W. (2000) Estonia's integration policies in a comparative perspective. In *Estonia's Integration Landscape: From Apathy to Harmony* (pp. 29–58). Tallinn: Avatud Eesti Fond & Jaan Tõnissoni Instituut.
Laitin, D. (1996) Language planning in the former Soviet Union: The case of Estonia. *International Journal of the Sociology of Language* (118), 43–61.
Laitin, D. (1998) *Identity in Formation. The Russian-Speaking Populations in the Near-Abroad*. Ithaca: Cornell University Press.
Laitin, D. (2003) Three models of integration and the Estonian/Russian reality. *Multicultural Estonia* (pp. 39–57). Tallinn: Integration Foundation.
Lauristin, M., Kaal, E., Kirss, L., Kriger, T., Masso, A., Nurmela, K., Seppel, K., Tammaru, T., Uus, M., Vihalemm, P. and Vihalemm, T. (2011) *Integration Monitoring 2011. Summary*. Tartu: University of Tartu, AS Emor, Praxis Center for Policy Studies.
Lauristin, M. and Vihalemm, T. (2009a) Introduction. In T. Vihalemm (ed.) *Estonian Human Development 2008* (p. 81). Tallinn: Eesti Koostöö Kogu.
Lauristin, M. and Vihalemm, T. (2009b) Summary. In T. Vihalemm (ed.) *Estonian Human Development Report 2008* (pp. 100–101). Tallinn: Eesti Koostöö Kogu.
Lauristin, M., Vihalemm, T., Kallas, K. and Jakobson, V. (2007) *Rahvussuhted ja integratsioonipoliitika väljakutsed pärast pronkssõduri kriisi.* [Ethnic relations and challenges for the politics of integration after the Bronze Soldier crisis] Saar Poll OÜ, Rahvastikuministri Büroo. Tallinn: Saar Poll OÜ.
Liiv, S. and Laasi, B. (2006) Attitudes towards the influence of the English language on Estonian. *Journal of Baltic Studies* 37 (4), 482–487.
Lindemann, K. and Saar, E. (2009) Non-Estonians in the labour market. In T. Vihalemm (ed.) *Estonian Human Development Report 2008* (pp. 95–99). Tallinn: Eesti Koostöö Kogu
Masso, A. and Vihalemm, T. (2005) *Võõrkeelte oskus ja kasutamine, seos sotsiaalse integratsiooni ja mobiilsusega Eesti uhiskonnas 2002–2003. Kvantitatiivne analüüs küsitluse, Mina. Maailm. Meedia. baasil.* [Foreign language knowledge and use in the framework of integration and mobility in Estonian society 2002–2003. Quantitative analysis of the survey 'I. The world. The media']. Tartu: Haridus- ja Teadusministeerium [Ministry of Science and Education].
Pettai, V. (1998) *The Ethnopolitics of Integration in Estonia and Latvia*. Akadeemiline Balti ja Vene Uuringute Keskus. See http://www.ut.ee/ABVKeskus (accessed September 2010).
Pettai, I. (2002) Estonians and non-Estonians: A typology of tolerance. In K. Hallik (ed.) *Integration of Estonian Society. Monitoring 2002* (pp. 27–39). Tallinn: Integration Foundation.
Poleshchuk, V. (2009a) *The War of the Monuments in Estonia: The Challenges of History and the Minority Population*. Aland Islands Peace Institute. See www.peace.ax (accessed September 2010).
Poleshchuk, V. (ed.) (2009b) *Chance to Survive: Minority Rights in Estonia and Latvia*. Moscow-Paris-Tallinn: Foundation for Historical Outlook.
Population and Housing Census 2011. See www.stat.ee/phc2011 (accessed 09 January 2013).]

Pujolar, J. (1997) *De què vas, tio?* [*What's up, man?*]. Barcelona: Editorial Empúries.
Pujolar, J., Balletbò, I.G., Tanyà, A.F., and Sanmartí, R.M. (2010) *Llengua i joves. Usos i percepcions lingüístics de la joventut catalana* [*Language and youth. Language use and perceptions by Catalan youth*]. Barcelona: Generalitat de Catalunya, Departament d'Acció Social i Ciutadania. Secretaria de Joventut.
Rannut, Ü. (2003) Impact of the language environment on integration and the Estonian language acquisition of Russian-speaking children in Estonia. In *Multicultural Estonia* (pp. 125–137). Tallinn: Integration Foundation.
Rannut, M. (2004) *Language Planning in Estonia: Past and Present*. CIEMEN Mercator Working Papers See www.ciemen.org/mercator/pdf/wp16-def-ang.PDF (accessed September 2010).
Shafir, G. (1995) *Immigrants and Nationalists. Ethnic Conflict and Accommodation in Catalonia, the Basque Country, Latvia and Estonia*. Albany: State University of New York Press.
Siiner, M. and Vihalemm, T. (2011) Individual multilingualism in the Baltic states within the European context. In *Estonian Human Development Report 2010/2011. Baltic Ways of Human Development: Twenty Years On* (pp. 135–137). Tallinn: Eesti Koostöö Kogu.
Siiner, M. and Dabašinskiene, I. (2011) Conclusions: Perspectives for (real) multilingualism in the Baltic states. In *Estonian Human Development Report 2010/2011. Baltic Ways of Human Development: Twenty Years On* (p. 138). Tallinn: Eesti Koostöö Kogu.
Skerrett, D. M. (2012) How normal is normalization? The discourses shaping Finnish and Russian speakers' attitudes toward Estonian language policy. *Journal of Baltic Studies* 43 (3), 363–388.
Soler-Carbonell, J. (2012) 'Llengües mitjanes' i 'llengües internacionals' a Catalunya i Estònia en l'era *glocal* [Medium-sized, and 'international' languages in Catalonia and Estonia in the glocal era. A comparative analysis of their speakers' language ideologies]. Una anàlisi comparada de les ideologies lingüístiques dels seus parlants. *Revista de Llengua i Dret* 57, pp. 207–248.
Verschik, A. (2005a) Research into multilingualism in Estonia. *Journal of Multilingual and Multicultural Development* 26 (5), 378–390.
Verschik, A. (2005b) The language situation in Estonia. *Journal of Baltic Studies* 36 (3), 283–316.
Verschik, A. (2007) Multiple language contact in Tallinn: Transfer B2 >/A1 or B1 >/A2? *The International Journal of Bilingual Education and Bilingualism* 10 (1), 80–103.
Vetik, R. (2000) *Democratic Multiculturalism: A new Model of National Integration*. Akadeemiline Balti ja Vene Uuringute Keskus. See http://www.ut.ee/ABVKeskus (accessed September 2010).
Vetik, R. (2003) The need to develop the integration model of Estonia. *Multicultural Estonia* (pp. 158–164). Tallinn: Integration Foundation.
Vihalemm, T. (2008) Estonia's linguistic capital. In M. Heidmets (ed.) *Estonian Human Development Report 2007* (pp. 63–67). Tallinn: Eesti Koostöö Kogu.
Vihalemm, T. (2009) Quality of life and Integration. In T. Vihalemm (ed.) *Estonian Human Development Report 2008* (pp. 81–108) Tallinn: Eesti Koostöö Kogu.
Vila i Moreno, F.X. (ed.) (2012) *Survival and Development of Language Communities: Prospects and Challenges*. Bristol: Multilingual Matters.
Woolard, K.A. (1989) *Double Talk: Bilingualism and the Politics of Ethnicity in Catalonia*. Stanford: Stanford University Press.
Woolard, K.A. (1998) Introduction: Language ideology as a field of inquiry. In B.B. Schieffelin, K.A. Woolard and P.V. Kroskrity (eds) *Language Ideologies. Practice and Theory* (pp. 3–35). New York/Oxford: Oxford University Press.
Woolard, K.A. (2008) Language and identity choice in Catalonia: The interplay of contrasting ideologies of linguistic authority. In K. Süselbeck, U. Mühlschlegel,

P. Masson (eds) *Lengua, nación e identidad. La regulación del plurilingüismo en España y América Latina* (pp. 303–323). Frankfurt am Main: Vervuert/Madrid: Iberoamericana.

Woolard, K.A. (2009) Linguistic consciousness among adolescents in Catalonia: A case study from the Barcelona urban area in longitudinal perspective. *Zeitschrift für Katalanistik* 22, 25–149.

Woolard, K.A. (2011) Is there linguistic life after high school? Longitudinal cases in the bilingual repertoire in metropolitan Barcelona. *Language in Society* 40 (5), 17–648.

Appendix

Original transcripts

Transcript 1

JA2ML1EST: Ja minul võib selline veel, võib-olla lisaksime, et sa oled nagu ühe väikese noh ütleme natukene ülle miljoni rahva liige, kes räägib tegelikult suhteliselt, ütleme, raskest ja õpetavad mõnes mõttes ka eksootilist keelt tänapäeva maailmas globaliseerimis maailmas, kus kõik on 'in English', eks, see on nagu minu jaoks, nagu omapärane huvitav ja et ta on ikkagi jah, nagu minu keel, ma ütlen.

Transcript 2

JA2FL1EST: Ütleme niimoodi, et me identifitseerime selle keelega, et see on meie nagu, osa identiteedist, ja mida rohkem, nagu on pärit maailmas ringi, eks ole. Oma väike keel, ja oma selle identiteed, see on natukene teistsugune, kui need suurem Euroopa või maailma identiteed. [...] Ikkagi see identiteediks küsimus, eks ole. Et tänapäevas maailmas on nii palju seda, kuidas öelda siis pealiskaudsed ükskõiksust, on ju¿ [...] Et see väikese oma see keel, oma kultuur, oma see ühiskond on kuidagi sukkest, et see ei ole nii anonüümne, või mis sa arvad¿

Transcript 3

JSC: Okay. Mis Sulle meeldib, mis Teile meeldib eesti keeles¿
JI2FL1EST: Jäääär.
JA1FL1EST: Ilus kõla.
JSC: Ilus kõla.
JÕ3FL1EST: Jüriöö ülestõus.
[...]
JSC: Mis Teile annab nagu erilist...
JR1FL1EST: Isamaa.

Transcript 4

JSC: Ты думаешь, что это важно - хорошо говорить по-эстоэстонски?

JE1ML1RUS: В Эстонии? Да, я думаю это важно. Сложно найти хорошую работы без этого, но это просто, если не говоришь на языке, на котором большинство говорят. Я это лично знаю, что если эстонский хорошо знаешь, у тебя больше хороших возможностей. И возможности, и круг общения расширяются, много много очень плюсов.

Transcript 5

JSC: Какой язык ты используешь, когда начинаешь разговор?
JE1ML1RUS: Эстонский. Больше и больше людей говорят по-эстонски в Эстонии. Те люди, которые русские, они как-бы тоже эстонский знают, а те люди, которые эстонцы, они часто русский не знают, поэтому, говоришь по-эстонски, и так и так поймут. Потом может быть ясно, лучше на русском говорить или нет. Но обычно видно, на самом деле, кто русский, кто эстонский.

Transcript 6

JE1FL1RUS: Начинаешь всегда по-эстонски, потом смотришь, если обслуживающий русский, то переходишь, хотя даже часто бывает так, что всё равно, говоришь на эстонском.
JSC: Да?
JA1FL1RUS: Даже если другой человек русский, всё равно говоришь по-эстонски.
JSC: Даже если он или она, заметили, что вы русские, всё равно говорите по-эстонски?
JA1FL1RUS: Да, всё равно.
JE1FL1RUS: Для многих просто принципяльно, те, кто работают в хороших фирмах, они как-бы, держывают свои места и старают всё равно и говорить по-эстонски с клиентами.
JM1FL1BILING: Тоже это не удобно переходить всё время.

Transcript 7

JE1FL1RUS: Я например работала в отеле, когда видят, что говорю по-русски, то меня сразу берут на работу, много людей приезжают из России, много туристов. Умные люди, они понимают, что это нужный язык. Это показывает, что это надо для биснесса, для цели.
JSC: То есть пока ещё мало эстонцев, кто считает, что русский язык - нужен?
JA1FL1RUS: Будем надеяться, что их больше.
JM1FBILING: Нет, правильно, я думаю, что молодёжь, они уже понимают это.

Transcript 8

This transcript was taken from a conversation in Catalan with students of Catalan language at the University of Tartu.

6 Multilingual Valencia: Linguistic Destruction and Reconstruction of an Urban Space[1]

Miquel Nicolás Amorós and Francesc Jesús Hernández Dobon

Introduction

Cities are, by definition, places where social life is constructed and the greatest number of communication exchanges occurs. Without entering into the debate on whether they are the most successful formula for organising the resources of civilization (Glaesser, 2011), what is certain in sociolinguistic terms is that they have become the main stage for linguistic interaction and the observatory from which this interaction is interpreted and feeds back on itself through the verbal behaviour of speakers.

The connections of cities on the Mediterranean, a site of confrontation, meeting and contact of languages, stand out among the various foci of urban civilization. In effect, within the arc of the fertile crescent, squeezed in between the Egyptian and Mesopotamian worlds, the Mediterranean Levant was the cradle of the three monotheistic religions, which, jointly with the Graeco-Roman world, moulded over the centuries what is the substratum of Western culture. This culture has be constantly rewritten along the shores of this inner sea shared by all factions of Jews, Christians and Muslims. The linguistic manifestations of this cultural base have been diverse. First, one must consider the reordering of orality that brought about the invention of the alphabet, soon used to record transactions in the Phoenician emporia, then scattered in all directions. And second, the diversification of languages and linguistic varieties. Endowed with writing, the great linguistic systems

(Greek, Latin, Aramaic, Hebrew, Arabic) served as a substrate for derived or related languages (the Romance, Germanic and Slav branches) and for the crossover languages, such as *sabir* or *lingua franca*, that assisted trade between navigators and merchants.

In any case, the history of the Mediterranean is a history of tumultuous waves (Porcel, 1996) washing over and leaving the main sea-ports: Tangier, Oran, Tunis, Alexandria, Haifa, Beirut, Smyrna, Salonica, the Piraeus, Venice, Naples, Palermo, Cagliari, Genoa, Toulon, Marseilles, Barcelona, etc. The linguistic history of the Mediterranean is, then, that of a network of port cities, subjected to the homogenising power of the period and at the same time multi-ethnic and mixed-race in their human structure and multilingual in the fabric of their day-to-day communication. On the Western shore of *Mare Nostrum*, in the Iberian Peninsula, right in the middle of what the Muslims called xarq-al-Andalus, the city of Valencia is one more link in this chain of cities, which are as likely to compete with each other as to press closer with cooperative bonds (Sanchis Guarner, 1981).

The aim of this text is to sketch the multilingual past and present of our city, Valencia, which inspires in us (it is best to say it at the start) conflicting feelings of love and disaffection, of recognition and strangeness. This thousand-year-old city, shaped linguistically in the 13th century, has always had intercultural and interlinguistic contacts, bonds that weigh down on the present where they connect to the flows of globalization and the aesthetic currents of liquid postmodernity.

The chapter is divided into three parts. In the first, we locate Valencia in its coordinates of time and space. We make a brief synopsis of the city's history and describe its urban topography, aiming to give only the essential data for a sociolinguistic evaluation of the city. In the second, we trace the linguistic possibilities of the urban population in relation to *valencià* (Valencian), the local variety of the Catalan language and the native language of the city. The third part shows the new perspectives for multilingual communication. As this is a fairly recent and as yet little studied phenomenon, the panorama we put forward has to be understood more as a perspective for future research, with the potential and drawbacks intrinsic to any work in progress. We close our explanation with some conclusions looking towards the future, dominated today by a mixture of expectation, fears and hopes. Throughout, we will alternate factual description with interpretation and reflection, derived from the tradition of critical sociology and cultural analysis. It should be said that we are aiming, above all, at a model reader with little information about the reality of Valencia, who needs to understand its context as well as the reality within that context. We hope that readers who are well-versed in the data or ideas expressed here will excuse us for going over familiar territory, and will focus on the arguments we put forward, with a view to debating the themes we have broached.

1. The Multilingual City of Valencia

1.1. The physical context

The city of Valencia is the political capital of one of the autonomous territories that make up the Spanish state. The name of this territory, *Comunitat Valenciana* (Valencian Community), was adopted in 1982 with the theoretical intention of overcoming the social-political conflict concerning the name, identity and characteristics of the native language which had erupted in the period of transition from the Franco dictatorship to the regime of representative democracy (1975–1983). As we will see later, the name is a term that has faded with time, although the conflict, with its opposed names, is far from having been fully resolved.

The entire territory of Valencia has a surface area of 23,255 km². The city of Valencia is also the capital of the province of the same name and at the same time a municipality that occupies an area of 134.65 km², of which only about a quarter is urban land. In 2011, it had 798,033 inhabitants, according to the population census, with a population density close to 6000 inhabitants per square kilometre. Given the marked mobility and fluidity of sociolinguistic exchanges, we will study both the city and the Metropolitan area, which with nearly 1,800,000 people is one of the 20 biggest conurbations in Europe. For over a decade, the city has been losing population, partly because of the movement of skilled workers and well-off families to the dormitory towns of the Metropolitan ring. This demographic trend has deepened further in the last five years due to the return of immigrants to their countries of origin; and, though this is still incipient, by the exodus of young professionals to other countries. The city core, however, continues to be the centre of trade and of university, cultural, financial and festive activity.

The city has 19 districts, which group a good eighty neighbourhoods and population nuclei (see Figure 6.1), distributed as shown in Table 6.1.

The following contrasts can be seen in the city's physiognomy:

(1) between the sea front of the city and its inland plain, which reaches a height of 15 metres above sea level;
(2) between, on the one hand, the old city (*Ciutat Vella*) and the oldest population nuclei (Russafa, Campanar, Saïdia, Grau, Cabanyal...), and on the other hand, the expansions, the neighbourhoods of mass immigration from the rest of the Spanish state and the axes of urban growth and symbolic projection of the city (City of Arts and Sciences, Neighbourhood of the Corts Valencianes/Nou Mestalla...);
(3) between the various districts that make up the urban grid and the population nuclei of the periphery, where there are still extensive agricultural lands that in some cases run directly into the city and in others, are quite distant from the historic nucleus. To the second category belong

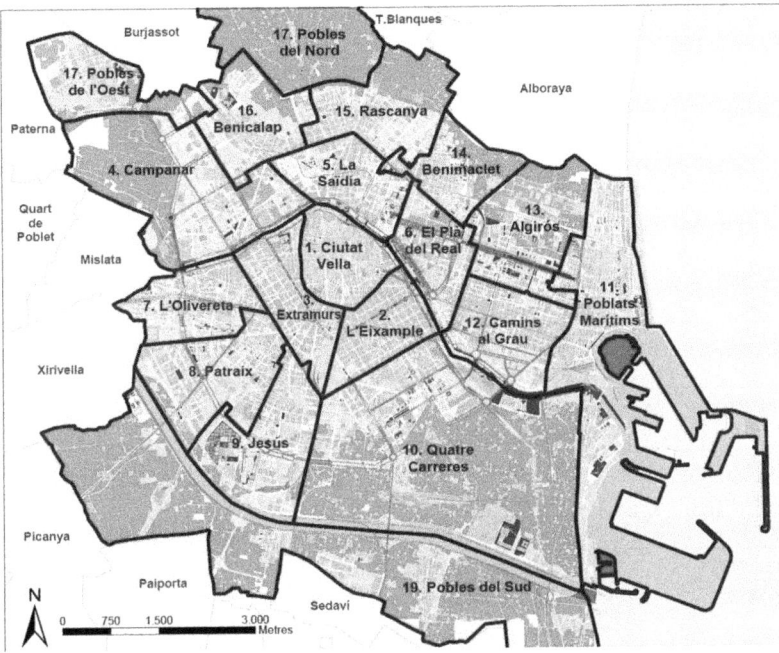

Figure 6.1 Source: Municipal Maps online http://mapas.valencia.es/WebsMunicipales/callejero/web_callejero.jsp?lang=es

the villages of El Palmar and El Perellonet, by the Albufera lake, the most important water ecosystem on the west of the Iberian peninsula and a major cultural reference in the life of city-dwelling Valencians.

As we will see, these urban divisions correlate with how much or how little the native language is rooted. The bourgeois neighbourhoods (the expansions, some of the neighbourhoods of new immigrants and those of the new urban lay-out) are more Spanish-speaking, whereas the artisan and worker neighbourhoods in the centre and the semi-agricultural periphery, which include the villages to the north and south and the old villages assimilated by the city, remain more faithful to the native language. And the more recent the period of urban development, the lower is the index of survival of the city's historic language.

As in so many other cases around Europe, and as it has no natural obstacles, the city has grown at the expense of its agricultural surroundings and thanks to the absorption of earlier independent towns such as Russafa, Benimaclet, and Patraix. These transformations were intensified in the process of uncontrolled development which was favoured during the later stages of the dictatorship and which continued during the transition to representative democracy. During the period of socialist municipal government,

Table 6.1 Neighbourhoods and population nuclei of districts of Valencia

District	Neighbourhoods and population nuclei
Ciutat Vella	Seu, Carme, Pilar, Mercat, Sant Francesc
Eixample	Russafa, Pla del Remei, Gran Via
Extramurs	Botànic, Roqueta, Petxina, Arrancapins
Campanar	Campanar, Tendetes, Calvari, Sant Pau
Saïdia	Marxalenes, Morvedre, Trinitat, Tormos, Sant Antoni
Pla del Reial	Exposició, Mestalla, Jaume Roig, Ciutat Universitaria
Olivereta	Nou Moles, Soternes, Tres Forques, Fuensanta, Llum
Patraix	Patraix, Sant Isidre, Vara de Quart, Safranar, Favara
Jesús	Raiosa, Hort de Senabre, Creu Coberta, Sant Marcel·lí, Camí Reial
Quatre Carreres	Montolivet, En Corts, Malilla, Font Sant Lluís, Na Rovella, La Punta, Ciutat d'Arts i Ciències
Poblats Marítims	Grau, Cabanyal-Canyamelar, Malva-rosa, Beteró, Natzaret
Camins al Grau	Aiora, Albors, Creu del Fondo, Penya-roja
Algirós	Illa Perduda, Ciutat Jardí, Amistat, Vega Baixa, Carrasca
Benimaclet	Benimaclet, Camí de Vera
Rascanya	Orriols, Torrefiel, Sant Llorenç
Benicalap	Benicalap, Ciutat Fallera
Poblats Nord	Poble Nou, Borbotó, Carpesa, Benifaraig, Massarrojos, Mauella, Cases de Bàrcena
Poblats Oest	Beniferri, Benimàmet
Poblats Sud	Torre, Faitanar, Forn Alcedo, Castellar-Oliveral, Pinedo, Saler, Palmar, Perellonet

attempts to order and regulate the growth of the city encountered considerable hindrance and resistance (Sorribes, 2007c). With the successive governments of the PP, Spain's conservative party, the city administration has favoured real estate speculation, hidden under the construction of major leisure facilities. Clear examples of this are the Palau de Congressos and the Ciutat de les Arts i les Ciències, which have built up their respective neighbourhoods in the form of low skyscrapers. Like any city that aspires to be a player in the unceasing market of postmodern international tourism, Valencia has had to give itself a skyline, albeit a modest one, complemented by a network of shopping malls, hypermarkets and leisure centres.

These initiatives have been supported by the organization, always paid for out of public funds, of major sporting events: the America's Cup, an urban circuit for the Formula 1 Grand Prix of Europe and international tennis and equine competitions. The official discourse speaks proudly of the city's position in the ranking tables of world cities with the highest numbers of visitors. However, the antagonism between private urban development interests and public defence of the *res publica* was made very clear in the political row over the future of the Cabanyal, an old artisan and fishermen's neighbourhood, which is a protected zone due to the heritage value of many of its buildings. The municipal plan drawn up by the majority conservative party envisaged the partial demolition of the neighbourhood, with the claimed purpose of making access to the sea front easier and quicker (Sorribes, 2007a, 2007b).

1.2. The historical roots

It is not easy to explain just how the linguistic past of a human community moulds the forms and habits of communication today. Apart from a few specialists, most speakers do not know that in the words, expressions and conventions with which they communicate daily, the echoes of the past are encrypted: the ways in which all the vanished generations communicated and constructed their lives. The idea that the present contains the entire past is clear, but is opaque at the same time. Assuming, then, the limitations of historiographic evocation, especially when the subject matter for this history, like verbal communication, is doubly elusive, we propose a minimalist sketch of Valencia as a multilingual city. The purpose is that some of the thin threads in this spool of sociolinguistic relationships should be recognized in the fabric of the present.

The name *Valencia* reveals the city's Latin origins. A Roman settlement from 138 BC, very little is known from written documents about its incorporation into the Tarraconense province, formed at the end of the Republican era – and still less of its pre-Roman past, which links it to the civilization of the Ibers, the 'Princes of the West'. Archaeological deposits, however, provide evidence of an emerging Roman colony, founded on a rocky island in the River Túria. With the passage of time, VALENTIA must have become an important landmark on the Via Augusta, which linked the north and southeast of Roman Hispania along the Mediterranean corridor.

The vulgar Latin that evolved in this part of the Empire gave way to an native Romance variety, shaped during the Visigothic period, which, like Roman times, is very scantily documented. In any case, the civilizing, religious and linguistic traces of Rome were lost during the centuries of Muslim domination. The mark of early Romanization was conserved in a few Mozarabic toponyms, such as Patraix, an ancient municipality that is now a neighbourhood integrated into Valencia's urban fabric. After the disintegration of the Caliphate of Cordoba, the invasion of Almohads and Almoravids assisted the re-Islamization of the *taifas* (kingdoms) into which the Iberian peninsula had been fragmented. In the early 13th century, when the Catalan-Aragonese King Jaume I began the conquest of the lands of Valencia, no trace remained of primitive Valencian Christianity, its institutions, or its Romance speech. Urban toponyms such as Boatella or Russafa remain from the Muslim period.

The Christian conquest marked a radical turning-point, a caesura between the Muslim past and the new frontier society, made up of Catalan and Aragonese settlers. Jaume I shaped the new country as a patrimonial kingdom, linked to the Catalan-Aragonese crown, but endowed with its own laws and institutions. In contrast to New Castile or Andalusia, territorial expansions won by Castile from Islam, the kingdom of Valencia was not an appendix of Aragon or Catalonia, but an *ex novo* political entity, fruit of the crusader mentality, in which the Muslims were essential for agriculture and for this reason were tolerated for almost four centuries more. The local variety of Catalan was the language of this peculiar society, in which the Christians were the ruling minority for a long time.

The ancient Balansiyya of the Muslims would be the *cap i casal* (central point) of the new country. This clichéd expression sums up the problem. The importance of the capital is so marked that, throughout the entire time that the country has existed as a political entity (until 1707), it was called *City and Kingdom of Valencia*. Of course, right down to today, there has been no shortage of voices critical of this hypertrophy of the city in relation to the territory as a whole. A city whose leaders have shown their inability to reflect the overall interests of the country and to represent them politically: a prosperous city, set on the central plain of lands with an agricultural and mercantile tradition, with an efficient irrigation network created by Romans and Saracens, which the Christians later expanded and improved.

The wealth of Valencia reached its peak in the 15th and early 16th century, when it benefited from the political and economic crisis that assailed Barcelona. This period saw the most important urban expansion and artistic and literary developments. It is the moment of greatness in literary creation, which gave great names to European culture, whether in its native language (Ausiàs March, Joanot Martorell) or in the Latin of the humanists (Joan Lluís Vives). By the end of the 15th century, Valencia was a lively city with a population of over 50,000, alongside Granada the most important in the peninsula and among the seven or eight leading cities of Europe.

However, a series of factors such as the shifting of the centre of gravity of international politics and the economy from the Mediterranean to the Atlantic hindered the continuance of this splendour, which in fact contained from the start the seeds of its own disintegration. In only a few decades, shaken by class antagonisms, re-feudalization, the fundamentalism of the House of Habsburg (Austria), anti-Semitism and Tridentine dogmatism, Valencia turned into a secondary city, subjected to the dominance of Castilian Spanish and to the interests of the elites who governed the Empire. When the Borbons reduced it by force of arms, they annexed it to Castile along with the other countries of the extinct Crown of Aragon, abolished its historical local rights and imposed the Castilian language in all spheres of public life.

Valencia and the country to which it gives its name were excluded from many of the characteristic transformations that spread through European societies in modern times. Recovery of the rhythm of history was not easy. And as neither politics nor cultural construction satisfied collective energies, these energies partly took refuge in economic growth. The 18th century was a period of repression and expansion of agriculture and trade. Valencia was no longer capital of a kingdom with its own rights created in the Middle Ages, but a lost region in the Levant of the Spanish monarchy. And in fact this monarchy was reluctant to follow the path of modernity and only accepted the most innocuous facets of the Enlightenment's rational discourse.

Historically, the economy of the city had been bound up with its status as administrative capital and agricultural centre. Since its Christian refounding in the 13th century, It was also home to a small craft industry that reached its greatest splendour in the 18th century with silk manufacture. In the 19th century, due to a variety of social-political and administrative changes such as regulatory development, controlled liberalism, ecclesiastical dissolution, and provincialization, a new enriched bourgeoisie emerged engaged in financial speculation and the export of citrus fruits and other agricultural products such as rice. Small-scale industry with food manufacturing, metalwork, textiles, footwear and furniture workshops appeared in the city and the belt surrounding it. Industrialization involved a series of processes: immigration off the land, the emergence of a steadily more aware and better-organized working class, increased literacy, and the appearance of mass culture products. The elites of the government bureaucracy and financial oligarchy based in Madrid sought to bring the city of Valencia under their aegis and reduce the influence of Barcelona, a city with which it shared a language and many cultural traits (CCCB, 2010).

In the political order, as well as this triangular play of attraction and repulsion between Valencia, Barcelona and Madrid, the city's partial industrialization increased the weight of people's political organizations. In the early 20th century, Valencia was a city where class struggle unions, particularly anarcho-syndicalist ones, and Left socialist and Republican parties disputed the hegemony of the conservative parties that propped up a decadent monarchy. During the Republican period and the Civil War Valencia was the home of the legitimate government for a year, until its evacuation to Barcelona. Because of the city's commitment to the democratic regime, it was fiercely repressed by the Francoist authorities once the war was over.

Undoubtedly, the Civil War and the Franco dictatorship are the most decisive episodes in the country's recent history. They have conditioned, and still condition to a high degree, the political dynamics, and social, cultural and artistic practices of the peoples of Spain. This is why it is legitimate today, when over three decades have passed since the death of the dictator, to ask ourselves about the conditions of the apparent dismantling of the totalitarian regime he forged. What is called the Transition has often been presented as a model example of an evolution to democracy without social fracturing. We have many arguments with which to refute this Arcadian story, which has become something of a foundation myth, a discourse to legitimize the political insufficiencies of the present. As we will see, one of the faces of this imposture is the interested politicization of the linguistic identity of *valencià* at the end of the Franco period.

1.3. The linguistic profile of the city

We have already seen that, despite its much longer existence, the genealogy of today's Valencia starts with the Christian conquest by Jaume I, the founder of a dynasty and probably the monarch best known and most loved by the Valencians. In sociolinguistic terms, and simplifying the complexity of diachronic processes, we can identify three great historical stages in the evolution of communication exchanges in the city of Valencia.

(1) From the 13th-century political origins to the 18th century.
As we have already said, the historic, native speech, to the city of Valencia and its kingdom, is a variety of the Catalan language brought by the conquerors who arrived with Jaume I and repopulated the country over many decades. As most of these repopulators came from the lands of western Catalonia, *valencià* belongs to the western block of the Catalan language.

The original names of the language, such as *romanç* or *pla* (Romance or plain), do not indicate its geographical origin. Throughout the period, we find a minority of literary-minded citizens, aware of the language's historic origins, who have borne witness to its unity with other Catalan-speaking territories. Awareness of the unity of the language is compatible with the fact that, as early as the 14th century when the name *català* began to be generalized, more local names such as *valencià* or *Valencian language* were used. These names are the expression of small-scale local pride in distinctive ownership, which some historians call the 'Creole complex'; but using them does not bring into question Valencia's linguistic unity with Catalonia and the Balearic Islands.

The kind of *valencià* spoken today in the city of Valencia and its immediate surroundings, the county of l'Horta, is called *apitxat* (compressed) because it is characterized by an 'apitxament' or narrowing of the vocal chords, which results in the muffled pronunciation of certain consonant sounds, for example *casa*, pronounced [kása] and not [káza]. It appears that in the 16th century most of the population spoke a *valencià* very like contemporary *apitxat*. A lettered minority knew Latin, Castilian Spanish and, in the Enlightenment, French. Under the Habsburgs, Castilian became increasingly predominant; but as this early Castilianization was horizontal and selective, it only affected the aristocracy and the literary elites (Ninyoles, 1995a).

(2) From the War of Succession to the Franco dictatorship.
The rout of the Habsburg dynasty and the coming to the throne of Philip V, the first king in the Borbon line, marked the start of the political persecution of Catalan in all spheres of public life. This persecution, with its contradictory options, rhythms and results, culminated with the repression of the Franco years.

Until well into the Industrial Revolution, at a time when most of the population were illiterate, the native language continued to be used, although Castilian steadily became more common: it was heard in the pulpit, the theatres, the courts and official announcements and in much expressions of oral literature. With extensive layers of popular classes becoming literate, knowledge of Castilian served as an indicator of class position. The *sainets* (farces) of Eduard Escalante, magnificently studied by Aracil (1966), reflect very well the phenomenon of social mobility by means of ambivalent mechanisms of humour. The generalization of this process is the consequence of social stratification and economic interests that were different from those prevailing in Catalonia. There the colonial crisis precipitated the articulation of a pre-nationalist discourse, centred on a language that was standardized by Pompeu Fabra. In the Valencian Lands, although the teaching of the Barcelona linguist could not be disputed and attracted many followers in the city of Valencia (Pitarch, 2011), political Valencianism did not succeed in becoming a broad social movement with a reach across different classes.

Francoism only exacerbated Castilianization, which became vertical and indiscriminate. The violence exerted against *valencià* was varying. In the first years of the dictatorship, as in other places with their own language, the streets of the city were filled with graffiti with the slogan 'Hable usted en cristiano' (Speak in Christian). This threatening expression was also common among the authorities of the regime. Pressure was exerted in many ways: in street names, in the communications media, in centres of education, and in entertainment, but perhaps the most effective way was through the unconscious assimilation of use patterns induced by mass indoctrination and systematic terror. Thousands of Valencian-speaking couples came to the city from the inland areas and 'decided' to bring up their children in the *language of the Empire* (i.e. Castilian).

(3) From the Transition to the current globalization of poverty.
History has accelerated greatly in the last four decades. Technological, economic, social-political and cultural change is deeper and faster than in any preceding period. Many cities have seen radical changes in their urban physiognomy, their human landscape and the social routines which, like linguistic communication, do not seem very visible, which means they can disappear without leaving a trace. In little more than 30 years, Valencia has changed from a backward city, lacking communications, cultural and leisure facilities or attractive monuments to being an open well-communicated urban centre with a broad range of hotels and increasing mobility of visitors for business, cultural and academic activities or simply as occasional tourists.

The sociolinguistic evolution that has accompanied this process is just as interesting and well worth studying. At the end of the Franco period, the political opposition to the regime succeeded in agreeing a programme of demands that were crystallized in the slogan 'Liberty, Amnesty and Statute of Autonomy'. The third of these terms called for government decentralization and recognition of linguistic rights for those communities with their own language. Demanding for *valencià* the same rights as those given to the State's common language placed on the table the problem of its identity: the name, the narrative of its origins and the symbols that made it visible. The question was to fill a centuries-old deficit, lasting at least from the 18th century, when diglossia was imposed on the city by force of arms, *valencià* had continued to be spoken, but had disappeared from the public stage.

Aware of the threat represented by this political change, the local representatives of the Franco regime (the authorities, senior civil servants, businessmen, media bosses and professional people) took advantage of the circumstances and led the political debate onto the terrain of emotional confrontation. The myth of the foreign invader was created for public opinion. Catalonia, with the connivance of pro-Catalanists within the country, aimed to impose their language, which was presented as totally different from *valencià*. What some have incorrectly called the *Battle of Valencia*, the social-political conflict about names and symbols that was unleashed from 1976 on, dominated the social and political life of the city until well into the following decade and has conditioned the political debate right down to today.

In the conflict, unitarists and secessionists faced off against each other, i.e. those who believed *valencià* belonged to the common trunk of the Catalan language and those who objected to this view. Both sectors called themselves, also incorrectly, *Catalanists* or *blavers*. Each had their symbolic repertoire (name of the territory, *País Valencià* – Valencian Land – or *Regne de València*, Kingdom of Valencia; *senyera*, autocton flag, standard without a blue fringe or with one, source of the pejorative term, *blavers*; hymn, *La Moixaranga*, a traditional tune, *versus* the Hymn of the 1909 Regional Exhibition).

The confrontation caused no fatalities, apart from a young demonstrator killed in Alicante in 1977. But the energy wasted was huge. And, more seriously, the political price has still not been paid. In fact, the symbols of linguistic secession were imposed in the debate on the Autonomy Statute for the Valencian Community (1982) and in its reform (2006), which sanctions them together with the official name of the territory. It is not at all easy to summarize the causes, manifestations and consequences of this conflict, which has needed the passage of time and generational change to find plausible explanations within the social sciences (Archilés, 2010; Flor, 2011).

In the argument about the name, identity and symbols of the language, both sides have achieved partial successes. The Constitutional

Court accepted the use of the term 'Catalan language' to refer to *valencià* in a 1997 sentence concerning the Statutes of the University of Valencia. Since then, the abundant case law has recognized openly the legal-referential equivalence of *català* and *valencià*. In addition, the Institut d'Estudis Catalans, Catalonia's top academic body and a scientific institution widely recognized throughout Europe, accepted the name *valencià* to refer to the Catalan language, over which it has had regulatory authority since 1976.

Sidestepping legal and scientific arguments, local and regional governments, which have been in the hands of the centre-right (PP) since 1991 and 1995 respectively, have sought to profit from the conflict. Thus, in summer 1998, Eduardo Zaplana, then President of the Generalitat (the Autonomous Government) of Valencia, asked the Valencia Council for Culture (CVC) to issue a dictate on the identity conflict. The document drawn up by the CVC, and passed on 13 July 1998, stated this:

> We must also say that, under the protection of the Statute of Autonomy and of the self-government that the Statute has made possible, we have seen recently a clear improvement in the level of esteem and social prestige of *valencià*, which is a favourable basis for seeking with optimism the necessary recovery of our language, so damaged at present by abandonment and neglect. Unfortunately, this improvement is impeded by the sterile conflict perpetuated among us, especially in the city of Valencia and its conurbation. A conflict about the name, nature and regulations of the native language of the Valencians that damages its health and adds to the difficulties in the process of recovery of the language that should identify and unite us as Valencians, instead of separating us. (*Official Gazette of the Generalitat of Valencia*, dogv, no. 3334)

This extract is highly significant. First, the linguistic conflict is not attributed to the process of Castilianization, which is usual in the relevant sociolinguistic bibliography, but to a dispute about 'the name, nature and regulations' of *valencià*, which, as we have just indicated, could have been partly resolved by respecting the legal and scientific pronouncements about it. Second, the extract falls into what it denounces: the continuation of the conflict. The name of the language is expressed in a customarily roundabout way (*the native language of the Valencians*), avoiding those other clearer formulations that, as stated by regulatory and cultural authorities, should conclude the dispute. Put another way, it wants to conjure away a conflict of lack of definition with further lack of definition. Third, it puts forward a bold thesis: the conflict is sterile, at least in the city of Valencia. The CVC advises that the dispute on names and symbols should be closed, so that the language can become the main collective element of cohesive identity. The conflict is sterile because it encourages social confrontation, especially in the capital. The extract sets up a counter-position: on the one hand, there would be a general recovery of the language, reflected in the text by expressions such as 'clear improvement', 'favourable basis', 'necessary recovery', would take place. On the other hand, the capital would suffer due to what is described in the extract as the 'sterile conflict' which 'damages health' and 'adds to difficulties': in short, the maintenance of 'abandonment and neglect'.

This dictate ushered in legislation that created the Valencian Academy of the Language (AVL) in the same year. The academy was finally constituted in 2001, with its permanent headquarters in the capital. This organism is more political than academic. Its apparent aim is to resolve the conflict once and for all, by bringing together representatives of the two opposing sides and providing major resources and regulatory power over all aspects of the native language. Under these conditions, the scientific and social legitimacy of the AVL was questioned. Over a decade after its creation, little is known of the AVL's activity and it is still controversial. It has little if any social visibility and so far has done practically nothing to provide an effective solution to the underlying social-political problem.

In effect, the threat of social fracture due to the identity conflict is the principal argument that successive Autonomous Community governments have wielded, in order to pose a short-term linguistic policy. During the Socialist period (1983–1995), the Llei d'Ús i Ensenyament del Valencià (LUEV), Act on the Use and Teaching of *Valencià* (1983) was passed and the social expansion of the language was based on three basic pillars: education, the mass media, and local government bodies. The PP governments (1995–2012) did not vary their approach greatly at first (Bodoque, 2009). However, as they have enjoyed large overall majorities since 1999, there has been a growing tendency to neutralize the timid advances and even to dismantle inherited government action (Pardines & Torres, 2011).

Of the three pillars of the linguistic recovery mentioned, only education has given clear returns and has maintained a mass of speakers competent in the language (see Section 2). In effect, the educational system, with the great support of Valencia's public universities, and particularly of the biggest, the University of Valencia, has advanced towards the partial Valencianization of state schools at all levels. Teaching of *valencià* and in *valencià* has also favoured the birth of a fragile network of culture industries, particularly publishers. The most important asset in this entire process is the associative social movement *Escola Valenciana*, which mobilizes thousands of teachers and students at all educational levels.

The sociolinguistic balance-sheet of the Autonomous Community's radio and television, created during the Socialist period (1989), is somewhat contradictory. On the one hand, access to the Valencian variety of Catalan in such powerful mass media is a historic achievement in itself. Nor should the role they have played in endowing *valencià* with dignity and in educating citizens linguistically be underestimated. But the fact that broadcasts have never been exclusively in Catalan, the low quality of programmes produced by the channels themselves and the sectarianism of news coverage, more and more accentuated under conservative control, have failed to meet the high expectations that their creation aroused. Much the same could be said of the scant use of *valencià* in the government bodies and courts based in the city.

On the other hand, the last twenty years have not just seen a critical deadlock in linguistic policy. Like so many other societies in Europe, Valencia has changed due to the combination of two interdependent processes:

- technological development linked to the spreading of computer networks;
- the economic and demographic changes characteristic of the stage of capitalism previous to the current crisis of the system.

In effect, between 1989 and 2006 there was strong economic growth (Boira, 2011, 2012). We have already highlighted Valencia's urban take-off, which was achieved on the basis of swallowing up hectares of agricultural land in one of Europe's most fertile alluvial plains. This growth required abundant imported labour. In reality, despite what the sterotypical xenophobe defends, migrations in the new globalization are not a consequence of the 'call effect', but of the demand of aged societies embracing the knowledge economy, which need a lot of labour for primary jobs (Piqueras Infante, 2005). This is the context within which we will discuss, in the following two sections, the linguistic interactions that organize the life of the city.

2. Language Competence and Use Among the Urban Population: The Castilian/Catalan Contrast

2.1. Prior considerations

Barring some exceptions, the studies on the status of Catalan and Castilian in the city of Valencia have used quantitative techniques and general data. The two data sources for analysing the linguistic competence and usage of the population of Valencia are (1) the population censuses and the municipal rolls and their updatings, of both the city itself and the towns in its Metropolitan area and (2) sociolinguistic questionnaires (Hernández Dobon, 2001).

Clearly neither source is perfect, since they record what individuals state about what they know and do, but do not reveal what individuals *really* know and do. For example, the common question in questionnaires 'do you read in *valencià*?', which in reality is asking about passive written competence, paradoxically receives lower percentages of affirmative answers than the question about whether the person in question reads signs in *valencià* in the street. This means that many people are saying nothing about their competence, but rather about whether in effect they read, for example, books in *valencià*. In addition, though, there's a further problem, already referred to. It is not the same to formulate the question 'Do you read in *valencià*?' as 'Do you read in Catalan?' or 'Do you read in the Valencian language?'. What for an outside observer may seem a trivial point refers to a certain social conflict at the heart of the city that has not been overcome.

A third difficulty lies in that sociolinguistic surveys (and from now on, population censuses too) and the publication of their findings are decided on by the corresponding authorities, which are subject to political decisions and budget restraints. This explains why the surveys conducted have not been at all systematic. As we lack coherent data series, analyses often have to recur to calculations or extrapolations that reduce the accuracy of the conclusions. For the same reason, the relationship between the city's sociolinguistic situation and other social variables (such as migratory movements, for instance) cannot be studied in the necessary detail. After these prior comments, we will now analyse the data available.

2.2. Linguistic competence

The results of the censuses and the municipal rolls are summarized in Table 6.2, where the percentages of population over three years old that can

Table 6.2 POC, AOC, PWC and AWC in the city of Valencia, censuses of 1991 and 2001 and rolls of 1986 and 1996

	Roll 1986 (A)	Census 1991	Roll 1996	Census 2001 (B)
POC	82.1%	86.93%	91.38%	88.5%
AOC	39.7%	43.27%	46.13%	43.3%
AOC/POC	48.35%	49.77%	50.48%	48.92%
PWC	36.34%	46.23%	44.72%	52.4%
AWC	6.7%	13.83%	18.28%	21.5%
AWC/PWC	18.43%	29.91%	40.87%	41.03%
	Absolute variation (B-A)	Relative variation (B-A)/A	Annual rate (C)	
POC	6.4%	7.79%	0.5%	
AOC	3.6%	9.06%	0.58%	
PWC	16.06%	44.19%	2.46%	
AWC	14.80%	220.89%	8.08%	

Source: INE, Statistical Office of Valencia City Council, Colom 2011 and own data. The annual rate is calculated with the formula $B = A (1 + C)^n$, where n is the number of years between A and B, i.e. 15.

understand *valencià* (passive oral competence, POC), speak it (active oral competence, AOC), read it (passive written competence, PWC) or write it (active written competence, AWC) are detailed. As can be seen, POC reached 88.5% in the last census, having risen slightly, at an annual rate of 0.5%, by almost 8 points in 15 years. AOC is just half POC, at around 43.3%, though it has also receded in recent years. Its annual rate is 0.58%, similar to that of POC. The PWC percentage is higher than AO's, but with a higher annual rate of 2.46%. Both censuses and rolls coincide that there are more people who can read in *valencià* than who talk it. Lastly, AWC reached 21.5% in the 2001 census, with a very high annual rate of 8.08%.

The two sociolinguistic surveys conducted by the Research and Sociolinguistic Studies Service (SIES)[2] offer a very broad range of replies. The respondent is asked if he/she understands, knows how to talk, knows how to read or knows how to write, with the following options: not at all, a little, quite well, perfectly, don't know/don't answer. For the following data we have grouped the 'quite well' and 'perfectly' options. In 1993 and 2006, the POC of inhabitants of the city who were of age dropped slightly less than 10 percentage points, practically the same as the increase in PWC. This discrepancy between oral and written competence became still more accentuated in the case of active competence. Whereas AOC increased little more than three points, active written competence (AWC) increased by more than 22 points. Oral competence varied by −10.87% (POC) and 3.39% (AOC), figures much lower than those for written competence, which are 19.41% (PWC) and 123.88% (AWC). The data indicate an annual increase rate of 6.39% in the number of people who state they can write in our language. These figures are presented in Table 6.3.

Although they are two different data sources, in one case including people over three-years-old and in the other those over 18, both find that the figures for oral competence behave very differently from those for written competence.

Table 6.3 POC, AOC, PWC and AWC in the city of Valencia, 1993 and 2006 surveys

	1993 (A)	2006 (B)	Absolute variation (B–A)	Relative variation (B–A)/A	Annual rate (C)
POC (quite well + perfectly)	89.65%	79.9%	−9.75%	−10.87%	−0.88%
AOC (quite well + perfectly)	54.45%	56.3%	1.85%	3.39%	0.25%
AOC/POC	60.73%	70.46%			
PWC (quite well + perfectly)	48.15%	57.5%	9.35%	19.41%	1.37%
AWC (quite well + perfectly)	18.00%	40.3%	22.30%	123.88%	6.39%
AWC/PWC	37.38%	70.08%			

Source: SIES: Sociological Surveys in the city of Valencia, 1993, 2006 and own data. The annual rate is calculated with the formula $B = A(1+C)^n$, where n is the number of years between A and B, i.e. 15.

Whereas the former oscillate slightly (with annual rates between – 0.88% and 0.58%), written competence has risen, and faster in the case of active competence (with a rate between 6.39% and 8.08%, depending on the source). There is a discrepancy between the two data sources in the relationship between passive and active competence. Whereas the data in the rolls and censuses pointed to a practically constant relationship at around 50% between AOC and POC, in the surveys the relationship was greater and increased to 70%. The discrepancy is still greater in the relationship between AWC and PWC, which is partly explained by the difference in the ages of the populations surveyed.

The data describe two processes: first, the stabilization of the number of people with oral competence and, second, a phenomenon we could '*escripturització* (i.e. raising the profile of the written form)', '*assignaturització* (i.e. converting it into a school subject)' or simply '*escolarització* (schooling)' of the language. The conclusion we can draw from the data on competence and the processes indicated is that the inhabitants of Valencia are divided, in two ways: not only is there a division between people who are competent and can understand, speak, read or write in *valencià* and those others who are not and cannot, but there is also a second division between those with active competence and those who have only passive competence or none at all. In the case of oral competence, this double division has varied little over time, which would mean that the city does not have the ability to shape new speakers in any real way. It should be noted that public spaces do not have an educational character. Written competence, which at the start of the statistical series had much lower percentages than oral competence, has increased markedly (both in its rates and in the proportion of active/passive competence), drawing close to the oral competence percentages.

The trend towards dualization due to convergence of the percentages of the two kinds of active competence is illustrated in Figure 6.2, which shows the (exponential) trend lines of the two variables, AOC and AWC, according to the census and municipal roll data sources.

The incapacity of public space to promote the competence of citizens can be seen if we make two more detailed analyses of the above data. First, we can compare the different degrees of competence of the native and the foreign populations. As can be seen, in the case of active competence the 16–64-year-old age-group does not reach more than 10% of the competence achieved by the native population. The table also shows the impact of teaching *valencià*, because the group of foreigners under 16 have competence percentages higher than the 16–64 age-group in all cases.

Taking into account the sociolinguistic surveys of the SIES for 1993 and 2006, and if we analyse the competence data of the various age cohorts and establish an expected variation, we obtain the results given in Table 6.5.

As can be seen, the competence recorded is superior to that expected in the case of AWC and solely in the 35–44 age-groups in the cases of AOC and PWC. For the other cases, the AOC and PWC groups over 45 and all POC

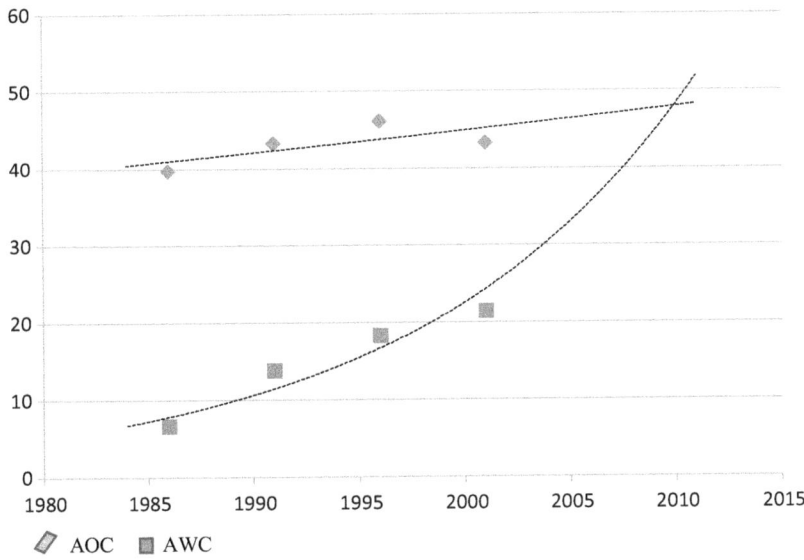

Figure 6.2 Trends: Provisional calculation
Source: Own data: Table 6.2.

Table 6.4 POC, AOC, PWC and AWC according to the 2001 Census. Native and foreign people, by age-groups and comparison

	Native			Foreign			Comparison		
	−16 years old	16–64	+64	−16	16–64	+64	−16	16–64	+64
POC	69.1	95.5	88.3	40.8	39.6	47.8	59%	41%	54%
AOC	33.5	48.3	41.1	10.4	4.6	10.1	31%	10%	25%
PWC	41.7	61.7	35.3	17.6	9.9	14.0	42%	16%	40%
AWC	25.6	25.6	7.0	8.3	2.5	1.0	32%	10%	14%

Source: Colom 2011, based on INE data: 2001 census.

groups, the results are lower than expected. The above table makes still clearer the differences in behaviour between oral and written competence.

2.3. Language use

Moving on to the use of the language (as can be seen in Table 6.6), according to the 1993 sociological survey 20.43% of the population spoke

Table 6.5 POC, AOC, PWC and AWC by age-groups, 1996 and 2003

POC	15–24	25–34	35–44	45–54	55–64	65
1993	93%	89%	92%	89%	87%	86%
2006	85%	81%	77%	80%	75%	80%
Variation			−13%	−11%	−15%	−8%
AOC	15–24	25–34	35–44	45–54	55–64	65
1993	51%	52%	54%	53%	62%	57%
2006	75%	57%	53%	50%	51%	52%
Variation			1%	−3%	−2%	−7%
PWC	15–24	25–34	35–44	45–54	55–64	65
1993	62%	52%	54%	54%	36%	25%
2006	84%	64%	59%	52%	45%	39%
Variation			4%	−1%	−9%	−2%
AWC	15–24	25–34	35–44	45–54	55–64	65
1993	38%	18%	16%	13%	9%	6%
2006	40%	40%	38%	27%	25%	26%
Variation			14%	10%	11%	16%

Source: SIES and own composition. The variation was calculated as follows. If we have three periods, A, B and C in the 1993 survey, we will calculate the expected value in the 2006 survey (13 years later) for C' as 3/10(A) + 7/10(B). We understand by variation the difference between the real value of C' and the calculated value.

Table 6.6 Use of the language in the city of Valencia, 1993 and 2006 surveys

	1993 (A)	2006 (B)	Absolute variation (B−A)	Relative variation (B−A)/A	Annual rate (C)
Use at home (always + generally in *valencià*)	20.43%	15.4%	−5.03%	−24.6%	−2.15%
Use in the street (with strangers) (always + generally in *valencià*)	7.02%	5.6%	−1.42%	−20.22%	−1.72%
Inhibition rate	65.64%	63.64%			

Source: SIES: sociological surveys in the city of Valencia, 1993 and 2006 and own data. The inhibition rate is the difference between use at home and in the street. The annual rate is calculated through the formula $B = A(1+C)^n$, where n is the number of years between A and B, i.e. 13.

always or generally in *valencià* at home, percentage that had fallen to 15.4% by 2006. This descent is an absolute loss of 5 percentage points or of 24.6% if we calculate the variation in relative terms. Thus, an increase of 3.39% in potential speakers has not been translated into an increase in effective speakers in the domestic environment: quite the opposite. Put another way, there are a few more people who say they can speak the language, but fewer people who understand it and who in reality speak it in private.

If we compare the use in private (at home) and in public (in the street with strangers) in the 1993 and 2006 surveys, we find that the level of inhibition of the language in public space was maintained, though of course with fewer speakers. The percentage of people who stopped using *valencià* at home always or generally in the 13 years between surveys is similar in relative figures to the percentage of people who stopped speaking the language in the street with strangers (–20.22%), which gives annual rates of about –2% in both cases (see Table 6.6). This means that, if this rhythm of descent is maintained, in about 20 years from the last survey (i.e. in about ten years from the date of this chapter), home speakers will have dropped beneath the threshold of 10% (see Figure 6.3).

In multilingual contexts it is clear that the percentage of people who use a language in private will be greater than in the public sphere in the case of a minority language and lower in the case of a majority language. If we define the 'inhibition rate' as the inverse of the relationship between use in the more private sphere and in the more public one, we find minimal variations between the results of the 1993 survey (65.64%) and the 2006 one (63.64%). This suggests that, out of every three people who use the language at home, only one uses it in the street with strangers.

Although the data show a fall in rates of use, social perception is quite different. According to the 2006 survey, the view of the city's inhabitants is that *valencià*, at the social level, was used 'more' than before (38.4%) or 'the

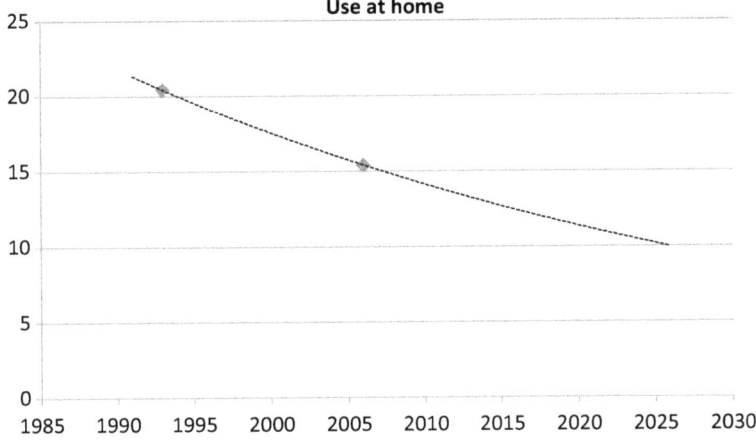

Figure 6.3 Predicted use of *valencià* at home
Source: own composition.

Table 6.7 *Valencià* is used/should be used

	More	Same	Less	Don't know/ don't answer
valencià is used socially...	38.4%	45.2%	14.6%	1.8%
Thinks that it should be used...	52.0%	41.3%	5.0%	1.1%

Source: SIES, 1993 and 2006.

same' (45.2%), replies much higher than 'less' (14.6%). Although the survey shows it is used less, very few people state that it *should* be used less (5%); on the contrary, over half the population think it should be used more (52%). See the results broken down in Table 6.7.

2.4. Valencia and l'Horta

The city of Valencia is located in the county of l'Horta. The capital and the towns surrounding it, known as the Metropolitan area of Valencia, make up a sociolinguistic region that has been studied in various surveys. Bearing in mind the distribution of population in Valencia and l'Horta, we can establish figures (of course, very provisional ones) for linguistic competence and use in the Metropolitan area.

The calculation is based on data from the Valencian Institute of Statistics (IVE) for the population of the counties on 1 January 2008, according to which the city of Valencia had 807,200 inhabitants, 52.77% of the population

Table 6.8 POC, AOC, PWC and AWC in the city of Valencia (2006 survey), in the Metropolitan area of Valencia and the city of Valencia (2005 survey) and calculation for the Metropolitan area

	City of Valencia (2006)	Metropolitan Area and city of Valencia (2005) (A)	Calculation Metropolitan Area (without the city)	Metropolitan Area and city of Valencia (2010) (B)	Annual rate
POC (fairly well + perfectly)	79.9%	75.7%	71.01%	73.4%	−0.61%
AOC (fairly well + perfectly)	56.3%	47.8%	38.30%	49.4%	0.65%
PWC (fairly well + perfectly)	57.5%	50.7%	43.10%	50.5%	−0.07%
AWC (fairly well + perfectly)	40.3%	27.9%	14.05%	29.8%	1.30%

Source: SIES: *Sociological surveys in the city of Valencia, 2006* and *Survey on knowledge and use of Valencià, 2005*.

Table 6.9 Language use in the city of Valencia (2006 survey), in the Metropolitan area of Valencia and city of Valencia (2005 and 2010 surveys) and calculation for the Metropolitan area

	City of Valencia (2006)	Metropolitan Area and city of Valencia (2005) (A)	Calculation Metropolitan Area (2005)	Metropolitan Area and city of Valencia (2010) (B)	Annual rate
Use at home (always + generally in *valencià*)	15.4%	22.4%	30.22%	17.0%	−5.36%
Use in the street (always + generally in *valencià*)	5.6%	9.2%	13.22%	8.1%	−2.57%
Inhibition rate	63.64%	58.93%	56.25%	52.35%	

Source: SIES: *Sociological surveys in the city of Valencia, 2006* and *Survey on knowledge and use of Valencià, 2005*. The inhibition rate is calculated as 1-(use in the street/ use at home). The annual rate is calculated with the formula $B = A(1+C)^n$, where n is the number of years between A and B, i.e. 5.

of the Metropolitan area (1,529,698), which also includes l'Horta North (214,758 inhabitants), l'Horta West (339,491 inhabitants) and l'Horta South (168,249 inhabitants). The annual rate is calculated with the formula $B = A(1+C)^n$, where n is the number of years between A and B, i.e. 5.

In Table 6.9 we have added the data from the 2010 survey, in which the trends already noted for the city of Valencia can be appreciated, such as the descent in POC and increase in AWC. However, in this case the changes are much more nuanced.

The figures in Tables 6.7 and 6.8 show that there are higher percentages of competence in the city of Valencia than in its Metropolitan area, but percentages of lower use and a greater inhibition rate.

2.5. The disconnection between competence and use

The belief that the increase in linguistic competence brought about by the teaching of *valencià* and in *valencià* would have positive effects on increasing use of the native language was not borne out by the data available. Not only is there a disconnection between competence and use, but there are distinct dynamics in oral and written competence. This is what we have called above the '*escolarització*' or 'schooling' of the language. This is why the age variable becomes significant.

Although we do not have sufficient data on the city of Valencia, the surveys conducted in the entire Autonomous Region allows us to establish the inverse relationship between linguistic competence and the presence of non-native population. For example, with the data from the general SIES studies of 2005 and 2010 and the corresponding reviews of the municipal rolls for the population aged between 25 and 64, we can calculate a correlation coefficient of POC and the presence of a foreign population of –0.65, and in the case of AOC, of –0.56 (Hernández Dobon, 2012).

These correlations can be logically explained by the weakness of public space as an educational tool. The effect of school is translated into increased written competence in the youngest cohorts, but only affects a part of the population. Thus, this favours a certain 'duality' in the population, due to two phenomena:

(a) A marked level of inhibition (relationship between the people who say they use the language in public space and in private, and those who use it only in private). This level may fall even lower, as the community using *valencià* goes down (in a situation of total duality, obviously it tends toward zero).
(b) A convergence in the trends linked to active competence.

3. A Compact View of Sociolinguistic Interaction in the City of Valencia

The description and analysis of the city of Valencia as a multilingual space must obviously include the series of interactions generated since the beginnings of the profound changes in the urban landscape of the past few years. This is a phenomenon shared with many other cities where urban growth, business opportunities, transport connections and community links have combined (Piqueras Infante, 2005). The result is that a range of ethnic minorities have now been added to the traditional population groups, and the primary ethnic profiles developed over centuries have been erased (with the possible exception of Gypsies) and replaced by barriers of class, corporate entity or professional identity. In the last 20 years, the city has welcomed these ethnic groups, who do not always respond to a single pattern of language use. Table 6.10 shows the main linguistic groups settled in the city.

Going beyond the data, which among other things require constant updating, the question is to establish that the presence of these ethnic-linguistic groups has introduced significant changes not just in economic activity, such as retail trade or the restaurant business, but also in the idiosyncrasy of certain neighbourhoods where their presence can be felt, and that the response to this phenomenon has been complex. This has occurred in the historic neighbourhood of Russafa, a lower-class area with a marked personality, where at the start of the 1990s a part of the Maghrebi colony settled and opened small food and hotel businesses. The attitudes of rejection by a part of the native population contributed to the propagation of the

Table 6.10 Foreigners in Valencia: Main nationalities

Ecuador	29,495
Romania	25,418
Colombia	18,073
Morocco	16,092
Bulgaria	14,502
Bolivia	13,472
United Kingdom	9146
Argentina	8877
Italy	7277
Algeria	6597
China	6403
France	6244
Ukraine	5992
Pakistan	5057

Source: INE, 2006 roll.

image of a neighbourhood in decline, but which later picked up momentum again and welcomed a number of new leisure and culture facilities.

It is clear that we lack a great deal of information about this new aspect of the city's sociolinguistic reality. Here we can do no more than point to a research perspective that would have to evaluate the subjects, the scenarios and the procedures for observation and analysis of the interactions of these subjects, and would not slip into mere measurement of communication exchanges. We stress the word 'communication' rather than 'language' because an ambitious study like this one needs to embrace the broader notion of communicative competence, representations and behaviour (which of course includes linguistic competence, representations and behaviour). We will limit ourselves to pointing out the lines of investigation that have to be borne in mind in the perspective of a study of multilateral linguistic studies, distinguishing three situations:

(I) The communication models of immigrants who have been stably settled in the city for a variable time;
(II) The communicative usage of the floating population whose stay is a brief one, for business, leisure or family reasons;
(III) The linguistic behaviour of academic exchange students.

(I) First, the new 'linguistic economy' that immigration creates should be looked at, with a complex description of 'submerged' linguistic communities and of their communication practice. Specifically, the following points should be analysed:

(a) The degree of internal cohesion, linked to the maintenance of their original languages, transmission rate, communication environments, creation of discourse (publications, radio and TV channels, presence in cyberspace), etc.
(b) The degree of competence and use and the linguistic attitudes created in the instrumental handling of Catalan and Castilian by different language groups settled in the city.
(c) The phenomena of code-switching and linguistic interference. A basic factor in this analysis is the growing passive and active competence in English that much of the world's population possesses today, by virtue of the technological communication that has reduced distances and drawn languages and cultures closer.

A full study of these characteristics would have to distinguish speakers' cultural and linguistic areas, within which the citizens of the same country are grouped. As is obvious, political-administrative reasons or national loyalty do not have the same weight in every context. The youngest nation-states of Africa are super-imposed on linguistic groups. And the reverse is also true: many ethnic and linguistic groups live together in the same country on the Gulf of Guinea or the coast of the Indian Ocean. The replies to the questions posed in (a) and (b) should refer to the following groups.

(1) Immigration from Latin America, divided between the communities that still conserve Amerindian languages (Quechua, Aymara, Guaraní...) and the two Romance languages exported by the Spanish and Portuguese. Following this schema, this immigration can be broken down into various national groups: Colombians, Ecuadorians, Argentinians, Brazilians, etc.
(2) Immigration from Eastern Europe. The people who arrive from countries that belonged to the Soviet bloc often come with asymmetrical competence, merely reproducing situations of linguistic conflict in their native context: for example, Romanians from the Magyar or German minorities, Ukrainians educated in standard Russian, Kosovars speaking Albanian and educated in Serbo-Croat, Poles who speak Czech or Byelorussian. These are some of the situations that we can find transferred to our country, i.e. one conflict superimposed on another, with an unstable background of communication flows and with an undisputable first common language.
(3) African immigration. The long list of ethno-cultural and linguistic groups from the African continent leads us to an initial sub-division. The first is the Mediterranean peoples of the north-west of the continent, and second comprises all the rest. In effect, immigration from the Maghreb starts with a particularity and historical, geographical and

cultural bonds that do not apply to the other areas. In addition, the peoples of the Maghreb have an interesting mix of languages and linguistic codes. Many of the communities from the north of Morocco, Algeria, Tunisia and part of Libya conserve their native language, *Amazig, berber* in the traditional pejorative name. *Amazig* is quite distinct from the Semitic linguistic family to which Arabic belongs, language with which these countries entered into contact at the start of the process of Islamization in the 7th century. In addition, within Arabic, the cultured or literary language, which is used in the reading of the Koran, needs to be distinguished from the regional varieties of vulgar Arabic or dialects. Over these two languages, still another is superimposed: the French of the European colonialists who exploited this extensive region for over a century.

The linguistic groups of sub-Saharan Africa also have a sociolinguistic panorama that is considerably more complex than what we might imagine with a reductionist Eurocentric vision. Alongside the older and more conservative native tongues, there coexist common languages, *pidgin* and creole speech and languages of the colonial superstratum that have ended up becoming naturalized and acquiring official status. A study such as the one we propose would lead us to distinguish, for example, Fula speakers, who might be Senegalese or Gambians, Wolof speakers, who could come from Senegal, Mauritania, Mali or Gambia; one of the Niger-Congo languages such as Mandinga or Soninke, spoken in the countries mentioned and in others in the area, such as Guinea, Guinea-Bissau or Ghana. Less numerous in Valencia, but not unknown, are speakers of Swahili, the East African language of the Bantu group, highly influenced by Arab, Portuguese and English superstrata. Swahili is spoken in the region of the Great Lakes, Kenya and Tanzania (Moreno Cabrera, 2004).

(4) Asian immigration. As with Africa, the study of the interactions between the host languages (Castilian and Catalan) and each group's own languages can be broken down into a fairly extensive list of languages. Like the case of Africa, too, we have to consider the confluence of the original languages of that vast continent, the European colonial languages and hybrid linguistic codes, which arise due to the requirements of international trade and politics, dominated for centuries by Westerners. Thus, from the Asian linguistic mosaic we would pick out just three main groups:

- communities from the Indian sub-continent, Hindu in religion and using, as well as English, Hindi as a supra-regional common language;
- the Pakistani community, Muslim in religion and speaking Urdu;
- the Chinese communities, who for their oral communication may use regional variations such as Cantonese, Wu, Min or Xiang, standard

Mandarin, which is the basis for classic written language, or Putonghua, a standard that also functions as a common communication language for many countries in South-east Asia, such as Singapore, Malaysia, Indonesia and Vietnam, among others (Moreno Cabrera, 2004).

(II) English, as the dominant common language of tourism and new business.

Clearly, the communication and language interactions occurring between occasional visitors and residents do not have the relevance of the interactions within the latter group, the stable population. This fluctuating population is very heterogeneous in itself, as it consists of a number of people with varying activities, including Spanish, European and non-European tourists, transport and communications workers, employees in many different services, people attending scientific or business meetings, and so on. Due to the intrinsic diversity of this group, it is very hard to measure it and establish a pattern of language ascription and communication situations.

If there is perhaps a common denominator of this group, it is that most people from outside Spain tend to use English as their usual common language. This is a growing trend and affects, to a lesser or greater extent, the language habits of hotel and restaurant workers, language services and retail trade in the city centre. A complete map of multilingual Valencia would have to pay attention to this phenomenon from the dual angle of language production (who is speaking and how, with what kind of formal repertoire, closer to or further from classic *pidgin* etc.) and of schemata of symbolic representation (what weight is given to international English, how it coexists in the terrain of symbols with other, native or foreign, linguistic codes, what personal and ideological consequences can be drawn from it all, and so on).

(III) Valencia as an academic destination.

The presence of foreign students in the city's two public universities, the UVEG and the UPV, creates a new front of inter-cultural and inter-linguistic contacts, with its own impact on the historic sociolinguistic conflict and the displacement of Catalan by Castilian Spanish in the many spheres of urban life. When students from EU member states on academic mobility programmes or from the US or other countries reach Valencia, they mostly have the same expectations regarding linguistic communication as they would have if they had gone to any other city in Spain. The degree of information on the bilingual reality of the city tends to be limited or even non-existent. Nonetheless, the presence of visiting students in courses taught in Catalan, especially at the UVEG, has not given rise to the problems that have been found in some universities in Catalonia. The language services of these two universities possess the data required for the study of this facet of multilingual Valencia.

4. Conclusions

Any reading of social data has to be linked to the social-political context that creates them. To make qualitative assessments, observation of a complex sociolinguistic reality such as the city of Valencia's has to be related to the historical, cultural and economic data and, of course, to the political bias of the municipal and regional governments that have succeeded each other over 30 years of democratic restoration. A restoration that, it should not be forgotten, was not born of a rupture with Francoism, but of its 'natural' continuity. As for the description supported by statistics, the limitations inherent to the paradox of the observer, exemplified in any scientific study, must be assumed. For sure, quantitative sociolinguistic measurement is indispensable, but is at the same time insufficient, as it is partial, uncertain and fragmentary.

In the end, in this summary we have combined the two approaches, with which we can formulate the following conclusions.

(1) A preliminary assessment of the sociolinguistic reality of the city of Valencia confirms for us the hybrid and contradictory nature of the contemporary multilingual city, crossroads where identities are reinvented and languages and social projects are counterposed (Ninyoles, 1995a, 1995b; Marí, 1996).
(2) Valencia is a paradigm of profound transformations, which are also found in inter-group linguistic communication. In little more than three decades, it has changed from being a parochial, provincial city, enclosed in the inertia of Francoist dependence and in which *valencià* played little if any role, to one characterized by the eruption of technological communication, in which the native language now has its own presence but has to compete on a playing field that is not level with Spanish, the State's language of reference, and with English, the main common language of tourism and large-scale economic operations.
(3) After centuries of subjugation, Catalan, the historical, native language that Valencians normally call 'valencià', the effects of a timid and partial policy of linguistic recovery, which started with the legislation passed in 1983 known as the LUEV, are beginning to be felt. The discreet advance of Catalan in the city and its surrounding areas has occurred through the combined action of school, radio and television (RTVV and TV3, Catalonia's main Catalan-language channel), the cultural subsystem in the native language, and other lesser initiatives, such as the language-promotion campaigns of some large town councils in the Valencian conurbation with progressive local governments.
(4) The surveys on competence and language use reveal that the city of Valencia shares a trend that can be seen in the rest of the País Valencià and even in Catalonia and the Balearic Islands: teaching has increased the competence of younger speakers, but the effective use of the

language outside the classroom is going backwards. This disconnection between competence and language use requires more accurate instruments of observation and, above all, the political will to correct it and re-balance the two sides of the social production of linguistic reality.

(5) There again, the linguistic advances in schooling and other areas are threatened by the presence of centre-right governments (PP) in the State as a whole, in the Autonomous Community and the Valencia City Council. This is the political formation that traditionally defends the interests of the Castilianized and Spanish-centralist elites, whose dislike for the Catalan language is self-evident. In addition, the disruption of linguistic policy occurs in the context of a social conflict and a conflict of identity which have never been satisfactorily resolved. Many professionals, teachers and people from the world of culture reject the constant attacks on *valencià*. The doubt is whether this civil society, of which the *Escola Valenciana* movement is a clear expression, will be able to prevent the urban *ghettoization* of Catalan, the stage preceding its virtual extinction.

(6) The political management of the city of Valencia in recent decades has developed in parallel a new kind of grandiloquent urban development and a destruction of the project of reconstructing the city and rebalancing the social deficits of its historic language. In this way of understanding the city, traditional urban planning and architecture are stripped of meaning in favour of the patterns of cultural homogenization. Globalization is accompanied by the appearance of what the anthropologist Marc Augé (1994) calls *Non-Places*, that is functional spaces (airports, shopping malls, museums, etc.), where the individual finds no elements of identification, where he/she cannot feel empathy or emotional closeness. These places are interchangeable and could be found anywhere else on the planet.

(7) As part of this process, Valencia is being relaunched into the world in parallel with the policy of the City Council and Autonomous Community of reducing the city's historic language to minority status. The dismantling of the educational network, of the small audiovisual ecosystem for *valencià* and local culture industries, especially publishing and the dramatic arts, is a serious step backwards as the native language tries to find its place inside the framework of modernity.

(8) The ruling discourse focuses precisely on the cliché of the modernity of the powerful languages, linked to progress and cyberspace (Spanish, English, Chinese), as opposed to the archaic and technologically obsolete character of native speech. In addition, its loss is justified by invoking what is won in exchange: connection with the rest of the world. *Valencià* continues to be the *apitxat* of the street, or else the more cultured and elaborate version taught in schools. It holds a subordinate position in the Autonomous Community's television channels and can

no longer oppose the State language, with which it has fought an uphill battle for centuries. Now, the conflict is mediated by a third actor in play, English.
(9) After two decades of 'runaway' growth (Giddens, 2000), in the middle of the last decade the crash of the finance-real estate bubble ushered in the current crisis, whose outcome is uncertain. If finally we succeed in emerging from the current situation, we will have to redefine shared social objectives, consensus values, the resources available and the productive structures. And in this joint endeavour, the roles of the languages that cohabit both on the city's virtual stage and in its physical reality will have to be assessed.

Notes

(1) This chapter has been supported by the Project research FFI2012-35502 'Globalization and social family multilingualism in European medium sized linguistic communities' (Spanish Ministry of Economy and Competitivity) GLOBLINMED.
(2) This study – and most of those conducted by language sociology in our country – has benefited from the surveys directed magnificently by Rafael L. Ninyoles, without whose work the analyses given here would have been impossible, though the deficiencies of the analyses are solely the authors' responsibility.

References

Aracil, L.V. (1966) El bilingüisme com a mite, in Aracil, L.V. (1982) *Papers de Sociolingüística* (pp. 39–57). Barcelona: La Magrana.
Aracil, L.V. (1968) Introducció to the edition of sainets (*farces*) of ESCALANTE, Eduard, *Les xiques de l'entresuelo. Tres forasters de Madrid*. Valencia: Garbí.
Archilés, F. (2010) El pensament nacionalista en l'obra de Joan Fuster. Unpublished PhD thesis, Universitat de València.
Augé, M. (1994) *Los No Lugares: espacios del anonimato. Una antropología de la sobremodernidad*. Barcelona: Gedisa.
Bodoque, A. (2009) *La política lingüística dels governs valencians (1983–2008): un estudi de polítiques públiques*. Valencia: Universitat de València.
Boira, J.V. (2011) *Valencia. La ciudad*. Valencia: Tirant lo Blanch.
Boira, J.V. (2012) *Valencia. La tormenta perfecta*. Barcelona: RBA.
CCCB (Centre De Cultura Contemporània De Barcelona) (2010) *Barcelona-Valencia-Palma. Una història de confluències i divergències*. Exhibition catalogue. Barcelona: CCCB/Diputació de Barcelona/Generalitat de Catalunya.
Colom, F. (2011) Desigualtats territorials en l'ensenyament a la ciutat de València. Unpublished PhD thesis. Valencia: Universitat de València.
Diari Oficial de la Genertalitat Valenciana, Llei 7/1998, de 16 de setembre, de la Generalitat Valenciana de creació de l'Acadèmia Valenciana de la Llengua, n° 3334 (21.09.1998), 14754-14764.
Flor, V. (2011) *Noves glòries a Espanya. Anticatalanisme i identitat valenciana*. Catarroja: Afers.
Giddens, A. (2000) *Un mundo desbocado: los efectos de la globalización en nuestras vidas*. Madrid: Taurus.
Glaesser, E. (2011) *Triumph of the City. How Our Greatest Invention Makes Us Richer, Smarter, Greener, Healthier, and Happier*. New York: Penguin.

Hernández Dobon F.J. (2001) El valencià a València. Unpublished PhD thesis. Valencia, Universitat de València.
Hernández Dobon F.J. (2012) Alarmant disminució de la competència i l'ús del valencià. *Arxius de Sociologia*, 27, 57–66.
Marí, I. (1996) *Plurilingüisme europeu i Llengua Catalana*. Valencia: Universitat de València.
Moreno Cabrera, J.C. (2004) *El universo de las lenguas*. Madrid: Castalia.
Ninyoles, R.Ll. (1992) *El País Valencià a l'eix mediterrani*. Valencia: L'Eixam.
Ninyoles, R.Ll. (1995a) *Conflicte lingüístic valencià*. Valencia: Eliseu Climent.
Ninyoles, R.Ll. (1995b) *Idioma i prejudici*. Valencia: Eliseu Climent.
Ninyoles, R.Ll. (1996) *Sociologia de la ciutat de València*. Alzira: Germania.
Pardines, S. and Torres, N. (2011) *La política lingüística al País Valencià. Del conflicte lingüístic a la gestió responsable*. Valencia: Fundació Nexe.
Piqueras Infante, A., coord. (2005) *Mediterrània migrant: les migracions al País Valencià*. Castelló de la Plana: Universitat Jaume Ir.
Pitarch, V. (2011) *Vicent Pitarch, l'autoritat admirada pel valencianisme*. Benassal: Fundació Carles Salvador.
Porcel, B. (1996) *Mediterrània. Onatges tumultuosos*. Barcelona: Proa.
Sanchis Guarner, M. (1981) *La ciutat de València. Síntesi d'història i geografia urbana*. Valencia: Ajuntament de València.
SIES (Servici d'Investigació i Estudis Sociolingüístics de la Generalitat Valenciana) (2006) Enquesta sociolingüística de 2006 a València. http://www.cece.gva.es/Polin/docs/sies_docs/dossiers/2007/Enquesta_sociolinguistica2006.pdf.
Sorribes, J. (2007a) *Les Valències. La urbs polièdrica*. Valencia: Faxímil.
Sorribes, J. (2007b) *Rita Barberá, el pensamiento vacío*. Valencia: Faxímil.
Sorribes, J. coord. (2007c) *València (1808–1991): en trànsit a gran ciutat*. Valencia: Biblioteca Valenciana.

7 Multilingualism in Barcelona: Towards An Asymmetrical Multilingualism[1]

Emili Boix-Fuster

> Barcelona's mother tongue is Catalan, not the Castilian Spanish standard for most of the country. (Allman, 1998: 45)

> He'd been warned that if he didn't want to fall into absurd and endless arguments, he should avoid the fierce linguistic struggles characteristic of Babelic cities not yet conscious of their true nature. Barcelona was now an endogamous and compulsive dichotomy. He'd adopted English as a lingua franca since leaving the country and, though he longed to savour his native tongue again, he made up his mind to stick to English in his dealings with strangers and service staff, whether private or public. It worked. You could find out much more this way than you would if you appeared more approachable and familiar. He understood what was being said by those who – confident that he spoke neither Catalan nor Spanish – shared secrets and swapped personal remarks. And he remained on the sidelines of linguistic disputes. You were like a stranger in a fools' paradise. The city was on the way to becoming a sort of officially bilingual Dublin, where everybody speaks Gaelic at school but really only uses English, though with an Irish accent, of course. (Sayonara Barcelona, Pijoan, 2007: 20)

Introduction

Barcelona is one of the most important multilingual cities in the Western world because of its sociolinguistic complexity. The city has played a prominent role in building a national culture and identity in Catalonia and revitalizing the country's historical language, Catalan, in a process known as 'language normalization and standardization'. I will first discuss the relationship between urbanization processes and the tendency toward linguistic homogenization, and then move on to consider the city of Barcelona, because it epitomizes the impact of urban development on the sociolinguistic situation of the Catalan-speaking territories, a medium-sized language community.

1. Urbanization and Multilingualism

Urban areas play a key role in processes of language homogenization throughout the world. This urbanization does not always entail homogeneity. It is becoming ever more apparent that 'a city is not necessarily an urban melting pot in which code and variety differences get smoothed out into a unique urban vernacular, but that a host of language varieties co-exist both in terms of social stratification and in terms of geographical dispersion' (Van de Craen & Baetens, 1987: 579). Research into this linguistic diversity needs to incorporate variables such as demographic evolution, religious traditions, sociopolitical factors, sociocultural institutions, educational structures and welfare organization, that is to say, it requires an interdisciplinary approach in which the focus is on language, but in which each discipline brings its own methodology, including the historical dimension. This need for an interdisciplinary approach is felt clearly when one draws up a list of potential questions which need to be answered in order to identify the linguistic repertoire of an urban community (Van de Craen & Baetens Beardsmore, 1987: 580–581):

How has the urban entity come about?

Has the bilingual element been incorporated into the city's bilingual life? What is the city's linguistic relationship to the rest of the country?

What legal, political and economic forces are reflected in the linguistic diversity of the city in question?

What are its linguistic components, how have statistics been compiled and how reliable are such statistics?

What are the city's different demographic components, how are its residence patterns distributed, is there a formation of linguistic ghettoes?

What sociological forces impede or enhance language contact or language shift, the maintenance of discrete linguistic varieties or their reduction?

What are the effects of migratory patterns, endogamy or exogamy on the linguistic forces present?

What attitudinal patterns characterize the different strata of society?

What is the 'street image' in terms of the linguistic environment of the different segments of the population, unilingual or multilingual?

What linguistic forces operate among the workforce?

How do schools, hospitals, churches, professional bodies, welfare, cultural associations, the police, the media, advertising and so on reflect the linguistic diversity of the local population?

Further guideposts should be added to understand multilingualism in Barcelona, because municipalities in Spain do not have much autonomy with regard to Catalonia's most general linguistic regulations. There is, however, a lack of general overviews of plurilingual Spain, such as those drawn up by McRae for Switzerland (1983). The principal factors to be examined should be as follows:

(1) historical and developmental patterns;
(2) the social structure of the language communities and the relationships between language divisions and other social divisions;
(3) the perceptions and attitudes of language communities and the expression of these attitudes in political life; and
(4) formal institutional arrangements concerning languages, including constitutional and legal provisions.

This long list of variables brings to mind the well-known story from India about the five blind men who decided to find out what an elephant was like. They all touched different parts of the elephant's body. The man who felt the trunk thought the elephant was like a snake; the one who felt a leg thought it was like a tree; the one who felt the ear thought it was like a fan, and so on.

To date, very few studies have encompassed such a vast array of sociocultural factors explaining language use, language knowledge and linguistic ideologies in urban areas. If one wants to understand the sociolinguistic situation of urban areas, the key question is 'What are the effects of the city on the language and on the relationships between languages?' Authors like Calvet (1994) and Mackey (2000) have tried to answer this question. Cities are more than the simple sum total of groups of different origins. They have a structure and organization that affect their linguistic repertoires. Urban agglomerations are a privileged vantage point from which to observe multilingualism. Urban culture has two important characteristics that we should recall here:

(1) a given spatial form, that is, spatial concentration of the population, and
(2) a given diffusion of a value system, that is, a cultural phenomenon.

Cities play a central role in processes of language change and language shift, because they are a starting point for innovations, and mainly because they are centres of power. They continuously form a synthesis of heterogeneous cultural contributions. Marí (1995) has clearly summarized the three main functions carried out by the city. First, the city works as a magnet, because it is a meeting point for diverse populations. Second, it is both an archive and a laboratory for the future. And third, the city is a lighthouse from which its melting amalgam is projected into the future and over time.

Cities are the destination where many thousands of migrants converge. The need to communicate explains the appearance of *lingua francas* in urban areas. Cities contribute to both unification and conflict. In bilingual families and in the graphic environment, for example, one can observe that cities are a linguistic battlefield, where linguistic varieties are worked out as indexes of identity.

Sociologists and anthropologists have largely neglected the role of language in urban areas. Sociolinguists have begun to study how people cope with social multilingualism *in vivo* and have also investigated *in vitro* interventions into this multilingualism. Language use *in vivo* is bottom-up use, emerging from spontaneous behaviour, whereas language use *in vitro* emerges from deliberate, conscious language policy decisions (Calvet, 1998). The power of the state intervenes in *in vitro* solutions, whereas bottom-up *in vivo* solutions are achieved in everyday social behaviour.

The effects of urban multilingualism are thus clear: the linguistic solutions proposed in the city are the ones that spread throughout a given country. In his book *Language Wars* (1987: 131) Calvet states again that 'cities work like a pump which accelerates the spread of growing languages'. In this volume, Calvet also makes the following prediction: 'A country will tend towards linguistic unification if it has both a high urbanization index and the country's biggest city as its capital' (1994: 138). Has Calvet's prediction been borne out by events? If one looks to the big Western cities, urbanization means linguistic homogeneity. In spite of the presence of important migrant groups with linguistic diversity, London, Paris, Buenos Aires, New York, Chicago and Berlin, for example, show a tendency toward a dominant language. The sociolinguistic landscape is much more complicated in non-Western cities where language diversity is much higher. Think of Calcutta, Mumbai and Singapore in Asia; La Paz, Asunción and Mexico in Latin America, or Lagos, Johannesburg and Dakar in Africa.

The main question is whether sustainable linguistic contact is possible in urban areas. Will only 'big' languages survive, assimilating the small ones? Sustainable linguistic contact is 'that which does not produce linguistic exposure or linguistic use in allochthonous languages at a speed and/or pressure – to a degree – so high as to make impossible the stable continuity of the autochthonous languages' (Bastardas, 2004: 8).

2. Multilingual Cities: The Case of Barcelona

Barcelona belongs to a special category of Western cities: those where for decades or centuries there has been a historical language conflict, that is, cities where two language groups feel that their languages are legitimate in the territory. In these cities, therefore, language use and language ideologies are controversial, and language becomes a key symbol of ethnic identity. For example, in Spain and in Catalonia some Spaniards have repeatedly derided Catalan as a vulgar dialect. Most Catalans, conversely, have proudly defended their separate language and feel their language has a historic homeland, an area that Catalan speakers see as their own. In multilingual cities like these, language is an open, everyday issue (see Carod-Rovira, 2012 for a recent example). In these multilingual cities, language is a problem of a kind monolingual people cannot really grasp. Joan Fuster, probably the best-known Valencian intellectual, once summarized the concern with language that affects communities that run the risk of losing theirs:

> A language is not the whole of society: it is, however, its keystone. The deposit of centuries, heritage of coexistence (*convivència*), framework of culture, the language is both axis and continuity for the life of a people, as a people. If the language is torn, bastardised or lost, the society is broken and sees its distinctive contours erased. Communities that have never suffered a severe linguistic crisis seldom realise that. Nobody thinks about health, they say, except the sick. (cited in Hall, 2001: 7)

Other authors (Larreula, 2002) have studied how some Catalan speakers actually experience 'linguistic pain' to defend their rights. Not surprisingly, in a society of this kind language becomes a source of debate, a symbolic tool in the process of nation-building. And most Catalan parties regard nation-building as part of their *raison d'être*. The exceptions are the *Partido Popular*, Spain's conservative party and now the governing party in Madrid, and an anti-Catalanist group known as *Ciudadanos*.

Examples of cities in the Western world that experience language conflict are Brussels (between Dutch and French), Montreal (French and English), and Bienne and Fribourg in Switzerland (German and French). In Spain, the biggest and most salient bilingual city is clearly Barcelona, where the conflict is between Spanish and Catalan. In her pioneering research on bilingualism in Barcelona, Woolard (1989) summarized the traits of both Barcelona as a city and Catalonia as a country.

The Catalan language community, with its almost 8 million Catalan speakers and roughly 4–5 million L1 speakers, represents an important segment of the Spanish population inside a multinational state (Linz, 1975). From a demolinguistic perspective, it is the largest minority in Europe. About half of the population in Catalonia is brought up in Catalan, and those not raised in the language can readily learn it.

Within the Catalan-speaking community, which includes Valencia, Andorra, the French department of Pyrénées-Orientales and the Balearic Islands, Catalonia is an anomaly. First, because despite being a region on the periphery that has long suffered political subordination and cultural and linguistic domination by the Castilian centre, Catalonia did not suffer from underdevelopment. In fact, industrialization came early.

Today Barcelona is a modern industrial city, the capital of Catalonia, a distinct polity, and an autochthonous political community within Spain. Barcelona is the centre of an urban area that is home to approximately 4 million people – 70% of the total population of Catalonia, the 'autonomous community' (*comunidad autónoma*) of which it is the capital. Its current linguistic repertoire is the result of two factors. On the one hand, it has suffered political subordination to central Spain, which has mainly been dominated by Castile, and on the other hand, the bulk of its working-class population comes from southern Spain, Latin America (therefore Spanish-speaking), and elsewhere, especially North Africa. Therefore, we find two sorts of minorities in today's Catalonia: first Catalans – and Catalonia within the Spanish state – and second, immigrant Castilian speakers within Catalonia, who share the language of the dominant Spanish state.

The contemporary vitality of Catalan as a vernacular language, despite centuries of institutional inferiority, is also unique among the minority languages of Western Europe and especially noteworthy in light of the repression exercised by two dictatorships (1923–1930 and 1939–1975), when there were concerted attempts to eradicate the language. As Woolard (1989) has pointed out, the Catalan case is a counterexample to the generalization that minority languages erode in complex industrialized urban societies. Catalan has been tenaciously maintained despite the institutional power and prestige of Castilian, not to mention its worldwide utility. Robert Hughes, the author of a recognized literary guide to the city, chose to give one chapter of his book the title 'Blind with Love for a Language'. The city's inhabitants may not dwell on these issues all day, but many have demonstrated their loyalty to the language. The city has also been the centre of language reform movements. The standardization of Catalan, fostered by the engineer and linguist Pompeu Fabra (Costa, 2009), emerged and spread from Barcelona, extending from there throughout the entire Catalan-speaking territory, mainly within Catalonia and to a lesser degree in Valencia and the Balearic Islands. This reform was possible because Catalan had, and still has, a clear, powerful urban centre. One can easily compare the fate of Catalan with that of its sister language, Occitan, the historical language of Southern France. Occitan has lacked an urban centre to foster the revival of the language and promote the creation of a standard variety. Neither Marseille, Toulouse nor Montpellier has ever played this key role, and as a result today Occitan has no standard variety and is almost extinct despite its glorious past. The loss of Occitan makes the revival of Catalan even more striking. In a volume on the history of Romance languages, Harris (1988: 2) points out that:

> It is no exaggeration to say that it is above all the fidelity of the majority of the inhabitants of the city, of all social groups, to their native tongue

which has ensured that its fate has been so unlike that of Occitan across the border in France; and indeed it is difficult to point to any language in Europe which has not become the official language of a nation-state which is as strongly placed as Catalan today.

Thus political and social elites have mobilized to back the cause of Catalan. The linguistic loyalty of Barcelona and its citizens has been a key factor behind the survival of the language in Catalonia. Salvador Giner (1987), president of the Catalan Academy of Sciences (the Institute of Catalan Studies), summarized the combination of localism and universalism that characterizes the city of Barcelona:

> More than a mere bond of kinship unites Barcelona with Catalonia: there is communion. To this day, the great, cosmopolitan Mediterranean city draws its identity and strength from the small nation where it has its roots. Its loyalty to the culture, the language, and the long and often difficult past of Catalonia is the source of its inspiration and uniqueness. Far from being a hindrance upon its projection towards the outside world, that loyalty goes a long way to explain the city's remarkable will to universality, its tireless love of work, its enterprising spirit.

The language policy of the municipal council has been in line with this pro-Catalan stance since the late seventies, when the second 20th-century dictatorship came to an end. Since then, from 1979 until 2011, the city was run by a centre-left coalition (Social Democrats, ex-Communists, and ERC, a pro-independence party). In 2002 (28 June), the plenary of the council approved the following declaration: 'The municipality of Barcelona undertakes to take the measures necessary to stimulate and promote the use of Catalan, its knowledge and its dissemination in order to achieve the full normalization of the use of the language among all citizens of the city' (Mataix, 2010). Based on this guiding principle, the city works with the *Consorci per a la Normalització Lingüística*, a Catalan government institute, to carry out programmes aimed at teaching Catalan and promoting its use. More recently, the Spanish Supreme Court ruled that the preferential use of Catalan in the municipality of Barcelona, intended to counterbalance the preference in favour of Spanish in Spain as a whole, was unconstitutional.

Of course detractors of Catalan normalization take a different view of this process, criticising the narrow-minded nationalism they claim lies behind it. Buruma, a Dutch observer (2001: 13) stated that because of its linguistic policy Barcelona 'runs the risk of becoming a more provincial city than it deserves to be, isolated in a language fog bank'. Spanish-speaking public employees, in particular, have felt under attack after being compelled to learn Catalan, that is, to become bilingual. In March 2006, a public opinion campaign targeted language policy in Catalonia. The campaign was instigated from inside and outside Catalonia and emerged from social sectors close to the *Partido Popular*, Spain's conservative party. The PP is a minority group in Catalonia (with some 18% of the vote) but the ruling party in Spain as a whole. These sectors ask for separate schools where teaching is in the mother tongue of students (at present the educational system is unified and does not split students up according to their first or preferred language). So far, however, there has been no significant language conflict: most Spanish speakers in Catalonia feel it is in their children's interest to learn Catalan.

To sum up, Catalan is by far the most used minority language in Europe. The notion of minority language is obviously dependent on the sociopolitical context. Danish, Estonian, Slovenian, Lithuanian, Slovak, Latvian, Finnish and Norwegian are in no danger of being classified as such – they are official languages of independent states – yet each of them has fewer speakers than Catalan. The fact remains that Catalan is spoken today in a country where it has authentic historical roots and a strong claim to linguistic supremacy (Webber & Strubell, 1991).

Of course, the sectors of the population most committed to Catalan nationalism do not see the future of the language in such a rosy light. Quim Monzó, a well-known Catalan writer, voiced a pessimistic view:

> If up to now Catalonia has not been a Bretagne or an Occitania, this is because Catalonia has a capital city like Barcelona, with a powerful bourgeoisie. But when this city stops being Catalan, the other parts of the country will fall like dominoes (*Poble Andorrà*, 4 February 1991).

3. Barcelona's Linguistic Repertoire

I will now describe the main characteristics of Barcelona's linguistic repertoire, namely knowledge of language, language use, linguistic identities, transmission of language from generation to generation, and finally geographical and social distribution.

What sort of bilingualism do we find in Barcelona? What is the social distribution of the two main linguistic groups? Research into these areas is still limited, but we can offer some tentative results.

(1) Language knowledge. First of all, how widespread is the use of each language? Which language do the city's inhabitants know better? The answer is Spanish. Everyone can speak it and does so when the situation requires. This is still not the case with Catalan, which still bears the scars of its repression under two 20th-century dictatorships. Many people cannot write in the language and feel unsure about it, and significant percentages of the population are still not able to speak it. Furthermore, the Francoist dictatorship made Spanish a native language in Catalonia for the first time in history (Rafanell, 2011). Spanish, according to the communicative measurements proposed by

Kuo (1979), is known by all inhabitants of Catalonia. Everyone is conversant with colloquial Spanish and it has become a native language in Catalonia following the massive arrival of population from the rest of Spain. One might add that everyone is obliged to know Spanish. Article 3 of the Spanish Constitution obliges all Spaniards to know it, stating that they have 'the right and the duty' to do so.

The conditions in which the massive influx of immigrants reached Catalonia between 1955 and 1975 (Farràs *et al.*, 2000: 157) are significant. Immigrants lived relatively segregated from the autochthonous population and did not receive education or social services in Catalan, which made acquisition of the local language extremely unlikely.

Since the return of democracy in the late seventies, Catalan has become an official language again, together with Spanish, which is the official language throughout Spain. Catalan has entered the educational system, the public administration, local and regional public services, and some sectors of the mass media, particularly the daily press, radio and television. As a result, knowledge of Catalan has increased significantly, as shown in Figure 7.1. In 1995 (Subirats, 2012), 3.8% of inhabitants of the Barcelona Metropolitan Region (BMR) could not understand Catalan, 26.7% understood the language but were not able to speak it, 29.5% could speak it but were not able to write it, and 40.1% could both speak and write Catalan. In 2006, 4.3% of inhabitants of the BMR could not understand Catalan, 23.2% understood the language but were not able to speak it, 21.4% could speak it but were not able to write it, and 51% could both speak and write Catalan.

The low percentage of writing in Catalan is a legacy of Spain's dictatorships. Only younger generations have learned the language at school and are

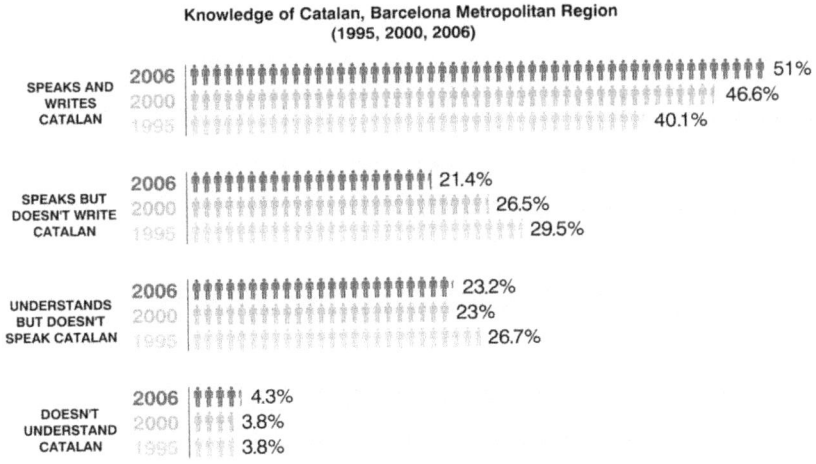

Figure 7.1 Knowledge of Catalan. Barcelona Metropolitan Region (1995, 2000, 2006)

proficient in both languages. Young people have a growing command of both languages; they can choose which they prefer to use, though social and economic pressure continues to give Spanish an edge. The slight increase in people unable to understand the language is due to the arrival of new immigrants from outside the Catalan-speaking territories. In 2009, for example, 18.1% of the inhabitants of Barcelona, that is, 295,000 people, had been born abroad (Mataix, 2010: 11).

(2) **First language.** As far as first language is concerned, we have data for the BMR for the period from 1990 to 2006, as shown in Figure 7.2. The data show a decreasing dominance of the Spanish-speaking group (53.4% in 1990 and 48% in 2006) and a decreasing minority of Catalan speakers (35.8% in 1990 and 32.1% in 2000). Thus, both linguistic groups are losing members in relation to the group of those who regard themselves as bilingual (9.8% in 1990 and 15.2% in 2000). So there is no Catalanization, in the sense of speakers adopting the language as their own, but rather an increase in family bilingualism. Catalan seems to be a select language (spoken more often in the most affluent segments of society), but the trend is toward it becoming a minority language.

(3) **Identification language.** We can only rely on data from the city of Barcelona as no data are available for the metropolitan region (BMR). However, the overall trend is likely to be very similar in both territories. As shown in Figure 7.3 (Mataix, 2010: 16–17), the percentage of citizens who regard Catalan as their language is higher than the percentage who see Catalan as their first language. It seems that Catalan enjoys some degree of social attraction: some Spanish-speaking citizens adopt Catalan as their identification language. This is not the case, however, among speakers of other languages. Thus 55.9% of Barcelona inhabitants have chosen Spanish as their first language, but only 48.2% have chosen it as their first identification language. Overall, though, Spanish remains the majority language and continues to play a pivotal role.

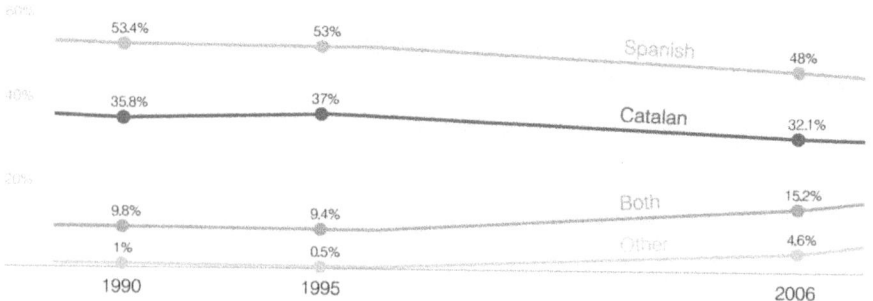

Figure 7.2 First language of the population (over 18). Barcelona Metropolitan Region (1990, 1995, 2006)

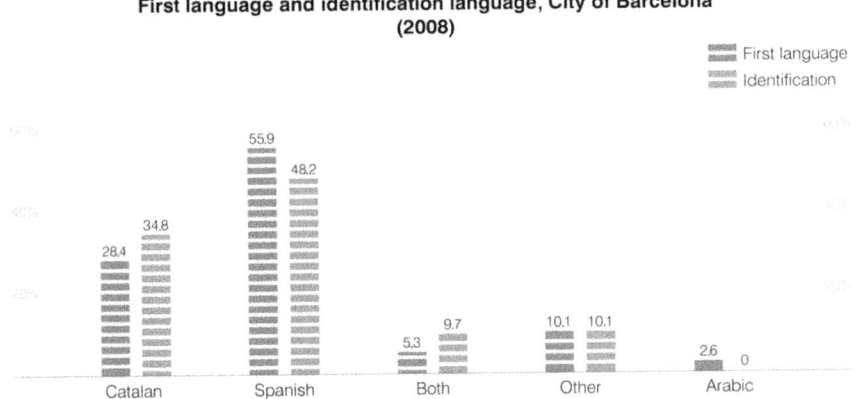

Figure 7.3 First language and identification language, City of Barcelona (2008)

(4) **Intergenerational language transmission.** What about patterns of intergenerational language transmission? In 1995 the majority of households in the Barcelona area were linguistically homogeneous: 29.1% used only Catalan in interaction between parents and children; 43.3% used only Spanish; 4.6% used both languages, and 0.1% used other languages, as shown in Figure 7.4. Couples tend to be rather homogeneous linguistically in Catalonia: whereas at random there would be 10% of homogeneous Catalan 1 couples, actually Catalan 1 couples represented 24% out of the total number of couples in 2008 (Sorolla, 2010). These figures are probably similar in Barcelona.

Eleven years later, in 2006, the majority of households in the Barcelona area were linguistically less homogeneous: 24.0% used only Catalan in interaction between parents and children; 31.1% used only Spanish; 7.9% used both languages, and 3.2% used other languages. The percentage of linguistically mixed households, in which each member of the couple has a different first language, increased from 11.9% in 1995 to 15.8% in 2006. In most bilingual households members of the younger generation regard both Spanish and Catalan as their own languages (the most common behaviour, which applies in 8% of households, is for each parent to transmit their own language to their children). Finally there are instances of so-called mutant households, in which the children learn a language that is not one of those spoken as a first language by the parents. In 2006, 13.3% of children learned both languages and 1% learned only Catalan. To sum up, based on recent qualitative research (Boix, 2009; Boix & Torrens, 2011), linguistic family trajectories show a tendency toward Catalan or bilingualism. In 1995, 72.4% of families were linguistically homogeneous (29.1% in Catalan and 43.3% in Spanish), whereas in 2006 only 55.1% were homogenous (24.0% in Catalan and 31.1% in

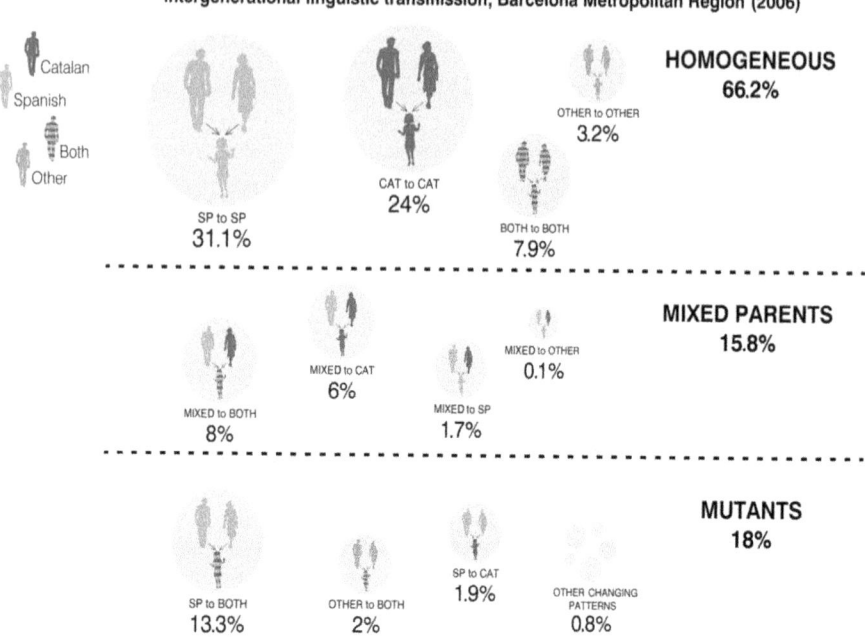

Figure 7.4 Intergenerational linguistic transmission, Barcelona Metropolitan Region (2006)

Spanish). The rest of the families showed some degree of linguistic hybridism. Catalan gains some new members in these bilingual households and even in homogeneous Spanish households, but this recovery does not offset the overall demolinguistic dominance of Spanish. The result of these intergenerational changes is a draw between the two main linguistic groups: 61.7% of families have some presence of Catalan, and 62.9% show a presence of Spanish, including in both groups those respondents who stated that they were bilingual.

(5) Geographical and social distribution of the linguistic groups. The social distribution of Catalan and Spanish (or Castilian) in Barcelona is sandwich-shaped. Spanish is the dominant language of both the highest stratum of society and the working-class population, whereas Catalan predominates slightly in managerial and skilled professions, in middle-class sectors. In 1995, for instance, Catalan was the language spoken to the mother by 40% of citizens throughout the city. In five neighbourhoods – Gràcia, Sarrià-Sant Gervasi, Eixample, Les Corts and Sants-Montjuïc – the percentage of Catalan as mother language was higher than average, whereas in other neighbourhoods the percentage was lower than the average (Ciutat Vella, Nou Barris, Sant Martí, Sant Andreu and Horta-Guinardó). This geographical distribution reflects the social distribution: the wealthiest districts are more Catalan-speaking and the poorest ones are Spanish-speaking, though in the richest districts there is a slight recovery of Spanish (Subirats, 2002; Boix-Fuster, 2002). In 2006, 50% of professional-class respondents in the BMR stated that Catalan was their language; 28.8% said it was Spanish, and 20.5% said both were (Subirats, 2012), as shown in Figure 7.5. Conversely, among young and adult members of the working class, 22.6% of respondents stated that Catalan was their language, 57.2% said it was Spanish, and 19.7% responded that both were their languages. Recent demolinguistic data confirm this sociolinguistic distribution of in the city (Ajuntament de Barcelona, 2014). In middle and upper middle-class neighbourhoods Catalan is the most used language (e.g. Gràcia: 54.4% Catalan, and 40.3% Spanish), whereas in working-class districts, Spanish is the most used language (e.g. Nou Barris: 20.9% Catalan, and 76.6% Spanish).

The two linguistic groups are still socially segregated, though political parties are constantly seeking to minimize this social cleavage (Rambla, 1993, working meetings of the Fundació Rafael Campalans [PSC], November 2005 to February 2006).[2] Marginalized groups still tend to be associated with Spanish (Woolard, 2003). There are no political parties that are organized along ethnolinguistic lines, though Catalan nationalist parties have a higher proportion of Catalan-speaking members and Spanish nationalist parties are voted for by a higher number of Spanish-speaking members. Recent novels are starting to reflect this ethnolinguistic divide in the Catalonia, including Puntí (2011) from the Catalan-speaking perspective and Pérez Andújar (2011) from the Spanish-speaking perspective.

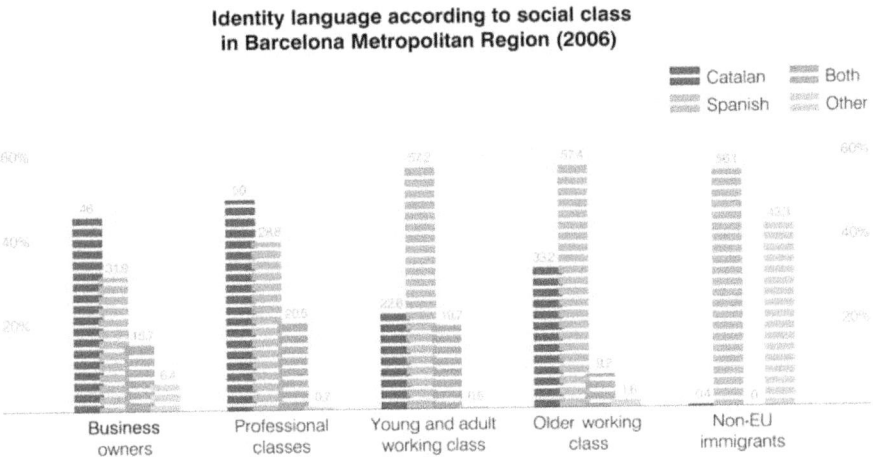

Figure 7.5 Identity language according to social class in Barcelona Metropolitan region (2006)

To sum up, knowledge of Catalan has increased dramatically in recent years. But the prestige of Catalan has not been sufficient to recruit new Catalan-speaking members from the Spanish-speaking immigrant population on a large scale. Many of them still do not regard Catalan as their own language (Subirats, 2002: 187). The Catalan language faces new challenges in the Barcelona area. Differences in the extent of Catalan use in the territory show that the spread of urbanization favours Spanish. In addition, the prestige of Catalan, the main language of the middle classes, is not sufficient to encourage its widespread adoption by the mainly Spanish-speaking working class. Subirats, a well-known sociologist, raises questions concerning the recently arrived population (Subirats, 2002: 187):

> The arrival of new immigration, a part of which has Spanish as their language, puts in doubt whether the Catalan language will have a sufficient demographic base to maintain itself as the language of an important part of the population if immigration strengthens the Spanish-speaking group.

4. The Legal Framework

All these demolinguistic changes have taken place within a particular legal framework, which goes some way to explaining the current linguistic landscape of Barcelona. Two laws (1983 and 1998) have regulated language use in Catalonia and Barcelona (McRoberts, 2001). The more recent one, passed with 80% of the votes in Parliament, gives priority to Catalan in institutional communications in the public sector. In other words, Catalan should be the normal and preferred language.

In the same vein, the proposal for reform of the Statute of Autonomy, passed by 90% of the members of the Catalan Parliament in September 2004, stated the following two points:

Article 6. Language

(1) The language proper to Catalonia is Catalan. As such, Catalan is the language of **normal and preferential** use in all Catalan public administration bodies and in the public media, and is, moreover, the language of normal use for teaching and learning in the education system.
(2) Catalan is the official language of Catalonia, together with Castilian, the official language of Spain. Each individual in Catalonia has the **right to use and duty to know these two official languages**. The public authorities of Catalonia shall establish the necessary measures to enable the exercise of these rights and the fulfilment of this duty.[3]

The municipality of Barcelona subsequently passed the *Reglament d´Ús de la Llengua Catalana* (2010), a set of regulations concerning language use in the city.

In accordance with the guidelines set out in the Catalan Statute of Autonomy, the municipal regulations give Catalan a slightly preferential status: 'Catalan is the language of Catalonia. It is therefore the official, normal and preferred language of the city council and should be used preferentially in its tasks and dealings'. In relation to dealings with citizens, the regulations state that 'Catalan should be used, without prejudice to a citizen's right to submit documents and make statements in Spanish, or to receive notifications in that language upon request'. With respect to oral communications, 'city council staff should use the Catalan language unless a citizen asks to be dealt with in Spanish. If necessary, city council staff may also use any language or means that facilitates communication'.

The regulations (Mataix, 2010: 10) contemplate the political option of choosing Catalan as the preferred language 'by creating public incentives so that those who do not know it end up learning it and regarding it as their "own" language'. This choice of Catalan as the default language contrasts with the preferential use of Spanish established in the legislation of Spain's central government.

Recent legal rulings have led to changes in these regulations. Catalonia's Supreme Court (TSJC) (*Nació digital* 31-05-12) rejected the preferential use of Catalan and established the requirement for 'normalised and parallel use of Spanish'. The rulings also stipulate that Spanish speakers should not have to explicitly request services in Spanish, because 'it is not acceptable that they should be required to express choices that are onerous or put them in an uncomfortable position'.

5. The Linguistic Landscape

Institutional communications are those communicated orally or in writing by an individual acting as a member of an institution (a public servant, for example), whereas *private communications* are those uttered by someone in his or her private life (Bastardas, 1996). Institutional communications are mainly given in Catalan or in bilingual form (Mataix, 2010).

The following are some examples of institutionalized language use in Barcelona, which does not show a diglossic pattern, in which each language corresponds to either high or low functions. We can also distinguish between public uses and private uses.

In institutionalized public domains the main intervening variable is the area of government involved. For example, the services of the central government in Catalonia use Spanish almost exclusively, since Catalan is not considered a Spanish national language. These services include immigration offices and branches of the central administration: social security, tax offices, the post office, the military, and so on. The judiciary system uses Spanish almost exclusively (as if burglars and thieves could not be Catalan speakers), because judges are not required to learn Catalan. Conversely, institutions that depend on the Catalan autonomous or local governments, though bilingual, give a slight preference to Catalan, the language of 'normal and preferred use'. To give another example, Catalan is the principal (though not exclusive) language throughout the educational system, especially in primary courses, where the immersion system is used. The goal is for all pupils to master the two official languages by the end of compulsory education, and so far the immersion methodology appears to be the most appropriate way to achieve this.

Street signs in Barcelona are exclusively in Catalan because they are the only ones authorized by law. Taped messages in underground carriages are given in Catalan, whereas written notices are trilingual (Catalan, Spanish and English). The main speeches given by the city's mayor are mostly in Catalan. The speech to mark the arrival of the 'Three Wise Men' (a Catholic celebration held on the eve of 6 January) is normally given in Catalan. Christmas announcements are given in many languages. The local Barcelona TV channel broadcasts mainly though not exclusively in Catalan, but the big Spanish private channels broadcast only in Spanish. Sessions of Parliament and the municipal council are normally held in Catalan. Political campaign ads, health information booklets and notification of fines by the municipality, however, are bilingual. Only very rarely are there public arguments about language choices or language negotiations. For instance, in September 2002, Valentí Fuster, a Catalan-speaking doctor working in the US, read the inaugural presentation for Barcelona's *festa major* (local festival held annually) and decided to give his talk half in Spanish and half in Catalan, because, he said, Spanish was the more widely-used language. This triggered reactions from the political parties. ERC, a pro-independence party, criticized the use of Spanish, whereas the PP applauded the bilingual option, which in its view should be the normal approach everywhere in Catalonia. A representative of the PP said (Fernández Diaz, 2002):

> Pluralism means recognising that ours is a linguistically, socially and culturally diverse society in which Catalans have two languages – Valentí Fuster reminded us of that – and that Catalan culture is the culture made by Catalans, regardless of how they express it, from the jota tortosina to the sardana, from the sevillana to castells (human towers).

The conservative party currently pays lip service to Catalan, rarely fostering its use, and more often contributing to its demise. The pro-Catalan parties, on the other hand, are reluctant to use the term bilingualism or promote generalized bilingualism because they are afraid this would result in Spanish-speakers remaining monolingual. Paradoxically, Catalan L1 speakers are the most bilingual, simply because they have no choice: legally and sociologically they are obliged to be bilingual. Both the linguistic context and the political context favour the learning of Spanish, the overall dominant language.

Spanish is also the dominant language in institutionalized private domains, but not the only one used in these settings. Though there are few studies available, in the workplace, in big companies and factories, Spanish is the first language. Church services (mainly Catholic) are in either language, with an important presence of Catalan thanks to the nationalist tradition of some sectors of the Catalan clergy. Conversely, most commercial and economic information, such as labelling of food, clothing and pharmaceutical products, is usually given only in Spanish. Most of the press is in Spanish. For example, the free press publishes approximately 20% of its articles in Catalan. Public announcements at the Barcelona football club stadium, which seats almost one hundred and twenty thousand spectators, are normally given only in Catalan. Posters and signs in the markets are in either Spanish or Catalan; they are rarely bilingual in a parallel, systematic way. Barcelona's two leading newspapers, *El Periódico* and *La Vanguardia*, are an exception to this pattern. Both publications decided to launch a parallel edition in Catalan with content identical to the original version in Spanish.

So far most of these language use phenomena are *in vitro*, that is, they are the product of planned decisions, in contrast to *in vivo* phenomena, which are more spontaneous. Of course, the linguistic landscape is much more complicated. In a restaurant, for instance, menus might be in Catalan, but the waiters speak to customers only in Spanish. The conclusion is that there is a pervasive fluid hybridism, with no strict rules or regulations. This sort of bilingualism works because a clear majority of the population is at least passively bilingual. Monolingual Spanish speakers (there are no monolingual Catalan speakers) hinder the use of Catalan.

In the society of Barcelona as a whole, however, *in vivo* messages and individualized communications are mainly in Spanish because it has a greater demolinguistic weight and because language norms encourage its use. The usual linguistic etiquette establishes that Catalan speakers accommodate to Spanish. They usually converge towards Spanish in bilingual encounters, though they will continue to speak in Catalan to a Catalan addressee in front of a Spanish-speaking participant. As we have already said, people are thus expected to be at least passively bilingual, that is, at least able to understand the other person's language. The similarity between the two languages in contact (Spanish and Catalan) makes this feasible. The distance between Catalan and Spanish is similar to that between Portuguese and Spanish. Only recently has research on the linguistic landscape of the city begun to be carried out (Comajoan & Long, 2012).

Funeral and death notices are in either Catalan or Spanish. Most of the small ads one finds on the noticeboards at supermarket exits are in Spanish. Most informal everyday conversations are in Spanish too. Finally, it is worth asking which language is used in speech addressed to non-identified interlocutors, for example, to ask for directions or ask the time. These utterances are good indicators of the use of a language in public places. The result of field work in central Barcelona suggests that both languages are commonly used in these interactions. In other words, it is supposed that the addressee will understand either language.

The current sociolinguistic situation at public universities in the Barcelona area epitomizes this sort of fluid bilingualism in Barcelona. The official pronouncements of rectors are usually in Catalan, because according to the Language Policy Act of 1998 Catalan is the 'normal' vehicle to be used in institutionalized communications. As everyone knows, 'normal' is an ambiguous term: 'normality' does not mean 'exclusivity'. Courses are taught in Spanish or Catalan, depending on the lecturer's individual choice, and students can choose to do their papers and exams in either language. So there is *productive* bilingualism (one can choose one's preferred language) but not *receptive* bilingualism (one cannot choose the teacher's or the student's language). This system implies that there is a passive knowledge of the two official languages. This is also a rather unique case of a bilingual university; only Freiburg in Switzerland and Ottawa in Canada have similar institutional practices. Theoretically this bilingualism might entail a disadvantage in that the city's universities might not attract the best students because some knowledge of Catalan is required. So far this has not been the case; local universities receive high numbers of study-abroad visitors. Other factors (the climate, the human atmosphere of the city, the night life, leisure opportunities, etc.) may compensate for the linguistic inconvenience.

This sociolinguistic landscape may appear fuzzy, because there is no clear-cut, dominant language for all social functions. The well-known diglossic pattern does not apply to the Catalan situation. For instance, I recently consulted forty city guidebooks for tourists and found that it is difficult for them to grapple with this complexity because they have to convey the idea of Catalan identity and the reality of multilingualism in very few words. Most point out that in this bilingual society, visitors can get by perfectly well with just Spanish. This is true, but the view of bilingualism in the city that they give is rather idealized: 'For the most part the two languages coexist with most people slipping from one to the other, depending on the person they are talking to' (*Insight City Guide*, 2005). At the same time, some guidebooks indicate that symbolically the pecking order is clear in most cases: Catalan first.

Let me add two final comments on the sociolinguistic landscape of Barcelona.

First, a reference to the 1992 Olympic Games will give an idea of patterns of language use in the city (DiGiacomo, 1999). The Games had four official languages. The presidential address was therefore read by the president of the International Olympic Committee, Joan Antoni Samaranch, a native of Barcelona, in English, French, Spanish and Catalan (Boix, 1993). But the four languages were used in different ways. Samaranch, himself bilingual in Catalan and Spanish, read his speech in English and French, each language clearly separated from the other. This was not the case with Catalan and

Spanish. Samaranch intentionally mixed the two languages in his speech, apparently in order to come across as both Catalan and Spanish before the local Catalan audience. His speech did not reflect everyday use of the two languages in the city. Today in Barcelona there is no equivalent to language mixing like the Spanglish spoken among Puerto Ricans in New York. The ethnolinguistic boundaries between the two main ethnic groups – those with Catalan as L1 and those with Castilian as L2 – are still clear-cut. There are occasional cases of code-switching between Catalan and Spanish, in particular for the purposes of humour. Recent research shows a growing number of translinguistic practices, especially among young people (Pujolar, 2011).

Second, it is worth briefly considering how urban bilingualism is reflected in literature and the mass media, a topic discussed in *Catalan Review* (Castellanos, 2004). Generally, as the German scholar Ute Heinemann (1998) points out, few novels have reflected the city's linguistic heterogeneity in their dialogue. A realistic novel that tried to mirror real language use in Barcelona would be bilingual. But this does not happen. Catalan-speaking readers might accept fragments in Spanish in the novels they read – they are bilingual and understand both languages – but they are not keen on language mixing. Conversely, Spanish-speaking readers (those from outside the Catalan-speaking territories) are usually monolingual in Spanish, so they cannot understand the nuances of bilingualism in the novels they read. A unique exception is *El amante bilingüe* [The bilingual lover] by Juan Marsé, where the two languages are often mixed in a way that is unlikely in everyday life.

These were the main sociolinguistic characteristics of Catalan and Barcelona society until 2006. Since the late nineties, a new phenomenon has emerged: the arrival of new migrants, especially from Latin America and Morocco. Their numbers are rising fast and the cultural gap between certain contingents of new immigrants, especially those from North and sub-Saharan Africa, and the host community is much wider. Their integration is further hindered by the precarious legal and economic situation in which many find themselves. In El Raval, a city neighbourhood in downtown Barcelona, almost half the population was born outside Spain. According to the GELA group, 250 languages are now spoken in Catalonia. In addition to generating many social problems, this new population poses a new sociolinguistic dilemma. Which language or languages will they learn? This is the old problem of allophones, to use the terminology of Quebec: which autochthonous group will they join, the Catalan one or the Spanish one? For the Latin American immigrants, who are already Spanish-speaking, the answer is clear: they choose Spanish. As Jacky Hall points out, they

> [...] are swelling the already large Spanish-speaking community, and those of other origins are understandably keen to learn, not Catalan, but Spanish, the language which is the basic requirement for interaction with

the central government immigration authorities and with potential employers both inside and outside Catalonia. The Catalan government's lack of jurisdiction in this field remains a major impediment to harmonious integration between newcomers and natives and, though there is no widespread friction at present, the phenomenon undoubtedly takes on added complexity when the host community itself is experiencing difficulties in defending its own linguistic and cultural rights. (Hall, 2001: 38)

Many efforts have been made to 'Catalanize' these new migrants. For instance, 5000 language pairs meet on a regularly basis and the autochthonous partner teaches the new immigrant Catalan. But the fact remains that for most of these new immigrants Catalan is not essential in their everyday lives. Therefore Catalans feel they may become a minority in their own territory if they do not succeed in spreading their language among newcomers.

6. Conclusions: Is There Language Conflict?

Is there a language conflict in Barcelona? Certainly there is none in the sense of frequent clashes between speakers of Catalan and Spanish. Of course, letters concerning linguistic issues are occasionally published in the newspapers. The press from outside Catalonia often launches harsh attacks on language policy in Catalonia, sometimes very provocatively, and without a serious understanding of what is really going on in everyday life in the country. Even the foreign press, through its correspondents in Madrid, is sometimes directly critical of language policy in Catalonia (see Ingendaay, 2006, for example).

But in present-day Catalonia there are no sharp ethnolinguistic boundaries between *Castilians* (those who usually speak Spanish, also known as Castilian) and *Catalans* (those who usually speak Catalan). There are, for instance, no political parties, jobs or major associations established according to linguistic alignments, even though there are linguistic tendencies: most choirs or trekking clubs use Catalan as their institutional language. Conversely, taxi drivers and trade union delegates usually use Spanish. Politicians seek to eradicate the tension-provoking pervasive dichotomy between Castilians and Catalans, using catchphrases such as 'All those who live and work here are Catalans' in order to play down the existence of two different cultural communities within Catalonia, even though in the eighties 'the two terms Catalan and Castilian [were] used as an exhaustive contrast set by the overwhelming majority of individuals in Barcelona' (Woolard, 1989: 43). Jacqueline Hall, a British resident in Catalonia, stresses the lack of open conflict in Catalan society (Hall, 2001: 50):

> In over 20 years in the country I have never witnessed any major incident, any display of real resentment or ill-will between Catalan and

Spanish-speakers beyond the banter and grumbling that are equally characteristic of any normal relationship between people with different backgrounds, viewpoints or tastes.

Nowadays it is increasingly commonplace to hear conversations in which each speaker uses his or her own language, confident that the other is likely to understand and accept the give-and-take involved. This 'passive bilingualism', as it is often termed, is possible thanks to the command of Spanish which Catalans have possessed for decades and thanks to the (usually more limited) familiarity with Catalan acquired by most resident Spanish speakers through the re-introduction of Catalan into the schools and the media.

Hall concludes as follows:

> There is little doubt that the way the language situation has evolved in recent years is conducive to a more balanced exercise of language rights between Spanish and Catalan speakers and thus to social harmony and *convivència*, but real equality seems a long way off.

Of course detractors of Catalan see the situation in a less positive light. Spain's main conservative party (PP) has severely criticized Catalan language policy on repeated occasions. The Spanish press (*El País*, 30–31 January 2005) and even the German press (*Frankfurter Allgemeine Zeitung*, 18 January 2005) describe Catalan language policy as oppressive. On a visit to Barcelona a few years back (14 February 2006), the then leader of the opposition party, Mariano Rajoy, said the sociolinguistic situation was similar to that under Franco's dictatorship, but the other way around: Catalan was now the privileged language. Rajoy is now Spain's prime minister.

Catalan speakers enjoy relatively high subjective ethnolinguistic vitality in Barcelona because of the high social position of its speakers[4] and the support of a sub-state government. So far many inhabitants of the city do not see loyalty to their historical language as an impediment to social advancement. Among other factors, this is because their allegiance to Catalan does not imply a lack of knowledge of Spanish: all Catalan speakers are fluent Spanish-Catalan bilinguals. The social attraction Catalan has for Spanish speakers who adopt it as their preferred or even first language is therefore understandable. Nevertheless, the demolinguistic dominance of Spanish is overwhelming. After the arrival of millions of non-Catalan-speaking immigrants, and despite the social attraction of Catalan, Spanish remains the most spoken and known language. As a result, new non-Spanish-speaking migrants tend to adopt Spanish as their language of communication. In other words, Spanish functions as a pivot language and Catalan runs the risk of being restricted to local, 'authentic' Catalans.

In my opinion, up until now the sociolinguistic landscape of Barcelona has been positive. The city's particular kind of bilingualism allows its citizens to master both languages: a world language, Spanish, and the historical language of the country, Catalan. The question is whether this urban multilingualism is sustainable, that is, to what extent are polyglottization and intercommunication among groups and persons compatible with the continuity and full development of all human linguistic groups?

It is not easy to describe and debate the sociolinguistic situation in Barcelona. Most inhabitants of the city think preserving their historical language, Catalan, yields significant benefits at the personal and group level, including enhanced self-esteem and positive self-image (Bastardas, 2004).

A certain social attraction of the Catalan language has been identified. Some Spanish speakers adopt Catalan as their preferred language, but at the same time new immigrants are adopting Spanish as their language. In other words, the demolinguistic weight of Spanish – the result of immense waves of migration and its hegemony in the legal and economic sphere – can hardly be offset by the better social position of Catalan speakers within Catalan society. Spanish plays a pivotal role.

Barcelona, one of the most complicated multilingual cities in a Western medium-sized language community, offers, at will or by chance, an example of linguistic sustainability, a positive example of tolerance and support for its linguistic minorities combined with loyalty to the historical language of the city, Catalan. If Barcelona loses its historical language, then Catalan will be lost everywhere.

Notes

(1) This chapter has been supported by the Project research FFI2012-35502 'Globalization and social family multilingualism in European medium sized linguistic communities' (Spanish Ministry of Economy and Competitivity). GLOBLINMED.
(2) 2012 elections, though, showed changing patterns, because they were polarized between unitarian Spanish parties and Catalan independentist parties. Some slogans during the campaigns tried to trigger internal ethnic confrontation.
(3) A watered-down version of this chapter, based on a compromise with the Spanish central government, reflects minor changes: 'Catalan is the official language of Catalonia, as well as Spanish, which is the official language of the Spanish state. All persons have the right to use both official languages, and the citizens of Catalonia have the duty to know them'. This duty to know Catalan was later rejected by the Spanish Constitutional Court in 2010.
(4) Catalan L1 speakers are mainly middle-class citizens. The deep economic crisis, that devastates Spain, might make this Catalan middle class shrink, and therefore Catalan speakers might recede.

References

Ajuntament de Barcelona (2014) *Enquesta de Serveis Municipals 2014. Resum de Resultats* [*Municipality Services' Survey, Results' Abstract*]. Barcelona: Ajuntament de Barcelona.
Allman, T.D. (1998) Barcelona. Star for the new Europe. *National Geographic* 194 (6), 42–59.

Arnau, P., Joan, P. and Tietz, M. (2001) *Escribir entre dos lenguas. Escritores catalanes y la elección de la lengua literaria* [Writing between two languages. Catalan writers and the literary language's choice]. Kassel: Reichenberger.
Bastardas, A. (1996) *Ecologia de les llengües. Medi. Contactes i dinàmica sociolingüística* [Ecology of Languages. Context and sociolinguistic dynamics]. Barcelona: Proa.
Bastardas, A. (2004) Toward 'linguistic sustainability': concepts, principles and problems of human communicative organisation in the twenty-first century. *Forum 2004. Dialogue on Linguistic Diversity, Sustainability and Peace*. See http:// www.linguapax. org/ congres04/indexan.html.
Boix, E. (1993) *Triar no és trair. Llengua i identitat entre els joves de Barcelona* [To choose doesn't mean to betray. Language and Identity among Young people in Barcelona]. Barcelona: Edicions 62.
Boix, E. (2009) *Català o castellà amb els fills? La transmissió lingüística en famílies bilingües a Barcelona* [Catalan or Spanish with the children. Linguistic transmission in bilingual families in Barcelona]. Sant Cugat del Vallès: Rourich.
Boix-Fuster, E. (2002) Barcelone 2000: un état de la question sociolinguistique [Barcelona 2000: a sociolinguistic state of the art]. *Terminogramme* 103–104, 213–244.
Boix-Fuster, E., Cots, G. and Rufo, G. (2011) Barcelona: A bivalent multilingual city. In R. Clément and C. Andrew (eds) *Cities and Languages: Governance and Policy. An International Symposium* (pp. 11–21) Ottawa: Invenire Books.
Boix-Fuster, E. and Milian-Massana, A. (eds) (2002) Aménagement linguistique dans les pays de langue catalane [Language planning in the Catalan-speaking countries]. *Terminogramme. Revue de recherche et d'information en aménagement linguistique et en terminologien*. 103–104.
Boix, E. and Torrens, R. (eds) (2011) *Les llengües al sofà. El bilingüisme familiar als països de llengua catalana* [Languages on the coach. Family bilingualism in the Catalan-speaking territories]. Lleida: Pagès editors.
Buruma, I. (2001) *El camino a Babel* [The path towards Babel]. Madrid: El Taller de Mario Muchnik.
Calvet, J.L. (1987) *La guerre des langues* [The war of languages]. Paris: Payot.
Calvet, J.L. (1994) *Les voix de la ville. Introduction à la sociolinguistique urbaine* [The voices of the city. Introduction to urban sociolinguistics]. Paris: Payot.
Calvet, L.L. (1998) *Language Wars and Linguistic Politics*. Oxford: Oxford University Press.
Carod-Rovira, J.L.L. (2012) La llengua de Barcelona [The language of Barcelona]. *Punt Avui* 29/IV/2012.
Castellanos, J. (2004) Barcelona en literatura: Imatges en conflicte [Barcelona in literature: Images in conflict]. *Catalan Review* XVIII (1–3), 131–148.
Comajoan, Ll. and Long, E. (2012) The linguistic landscape of three streets in Barcelona: Patterns of language visibility in public space. In D. Gorter, H.F. Marten, L. Van Mensel and G. Hogan-Brun (eds) *Minority Languages in the Linguistic Landscape* (pp. 183–203). Basingstoke: Palgrave Macmillan.
Costa, J. (ed.) (2009) The *Architect of Modern Catalan: Pompeu Fabra (1868–1948)*. Amsterdam: John Benjamins.
DiGiacomo, S.M. (1999) Language ideological debates in an Olympic city: Barcelona 1992–1996. In J. Blommaert (ed.) *Language Ideological Debates* (pp. 105–142). Berlin: Mouton de Gruyter.
Farràs, J., Torres, J. and Vila, F.X. (2000) *El coneixement del català.1996. Mapa sociolingüístic de Catalunya* [Knowledge of Catalan 1996. Sociolinguistic map of Catalonia]. Barcelona: Generalitat de Catalunya.
Fernández Diaz, A. (2002) Intervenció del president del Grup Popular a l'Ajuntament de Barcelona. Debat d'orientació política general del Govern [Intervention by the president of the Popular Party at the City Council of Barcelona], 2 October 2002.

Giner, S. (1987) Barcelona and its people. In *Homage to Barcelona. The City and its Arts (1888–1936)* (pp. 141–147). Barcelona: Ajuntament de Barcelona.
Hall, J. (2001) *Convivència in Catalonia: Languages Living Together*. Barcelona: Fundació Jaume Bofill.
Harris, M. (1988) Introduction. In M. Harris and N. Vincent (eds) *The Romance Languages* (pp. 1–25). Oxford: Oxford University Press.
Heinemann, U. (1998) *Schriftsteller als sprachliche Grenzgänger. Literarische Verarbeitung von Mehrsprachigkeit, Sprachkontakt und Sprachkonflikt in Barcelona* [Writers as border crossers. Literary elaboration of multilingualism, language contact and language conflict in Barcelona]. Vienna: Praesens.
Ingendaay, P. (2006) Die Sprachpolizei rät. Gängelei und Säuberung: Katalonien bedrängt Spanien [Languae policy advices. Child talk and cleansing. Catalonia harasses Spain]. *Frankfurter Allgemeine Zeitung*. 18 January 2006.
Insight City Guide. Barcelona (2005) APA Publications.
Kuo, E.C.Y. (1979) Measuring communicativity in multilingual societies: The case of Singapore and West Malaysia. *Anthropological Linguistics* 21 (7), 328–340.
Larreula, E. (2002) *Dolor de llengua [Language pain]*. València: Tres i Quatre.
Linz, J.J. (1975) Politics in a multi-national society with a dominant world language: The case of Spain. In J.G. Savard and R. Vigneault (eds) *Les états multilingues. Problèmes et solutions*. Québec: Les Presses de l'Université de Laval, 367–444.
Mackey, W.F. (2000) Les langues dans la cité [The languages of the city]. In *Terminogramme. Revue de recherche et d'information en aménagement linguistique et en terminologie* 93–94, 9–30.
Marí, I. (1995) La capital internacional de la llengua catalana [The international capital of the Catalan language]. In *17 per Barcelona. Presentació de Miquel Roca* (pp. 159–181). Barcelona: Columna.
Mataix, T. (2010) *Estudi sobre els usos multilingües a l'Ajuntament de Barcelona. Criteris i aplicación multilingüe en la relació entre el ciutadà i l'administració* [Research on the multilingual uses in the municipality of Barcelona in the relationships between citizens and the public administration]. Barcelona: Consorci per a la Normalització Lingüística de Barcelona.
McRae, K.D. (1983) *Switzerland. Conflict and Compromise in Multilingual Societies*. Waterloo, Ontario: Wilfried Laurier University Press.
McRoberts, K. (2001) Catalonia. *Nation Building Without a State*. Oxford: Oxford University Press.
Pérez Andújar, J. (2011) *Paseos con mi madre*. Barcelona: Tusquets.
Pijoan, J. (2007) *Sayonara Barcelona*. Barcelona: Proa.
Puntí, J. (2011) *Els castellans [The Castilians]*. Barcelona: L'Avenç.
Pujolar, J. (2011) Catalan-Spanish language contact in social interaction. In Ll. Payrató and J.M. Cots (eds) *The Pragmatics of Catalan* (pp. 361–385). Berlin: Mouton de Gruyter.
Rafanell, A. (2011) *Notícies d'abans d'ahir [The day before yesterday's news]*. Barcelona: Acontravent.
Rambla, F.X. (1993) *Factors de la distribució territorial de l'ús del català a la conurbació de Barcelona [Factors explaining the spacial distribution of the use of Catalan in the Barcelona área]*. Barcelona: Generalitat de Catalunya.
Reglament d'ús de la llengua catalana (2010) *Butlletí Oficial de la Província de Barcelona*, núm.38, 13 January 2010.
Sorolla, N. (2010) Famílies lingüísticament mixtes segons l'enquesta EULP08 [Linguistically mixed families in the survey EULP08]. *Butlleti Cercle XXI* 8 (20-XII-2010). http://www.cercle21.cat/ca/butlleti/8/index.html (accessed 9 April 2015).

Subirats, M. (1998) Trets culturals: educació, llengua i hàbits de lleure [Cultural traits: education, language and leisure habits]. In O. Nello, A. Recio, and M. Solsona (eds) *La transformació de la societat metropolitana. Una lectura de l'enquesta sobre condicions de vida i hàbits de la regió metropolitana de Barcelona (1985–1995)* [*The transformation of the metropolitan area. A Reading of the survey on the life conditions and habits in the Barcelona area*] (pp. 69–91). Bellaterra: Institut d'Estudis Metropolitans.

Subirats, M. (2002) Els trets lingüístics [Linguistic characteristics]. In S. Giner (ed.) *Enquesta de la Regió de Barcelona* [Survey of the Barcelona área. General rapport]. *Informe general*. Barcelona: Diputació de Barcelona. Àrea Metropolitana de Barcelona, 180–187.

Subirats, M. (2012) La llengua catalana: de la marginació al mestissatge. In *Barcelona: de la necessitat a la llibertat. Les classes socials: de la necessitat a la llibertat. Les clases socials al tombant del segle XXI* [*Barcelona: from necessity to freedom. Social clases al the turn of the XXIst century*]. Barcelona: L'Avenç.

Van de Craen, P. and Baetens Beardsmore, H. (1987) Research on city language. In U. Ammon (ed.) *Sociolinguistics: An International Handbook of the Science of Language and Society* (pp. 579–584). Berlin: Walter de Gruyter.

Webber, J. and Strubell, M. (1991) *The Catalan Language: Progress towards Normalisation*. Sheffield: The Anglo-Catalan Society.

Woolard, K.A. (1989) *Double Talk. Bilingualism and the Politics of Ethnicity in Catalonia*. Stanford: Stanford University Press.

Woolard, K.A. (2003) We don't speak Catalan because we are marginalized: Ethnic and class meanings of language in Barcelona. In R.K. Blot (ed.) *Language and Social Identity* (pp. 85–103). Westport. London: Praeger.

8 Language in Copenhagen: Changing Social Structures, Changing Ideologies, Changing Linguistic Practices

Marie Maegaard and J. Normann Jørgensen

Introduction

Copenhagen has undergone major societal and linguistic changes during the latest century. Some changes are general to Denmark, while others are specific to the Copenhagen community. In the following we present a brief overview of some of the historical developments that have led to the present demographic and linguistic situation in Copenhagen. We focus on minority language groups and their status in Copenhagen and in Danish society in general. At the same time, throughout the chapter our main focus is the disappearing division between high and low Copenhagen speech, which accompanies the emergence of new types of linguistic variation.

The History of the Copenhagen Speech Community

Three historical developments have played particularly important roles in shaping the sociolinguistic reality of Copenhagen. The first of these is the centralization that took place with the absolute monarchy's administration of the country, especially the part that is now Denmark proper. This development began in the 1660s as a consequence of military defeat. The second crucial development happened in the second half of the 1800s and led to Copenhagen's expansion in both geographical terms and number of inhabitants. Ideologically this period was also characterized by a Danish military defeat, this time in 1864. The third development took place after World War II, which incidentally began with another defeat and saw no glorious Danish participation. This led to the greatly expanded range of linguistic resources represented in Copenhagen, with a range of recently immigrated minority groups.

In the period of absolute monarchy, the state of Denmark suffered a range of military defeats that cut the geographical size of Denmark (excluding the North Atlantic parts) down to its present size. While the country was decreasing in size a homogenization was also going on with respect to cultural and linguistic variation within the population. At the time the Danish elite still saw the country as a European player. The elite was to a large extent of German descent, and apparently a range of languages were spoken in Copenhagen before the mid-1600s. A near-complete defeat by the Swedish king in 1659, however, led to a coup in which the Danish king, supported by the Copenhagen bourgeoisie, deprived the traditional landed nobility of its power to govern locally. The landed nobility was based locally, connected to the land, and to a certain extent was also linguistically local by speaking the local dialects of its home areas. During the first years of absolute monarchy, the old nobility lost its positions as local rulers and was substituted by a new elite. The men in this elite were educated at the university in Copenhagen. They were not locally born, but they reported to – and were loyal to – the king in Copenhagen. Copenhagen soon became the centre of gravity, first of all politically, but also culturally and economically. The city came to stand for the prestigious, the powerful, the educated and the rich.

Linguistically, the Copenhagen dialect gradually became the prestige variety, a national standard speech developed in the 1700s (e.g. Pedersen, 2005, 2009). Ideologically, the Danish elite turned nationalist in the 1700s, and by January 1776 a citizenship law was issued that denied Germans access to higher positions in the administration. This was one of a number of nationalist political moves that accompanied the gradual reduction in Denmark's size and political power in Europe.

High and Low Copenhagen Speech

Linguistically, Copenhagen Danish has been the standard since then and has gradually spread to all corners of Denmark. In the second half of the 1900s, this development accelerated, and the classical local dialects all but disappeared (Pedersen, 2003). Meanwhile, Copenhagen Danish developed into two separate sociolects.

Until around 1700, there were few differences within Copenhagen speech: people spoke the local dialect, as people did elsewhere in the country. During the 1700s, a development within Copenhagen Danish led to two separate sociolects one correlated with relatively high social status, and one correlated with relatively low social status. The H-Copenhagen sociolect advanced the change, particularly the sound change, whereas the L-Copenhagen sociolect maintained the older, shared forms, especially when these forms were not supported by the written language; that is, the socially motivated changes reflect the fact that the high status speakers were more comfortable with the written language.

The differentiation accelerated during the 1800s. Most of the changes, though not all, originated in L-Copenhagen speech and gradually spread to H-Copenhagen speech. By 1900 there were many and distinct differences between the two sociolects, and it was hardly possible to say very much without giving away one's social class (Brink & Lund, 1974: 58–59). During the 1800s, Copenhagen became overpopulated, and in 1857 the ramparts were in principle abolished to make room for the city's expansion. The removal was complete by 1872. This is the second development in the sociolinguistic reality of Copenhagen, as we mentioned earlier. The rapid urbanization led to the construction of low-quality housing, and by 1900 Copenhagen saw the greatest differences in living conditions between the classes at any time.

In ideological terms, the defeat by Prussia in 1864 led to the development of self-understanding among Danes who described the country as a small, defenceless, peaceful place surrounded by enemies. Denmark was seen as a homogeneous, but first and foremost small, country. An often-quoted expression by the nationalist poet Grundtvig (1820) describes the Danes: 'few have too much and fewer too little'. However, a feeling of belonging to a Nordic (or Scandinavian) communal entity also developed, and gradually Denmark came to see itself as a Nordic country rather than a European power. A certain animosity towards non-Nordic people gradually grew, particularly directed towards Germans.

This eventually led to a movement towards equality that characterized not only Copenhagen but also Denmark as a whole until 2000. It is characteristic of the 1900s that the considerable differences between H-Copenhagen speech and L-Copenhagen speech diminished to the extent that they are hardly discernible in the younger generations. Throughout the 1900s, most of the changes involved the H-Copenhagen speech approaching the L-Copenhagen speech. New developments also mainly originated in L-speech and gradually spread into H-speech. As the differences between the two sociolects diminished, L-Copenhagen became more like a young national standard, and H-speech more like a conservative national standard.

The national standard

H-Copenhagen speech spread as the prestigious and powerful way of speaking Danish, and eventually became the national standard. By 1800,

H-Copenhagen forms could be heard in the cities, although few, if any, people born and raised outside Copenhagen would use only H-Copenhagen forms.

The drive in the educational system was against the local ways of speaking. Dialects were considered rural and characteristic of peasantry. This approach has continued unchallenged until the late 1900s (Kristiansen, 1990), at which time the classical dialects were almost extinct and therefore no longer amounted to any challenge to the H-Copenhagen national standard. Today a lot of lip service is paid to the classical dialects, but they are taught nowhere. Teaching material teach about them more than in passing are rare. By the end of the 1900s the partial merger of the two Copenhagen sociolects resulted in the young national standard becoming the variety of prestige, generally associated with 'dynamism' and youth, while the conservative standard is associated with efficiency and power (Kristiansen, 2009).

Copenhagen Today

Today the population of the urban area of Copenhagen is around 1.2 million (Danmarks Statistik, 2010). The urban area is defined by measures of population density. However, the population of the entire Copenhagen region is approximately 1.7 million, which amounts to one third of the Danish population. For comparison, the second largest city in Denmark, Århus, has 300,000 inhabitants. With regard to population size as well as in many other ways, Copenhagen has a dominant position.

The history of Copenhagen, together with its size, and its political, administrative and cultural institutions, gives Copenhagen a very dominant position in the Danish economic and business life. Administratively, Denmark is also strongly dominated by Copenhagen – there are elected local governments, but their influence on the economy or other aspects of society is minimal compared to that of the national political bodies, the government and the parliament. The supreme court is also placed in Copenhagen, as are all the ministries and major national administrative institutions, including the national bank. The same is true for culture. The national museums, the national opera house, the national ballet and the national theatre are all in Copenhagen.

Copenhagen is divided into districts which have some rather minimal influence on certain matters within the district such as local cultural or citizens' initiatives. By and large, the city of Copenhagen (some 0.7 million people) is run by the city government which, since the coup in 1660, has had a special status compared to other regional or urban units in the country. The city electorate is traditionally more leftist than the national electorate, and Copenhagen has had a Social Democratic supreme mayor for more than 100 years. The city government, however, is shared among the major parties in a collective arrangement by which the supreme mayor shares power with six other mayors with different responsibilities. The responsibility for education has for some years been with one or the other of the socialist parties. However, in 2010 it was taken over by the Social Democrats, the office of minority teaching was closed (see below), and in 2013 the responsibility for education was taken over by a right wing party (Venstre).

Minority Language

In the second half of the 1900s, Denmark experienced an increasing immigration in addition to the near-elimination of the classical dialects. In the late 1960s, labour migrants began arriving in the thousands, mainly from the Middle East and Yugoslavia. In the 1970s, groups of refugees began to join the migrant labourers, including Chileans and Kurds. The majority of the newly arrived citizens settled in the cities, many of them in Copenhagen. Gradually, the new citizens, especially the labour migrants, reunited with their families by settling permanently in Denmark. This is the third development with respect to the language status of Copenhagen that we mentioned earlier.

In the beginning of the 1990s the number of people of ethnic minority background (defined in a certain way by the city council) was around 10% of the population. In 2013 it was 22% of the entire population, and in Copenhagen elementary schools it was 30% (Copenhagen City Council, 2013). This means that in the younger population having a minority background is very common, whereas it is less common among the older citizens. The largest minority population groups in Copenhagen are: Citizens of Turkish descent (c. 40,000), Pakistani (c. 20,000), Polish (c. 13,000), German (c. 10,000), Iraqi (c. 9000), Swedish (c. 9000), Iranian (c. 8000), British (c. 7000). As is evident from Guus Extra's Chapter 1, in this volume, counting such things as ethnic background is difficult and problematic. In this case, the numbers show which citizens have migrated from a different country, or have parents who both did. Whether or not the individuals themselves *feel* that they belong to a certain minority group is not taken into consideration. For instance, many of the people who are counted as having a Turkish background feel that they are Kurdish, and definitely not Turkish. This way building statistics on nationality is not a satisfactory solution, but it is the way it is done by the administration in Copenhagen.

In Copenhagen there is a larger concentration of linguistic minorities than in the rest of Denmark. There are no surveys of language skills and language use in people's private lives, but it is assumed that at least 140 languages are represented by mother tongue speakers in Copenhagen

(Risager, 2009). Some minorities include enough people to be able to set up organizations or even schools, but they only have an impact on public life through Danish (or English in a few cases).

The linguistic consequences of the movements of people that have taken place since the 1960s have been moderate in the sense that very little concrete influence on Danish, viz. the Copenhagen standard, has been noticed, nothing in terms of grammar and only a few loanwords. With the exception of English (see below), non-Danish language is very rarely heard in public or media interaction. This means that the increased linguistic diversity of the city population has not had any impact on the status of Danish as the common and standard language. The English language, on the other hand, is very dominant in Denmark – and in Copenhagen – but this is for different reasons than immigration from English-speaking countries, as is clear from the list given above (where the number of people of British minority background is quite low, which is also the case with American and Australian backgrounds).

In Copenhagen the first reaction to immigration was to set up a school reception system through which the children of migrant labourers and refugees were placed in special minority classes focused exclusively on learning to speak (and read) Danish. Simultaneously, the children were offered mother tongue classes a few hours per week, but always removed from their 'regular' schooling (i.e. the reception classes) in time and often also in place. This Copenhagen system became the backbone of minority students' schooling in the whole country. The reception methods became more varied, but never failed to focus on the Danish language. In compliance with EU council directive 77/486, the state guaranteed the teaching of minority languages as mother tongues, and the local communities were obliged to offer such classes.

In 2001 the national government of Denmark was won by a group of conservative parties, supported in parliament by the Danish People's Party (Dansk Folkeparti). Part of this party's program is that 'Denmark is not an immigrant country and never has been. Thus, we will not accept transformation into a multiethnic society' (Danish People's Party, 2011). One of the first actions of this new government was to abolish mother tongue teaching of minority languages. For several years the community of Copenhagen continued, not without success (Gimbel et al., 2000; Jørgensen & von Haffner, 2002), to a large extent because an office of professionals was set up to organize the teaching of minority students. However, in 2010 this office was closed, and Copenhagen joined the rest of the country in ignoring the mother tongues of the minorities.

Another important development took effect in 2010, namely the abolishing of publically supported interpreters for minority patients in the health sector and judicial system. Residents who have spent more than a given number of years in Denmark are no longer entitled to financial support for an interpreter, and they must, if they need one, pay for the interpreter themselves.

As mentioned above, in the Copenhagen school system, roughly 30% of the students are linguistic minority students. A considerable proportion of the young generation in Copenhagen has daily access to other languages than Danish (and English). However, this is only reflected in the mediated public sphere in programs that are specifically for minorities. Nevertheless, some young members of the linguistic minorities make an impact, namely by apparently leading some of the new developments, including new and ongoing sound changes in Copenhagen Danish (see below).

English

Two language policy documents issued by the Ministry of Culture (2003, 2008) formulate the language view and the goals of the government that ruled from 2001. The main concept of this is 'parallel languages', by which it is meant that all important public and scientific work must be available in both Danish and English. The idea is that Danish is 'threatened' by English, and this policy is considered a bulwark against the eradication of Danish from public life and learning.

One perhaps unintended consequence of this is that Danish students began focusing on learning English and abandoning all other languages in droves. The business school of Copenhagen has closed down MA programs in languages such as Italian, and the high schools reported that the proportion of students who took a third language in high school dropped from more than 40% to less than 10%.

This means that the vast majority of people in Copenhagen today will know some, or very much English. It is difficult to move through Copenhagen without encountering spoken and written English. The default reaction of many Copenhageners when they hear people speaking a language other than Danish is to reply in English. This even applies to some cases where the interlocutor is Scandinavian – Swedish, Norwegian, or Finno-Swedish. Anecdotal evidence has it that some Copenhageners will answer in English even when they hear accented Danish.

Cinemas and Danish television do not dub foreign productions, but subtitle them. This means that a lot of English comes across in these media, as movies produced with English dialogue are popular. Some Scandinavian, German or French productions also regularly make it into the media, and once in a while a production from elsewhere is released on the market. On these occasions, languages other than Danish and English are publicly used. This is perhaps more so in Copenhagen than elsewhere in the country, because the city has a number of small, upscale cinemas.

Variation in Spoken Danish in Copenhagen Today

As mentioned above, the distinction between the two Copenhagen sociolects, H-Copenhagen and L-Copenhagen speech, has almost disappeared. This is probably mainly due to societal changes. From the 1960s onwards Denmark witnessed very rapid economic development. Together with the Danish welfare system, this has produced a society that is at the same time both economically very wealthy and very equal (OECD 2008, 2010). According to the OECD, Denmark is the most economically equal society in the world, in terms of income distribution (OECD, 2008). One consequence of this is that traditional concepts of social class lose their importance. Economic wealth cannot be seen as the most significant parameter regarding class and social status. Linguistically, this means that the former differences between high and low Copenhagen speech are no longer relevant, since the classes that they used to be associated with no longer exist in the same way. However, new social distinctions have emerged in Denmark, and one of the most important has to do with constructions of ethnicity. The ideology of 'Danishness' has changed in recent years, and an 'us' vs. 'them' distinction has become very important in some parts of the majority population. This can be seen in official documents from the Ministry of Refugee, Immigration and Integration Affairs (e.g. 2009), where definitions of 'foreigners' and 'Danes' are made explicit. The definitions are not based on nationality, but on other criteria, such as parents' nationality and place of birth. Thus, according to the Danish authorities, 'foreigners' may very well have Danish citizenship and be born and raised in Denmark.

As mentioned above, the increase of citizens with a non-Danish linguistic background has not resulted in any weakening of Danish as the most important language in Denmark and in Copenhagen. However, the heterogeneity of the younger population regarding cultural and linguistic background has led to changes in processes of linguistic change in Danish. It has been described in many places that primarily speakers of lower socioeconomic background have lead the linguistic changes in Danish. However, with the increasing economic equality, and the increasing linguistic and cultural diversity, new groups of speakers seem to be the linguistic innovators in Copenhagen. We will report from an ethnographic study that examines how linguistic practices are imbedded in social structure in a diverse school environment in Copenhagen.

The study is a recent sociolinguistic investigation among Copenhagen youth that examines the relationship between social categories, social practice, and linguistic practice (Maegaard, 2007, 2009, 2010). The study builds on seven months of ethnographic field work among 83 young people (15–16 years old) in a Copenhagen school. The fieldwork consisted mainly of participant observation and interviews with the students. The focus was both linguistic and social. The linguistic focus was on new phonetic developments in Copenhagen speech, whereas the social focus was on social categories and practices that were socially meaningful and important to the social order in the school, to create a basis for analyses of connections between social practice, categories and linguistic variation. The social analyses led to distinctions between the categories of 'Danes' and 'foreigners', 'girls' and 'boys'. Furthermore, they resulted in the division of the young people into eight groups, based on analyses of clusters of the social practices that they engaged in.

The distinction between 'girls' and 'boys' is the most important distinction with regard to friendship networks among the students. Membership in these two categories is not negotiable in this community – either you are a girl or a boy, and even though gender identities can be performed in many different ways, the gender distinction is crucial to the social order in school. There are hardly any friendship networks that involve both girls and boys, unless they are of a romantic character. This is similar to results from many other Danish ethnographic studies among young people in schools or sports clubs (e.g. Madsen, 2008; Quist, 2005; Staunæs, 2004).

The distinction between 'foreigners' and 'Danes' is of a different kind. It may seem strange that such radical terminology exists among students who have spent the last ten years together in the same class (most of them at least). However, this distinction is fundamental in contemporary Danish society, and it is found even in official documents from the government. The distinction between 'foreigners' and 'Danes' or similar distinctions, has been documented in several other recent sociological or sociolinguistic studies among Copenhagen youth (Ag, 2010; Madsen, 2008; Quist, 2005; Stæhr, 2010; Staunæs, 2004). In our analyses of this specific community (the 9th graders in the City School) we will use the same terminology as the students. In other words, we will continue to refer to 'foreigners' and 'Danes' since these are the labels given to the categories by the students themselves.

Membership of the category 'foreigners' is not determined by criteria such as mother tongue or nationality. Such criteria play a part in the categorization, but they interact with other factors. Physical appearance is one important factor (all 'foreigners' are brown-eyed and dark-haired), but it is not enough to determine a student's category membership. The crucial factor is how individuals *act* in the social field. There are students who by some criteria could be categorized as 'foreigners', 'students with an ethnic background different from Danish', 'bilinguals', 'immigrants' etc., who are not categorized as 'foreigners' in school, because they do not participate in the same practices as the 'foreigners'. The clusters of practices that separate one category from another are described thoroughly elsewhere (Maegaard, 2007, 2010). Here, to give an impression of the social world of the students, we list the analysed practices and the labelled clusters that they form.

Table 8.1 shows the social practices that we analysed. The practices were selected because ethnographic fieldwork revealed that they were important to the social order in school. For every informant, the recurring pattern of engagement in distinct social practices was analysed. On the basis of this analysis the informants were ascribed to one cluster of practices – a style cluster. The style clusters are sets of practices that go together in the construction of a specific social identity or persona (Maegaard, 2010: 191 ff; Quist, 2008: 51). For example, the 'nerdy boys' engage in practices very different from the 'tough foreign boys and Danish boys hanging out with foreigners'. It is a basic assumption underlying this study that linguistic practice and other social practices are related, and that it is the repeated enactment of certain actions that construct and re-construct social meaning. One example of this could be clothing. Wearing a black leather jacket, for example, is commonly recognized as a symbol of 'toughness', 'rebellion' or 'opposition', whereas wearing a tweed jacket has very different connotations for many people. In this way, different styles of clothing can be part of the construction of different social meanings. This is not controversial. However, when it comes to linguistic practice, and even phonetic variation, this kind of relation (between variation and social meaning) may be more surprising. Furthermore, the relation between language and social meaning can be quite explicit to the language users themselves. The example below is from an interview with one of the boys in the City School. He is talking about a specific pronunciation of *t* (palatalization), and has just explained that many of the boys in school use this feature. Then the interviewer asks about the girls:

Interviewer: do any girls use it (.) do you think
er der nogle piger der bruger det (.) tror du
Kenneth: nah (.) not that I know of
næh (.) ikke hvad jeg har lagt mærke til
Interviewer: no
nej
(.)
Kenneth: it's mainly the boys because they want to be tough
det er mest drengene for at være seje
Interviewer: okay
okay

In this extract, Kenneth makes a direct connection between a certain pronunciation of *t* and 'toughness'. He states that boys use this phonetic feature to be 'tough'. Therefore, in his interpretation, the feature not is only

Table 8.1 Ten analyzed student practices

Social practices
Smoking
Use of alcohol
Whereabouts during school breaks
Leisure activities
Job (after school)
Lunch (type and where it is bought/eaten)
Way of walking
Whereabouts in the city
Clothing
Interaction with the other gender

used more frequently by boys than by girls, or more by 'tough' kids than by the rest, but in fact it *constructs* 'toughness'. In this understanding, phonetic features can help construct speakers as for instance more or less 'tough', 'clever' or 'funny'.

When analysing the students' practices we found that they cluster together into different style clusters. The analysis of the ten student practices in Table 8.1 led to the construction of eight different clusters of practices that different students engage in. If a student engages in more than eight practices that are part of a certain cluster, the student is ascribed to that style cluster. In Table 8.2 we present an example of one such style cluster, namely the 'nerdy boys'.

Table 8.2 Practices constituting the 'nerdy boys' cluster

Social practices	'Nerdy boys'
Smoking	Do not smoke
Use of alcohol	Drink alcohol
Whereabouts during school breaks	Stay in classroom during breaks
Leisure activities	Play computer games, go to scout meetings, role plays
Job (after school)	No job
Lunch (type and where it is bought/eaten)	Bring packed lunch from home
Way of walking	–
Whereabouts in the city	Local use of the city
Clothing	No mainstream fashion clothes. Jeans, neither narrow, nor baggy, sweatshirts in bright colours, untrendy trainers
Interaction with the other gender	No interaction with girls at school

A boy who engages in eight of these practices is categorized as a 'nerdy boy'. The vast majority of the students could be ascribed to a specific style cluster, but of course some students did not fit any of them.

The linguistic analysis led to the selection of 10 phonetic variables that are shown in Table 8.3. They are divided into (1) variables that are known from previous studies to be associated with the dichotomy between High Copenhagen and Low Copenhagen, (2) variables that are known from previous studies to be associated with the dichotomy between younger speakers and older speakers, and (3) variables that have not previously been analysed sociolinguistically (or at all) before. Table 8.3 shows the non-standard variants and examples of words in which the specific variant can occur.

The variables are selected on the basis of previous studies of variation in spoken Copenhagen and Danish in general (Brink & Lund, 1975; Brink *et al.*, 1991; Grønnum, 2005; Holmberg *et al.*, 1992; Jørgensen, 1980; Jørgensen & Kristensen, 1994) and on the basis of the variation that the fieldworker (Maegaard) noticed in the speech of the young people in the school.

The linguistic analysis involved an auditory analysis of 64 interviews with regard to the 10 variables.

The distribution of variants into categories based on constructed gender and ethnicity distinctions are shown in Table 8.4. As can be seen from the table, 'lengthening of short vowel' is the only variable in which the 'Danes' are in the lead, and the 'foreign' girls or boys are not. With regard to all the other variables, either the 'foreign' boys or 'foreign' girls are the most extreme.

Table 8.3 Phonetic variables selected for the quantitative analysis. For each variable three example words are listed

Traditional high/low-variables	Traditional young/old-variables	Non-traditional variables
'Lengthening of short vowels' Low 'snakke', 'gruppe', 'klasse'	Raising of (e) before velar nasals: [eŋ] (Young) 'tænke', 'engelsk', 'penge'	Devoicing of initial r: [ʁ̥] 'rimelig', 'rød', 'ryge'
Affrication of initial t: [t͡s] (Low) 'ti', 'tusind', 'teori'	Fusion of [ð] and the preceding vowel V into [ᵛð] (Young) 'tid', 'hvad', 'sidde'	Dentalization of s: [ʂ] 'sidste', 'cykel', 'sejt'
Backing of the nucleus of the aj-diphthong: [ɒj] (Low) 'haj', 'lege', 'hejse'		Palatalization of initial t: [tʲ] 'ti', 'tusind', 'teori'
Fronting of the nucleus of the aj-diphthong: [aj] (High) 'haj', 'lege', 'hejse'		
Postalveolar [ʃ] for standard [ɕ] (High) 'sjov', 'speciel', 'charme'		

Lengthening of short vowels can be said to be the only Low Copenhagen feature studied in this material, since the other Low feature, the affricated /t/, has not been a feature associated with Low speech for quite some time now (Brink & Lund, 1975: 353–355). This means that the only Low Copenhagen feature in the study shows a very different pattern from the other features. The 'Danish' boys and girls use this feature far more than the 'foreigners'.

The 'foreign' girls have the highest use of [s̺], [t͡s] and [aj], while the 'foreign' boys have the highest use of [tʲ], devoiced /r/, fusion of [ð] and the preceding vowel, [ʃ] and [eŋ]. This means that speakers in these two categories use the opposite variants, for most of the variables: when the 'foreign' boys make frequent use of a given variant, the 'foreign' girls have low use – and the other way around. It is worth noting that the extreme use of variants among 'foreigners' is not restricted to the non-traditional variables, but also applies to the traditional variables. It seems that this is not merely a question of the 'foreigners' inventing new variants, but of them using existing variation to construct social meaning through opposition. This becomes clearer when we look at the variation in relation to the style clusters.

If we look further at the different style groups and their use of the phonetic features, we see a more detailed pattern than that shown in Table 8.4.

If we see linguistic variation as social practice, we would expect the language use of students belonging to different style groups to be different. In Table 8.5, the pupils are categorized according to which style cluster they could be said to draw upon in their persona construction. This pattern is more fine-grained and detailed in many ways, and the pattern from Table 8.4 concerning constructions of gender and ethnicity is also found in this analysis: the 'foreign' girls in style group 1 use the opposite variants to style group 5, the 'tough foreign boys and boys hanging out with foreigners' (except regarding the use of devoiced /r/ which girls and boys use similarly). Again, these

Table 8.4 Frequency of non-standard variants according to categories based on constructions of gender and ethnicity distinctions

	Foreign girls %	Dan. girls %	Dan. boys %	For. boys %
[s̺]	23.3	6.0	0	15.8
[t͡s]	57.5	15.2	1.0	15.8
[tʲ]	0	0.8	7.3	15.0
[ʁ̥]	16.3	4.8	4.4	23.3
Length of short V	0	21.7	21.1	11.9
[ᵛð]	41.5	60.2	59.1	75.5
[ʃ]	11.8	20.7	53.6	98.1
[eŋ]	0	29.5	56.3	55.6
[aj]	73.3	15.3	8.4	0

Table 8.5 Frequency of non-standard variants according to style clusters

	Gr 1 Foreign girls	Gr 2 Decent Danish girls	Gr 3 Tough Danish girls	Gr 4 Alternative girls	Gr 5 Tough Ethnically mixed boys	Gr 6 Decent Danish boys	Gr 7 Tough Danish boys	Gr 8 Nerdy boys
[ṣ]	22.5	10.7	0	0	7.9	0	0	0
[ts]	57.5	27.5	6.7	8.3	8.3	1.3	0	2.5
[tʲ]	0	1.1	1.7	0	12.5	6.3	4.4	0
[ʁ̥]	16.3	5.0	15.0	8.3	12.1	6.3	4.4	0
Length of short V	0	22.5	26.1	2.3	11.8	3.0	38.0	40.0
[ˀð]	41.5	53.8	56.7	77.8	69.0	61.6	52.0	53.3
[ʃ]	11.8	15.3	40.0	33.3	95.4	48.1	34.1	60.0
[eŋ]	0	25.8	0	0	64.7	50.0	66.7	33.3
[aj]	73.3	21.2	0	0	0	27.3	3.8	0

two groups are the most extreme language users with regard to all the variables, except for the lengthening of short vowels.

Another interesting thing to note here is how social category and practice seem to fit together. The 'Danish' boys in style group 5 ('the tough foreign boys and Danish boys hanging out with foreigners') use the [tʲ] and [ʃ] variants approximately as much as the 'foreign' boys, and far more than the other groups of boys. Thus, there is a connection between language use and other social practices, in that the boys in style group 5 are categorized in the same group precisely because they participate in the same practices.

On the other hand, the devoiced /r/ is especially used by 'the foreign girls', 'foreign boys and Danish boys hanging out with foreign boys' and 'the tough Danish girls'. However, the 'Danish' boys in style group 5, who participate in the same practices as the 'foreign' boys, do not use devoiced /r/ very much. Actually, they use it even less than the 'Danish' boys who are not part of style group 5. It is possible that the 'Danish' boys in style group 5 do this to signal that after all they are not 'foreigners'. Consequently, even though it is possible to distinguish between different groups based on the practices they engage in (as in Table 8.5 above), the abstract category membership (such as boy, girl, 'Dane', 'foreigner') is still important. Thus, it seems that the style groups should not function as the only description, but that this analysis supplements an analysis based on social categories.

The linguistic analysis shows that the variation is connected both to social categories and to practices. In principle, relations that have been found among the pupils from the City School could turn out to be entirely locally bound, which means that we could not expect to find the same relations in other places in Copenhagen. To establish whether or not this seemed to be the case, a verbal guise study was carried out. This showed that other young people in Copenhagen connected the same type of social meanings to the linguistic variation as those seen in the City School. Furthermore, very similar perceptual results were found in different schools in Copenhagen (Maegaard, 2010).

Conclusions

The distinction between High and Low Copenhagen speech has more or less disappeared, or has been transformed into a new distinction that is connected to constructions of ethnicity. Some of the features associated with former Low Copenhagen speech are used by 'foreign girls', some by 'foreign boys', and some by 'Danes'. The same is true for features associated with former High Copenhagen. Young people in Copenhagen use the existing variation in new ways, and with new social meanings. At the same time, they use new features that have not previously been described as part of Copenhagen (or Danish) varieties.

The new social distinctions in Danish society have led to new linguistic distinctions. It is tempting to interpret this as yet another class division between 'high' and 'low'. Yet, this is not a straight-forward interpretation. The 'foreigners' are not necessarily lower class, measured in terms of socioeconomic class and, similarly, the 'Danes' are not necessarily higher class. However, ideologically, 'foreigners' are associated with lower class. This is seen in public discourse, in which politicians, journalists, teachers and others frequently refer to 'foreigners' or 'immigrants' in connection with unemployment, crime, educational problems and so forth. Thus, at the ideological macro-level, 'foreigners' are seen as problematic individuals who do not contribute to society, and are associated with a very low degree of prestige. At the same time, in local communities, 'foreigners' are often associated with attributes that are prestigious at local micro-level. This may involve toughness, cleverness, ambitions, attractiveness etc. as we have seen in several studies from Copenhagen schools (Madsen, 2008; Maegaard, 2007; Stæhr, 2010). All this means that issues of class, prestige and ethnicity are highly relevant in contemporary Danish society, and perhaps particularly in Copenhagen. Social constructions of class, prestige and ethnicity have changed, and they are interrelated in complicated ways at different levels of discourse. Furthermore, they are related to linguistic variation in the ways that we have described in this chapter.

All in all, we have argued that the increasing diversity in the Copenhagen population has not lead to any challenges towards Danish as the standard language of Denmark and Copenhagen. In our view nothing is threatening the Danish speech community more than itself. And by that we mean that the uniformitarian ideology of Danish speakers, trying to preserve Danish as it was, is at best a lost case. However, we also know, that typical characteristics of living languages are that they change, and that they are in contact with other languages. In that respect, the problematization of minority language speakers is both sad and disturbing. The challenges that Denmark is facing at the moment are to do with ethnocentrism and a lack of openness towards other languages – apart from English. But also here, we see a tendency towards a unified, standardized norm where speaking English is regarded as essential in a globalized world. However, this argument seem to only hold for English, and no other language, which means that in Denmark every year less young people choose to study another foreign language than English.

This is a picture of a very normative, standardized language community, whith very little variation, and with very low tolerance of it. However, it looks as if things will change with the large younger population in Copenhagen that has minority background. Diversity will eventually be much more visible, not only for the youngest generations, and perhaps in time, this will result in a less normative linguistic climate.

References

Ag, A. (2010) Sprogbrug og identitetsarbejde hos senmoderne storbypiger. [Language use and identity work among late modern urban girls] Københavnerstudier i Tosprogethed 53. Copenhagen: Aarhus University.

Brink, L. and Lund, J. (1975) *Dansk rigsmål. [Danish Standard Language]*. København: Gyldendal.

Brink, L., Lund, J., Heger, S. and Jørgensen, J.N. (1991) *Den Store Danske Udtaleordbog [The Comprehensive Danish Pronunciation Dictionary]*. Copenhagen: Munksgaard.

Copenhagen City Council (2013) Statistics: Population and origin. https://subsite.kk.dk/sitecore/content/Subsites/CityOfCopenhagen/SubsiteFrontpage/Press/Facts OnCopenhagen/Statistics/~/media/65D726C9A92146B895D15B31F649C34E.ashx (accessed 2 April 2015).

Danmarks Statistik (2010) Nyt fra Danmarks Statistik – Byopgørelsen 1 January 2010.

Danish People's Party (2011) Political Program. http://www.danskfolkeparti.dk/The_ Party_Program_of_the_Danish_Peoples_Party.asp (accessed 10 April 2013).

Gimbel, J., Holmen, A. and Jørgensen, J.N. (2000) Det bedste Københavns Kommune har foretaget sig hidtil. Beskrivelse og evaluering af sproggruppeforsøg i skoledistrikterne 6 og 12 i Københavns Kommunes Skolevæsen 1996–1999. [The best thing Copenhagen City Council has done so far. Description and evaluation of language group initiatives in school districts 6 and 12]. Københavnerstudier i Tosprogethed bind 31. Copenhagen: Danmarks Lærerhøjskole.

Grundtvig, N.F.S. (1820) Danmarks Trøst [Comfort of Denmark]. First published in 1820. Available online: http://danmarkshistorien.dk/leksikon-og-kilder/vis/materiale/n-f-s-grundtvig-danmarks-troest-1820/ (accessed 10 February 2011).

Grønnum, N. (2005) *Fonetik og Fonologi – Almen og Dansk [Phonetics and Phonology – general and Danish]*. Copenhagen: Akademisk Forlag.

Holmberg, H., Gregersen, F. and Pedersen, I.L. (1992) The sociophonetics of some vowel variables in Copenhagen speech. In F. Gregersen and I.L. Pedersen (eds) *The Copenhagen Study of Urban Sociolinguistics* (pp. 107–231). Copenhagen: C.A. Reitzels Forlag.

Jørgensen, J.N. (1980) Det flade a vil sejre. En undersøgelse på sociolingvistisk grundlag af visse københavnske sprogforhold [The flat *a* will conquer. A sociolinguistic study of certain Copenhagen language traits]. *SAML* 7. Department of Applied and Mathematical Linguistics, University of Copenhagen, 67–124.

Jørgensen, J.N. and Kristensen, K. (1994) *Moderne sjællandsk. En undersøgelse af unge sjællænderes talesprog* [*Modern Sealandic. A study of young Sealanders' spoken language*]. Copenhagen: Reitzel.

Jørgensen, J.N. and von Haffner, B. (2002) Seks år med sproggruppe-klasser – en efterundersøgelse af holdninger og erfaringer i forbindelse med Københavns Kommunes skolevæsens sproggruppeprojekt 1996–2002 [Six years with language group classes – a follow-up study of attitudes and experiences regarding Copenhagen school authorities language group project 1996–2002]. Københavnerstudier i Tosprogethed bind 34. Copenhagen: Aarhus University.

Kristiansen, T. (1990) Udtalenormering i skolen [Pronunciation norms in school]. Copenhagen: Gyldendal.

Kristiansen, T. (2009) The macro-level social meanings of late-modern Danish accents. *Acta Linguistica Hafniensia* 41, 167–192.

Madsen, L.M. (2008) Fighters and Outsiders: Linguistic Practices, Social Identities, and Social Relationships Among Urban Youth in a Martial Arts Club. PhD thesis. Copenhagen: University of Copenhagen.

Maegaard, M. (2007) Udtalevariation og -forandring i københavnsk. En etnografisk undersøgelse af sprogbrug, sociale kategorier og social praksis blandt unge på en københavnsk folkeskole [Phonetic variation and change in Copenhagen speech. An ethnographic study of language use, social categories and social practice among young people in a Copenhagen school]. *Danske Talesprog* 8, 1–179.

Maegaard, M. (2009) How many standards? Investigating 'the double standard model' in the light of evaluative patterns from a young urban community. In M. Maegaard, F. Gregersen, P. Quist and J. Normann Jørgensen (eds) *Language Attitudes, Standardization and Language Change* (pp. 131–148). Oslo: Novus.

Maegaard, M. (2010) Linguistic practice and stereotypes among Copenhagen adolescents. In P. Quist and B.A. Svendsen (eds) *Multilingual Urban Scandinavia* (pp. 189–206). Bristol: Multilingual Matters.

Ministry of Culture (2003) Sprog på spil. Et udspil til en dansk sprogpolitik [Language at play. Initiative for a Danish language policy]. See http://www.kum.dk/graphics/kum/downloads/Publikationer/Sprog_paa_spil.pdf (accessed 10 March 2010).

Ministry of Culture (2008) Sprog til tiden, rapport fra Sprogudvalget [Language on time, report from the Language council]. Copenhagen: Ministry of Culture.

Ministry of Refugee, Immigration and Integration Affairs (2009) Tal og fakta – befolkningsstatistik om indvandrere og efterkommere. Juli 2009 [Numbers and facts – demographic statistics about immigrants and descendants. July 2009].

OECD (2008) Growing Unequal? Income Distribution and Poverty in OECD Countries. OECD Publishing. See http://www.keepeek.com/Digital-Asset-Management/oecd/social-issues-migration-health/growing-unequal_9789264044197-en (accessed 10 March 2013).

OECD (2010) National Accounts at a Glance 2010. OECD Publishing. http://dx.doi.org/10.1787/na_glance-2010-en (accessed 5 September 2011).

Pedersen, I.L. (2003) Traditional dialects of Danish and the de-dialectalization 1900–2000. *International Journal of the Sociology of Language* 159, 9–28.

Pedersen, I.L. (2005) Processes of standardisation in Scandinavia. In P. Auer, F. Hinskens and P. Kerswill (eds) *Dialect Change: Convergence and Divergence in European Languages* (pp. 171–195). Cambridge: Cambridge University Press.

Pedersen, I.L. (2009) The social embedding of standard ideology through four hundred years of standardisation. In M. Maegaard, F. Gregersen, P. Quist and J. Normann Jørgensen (eds) *Language Attitudes, Standardization and Language Change* (pp. 51–68). Oslo: Novus.

Quist, P. (2005) Stilistiske praksisser i storbyens heterogene skole [Stylistic practices in the urban heterogeneous school]. PhD dissertation, University of Copenhagen.

Quist, P. (2008) Sociolinguistic approaches to multiethnolect: language variety and stylistic practice. *International Journal of Bilingualism* 12 (1–2), 43–61.

Risager, K. (2009) Et eksempel på en pluralistisk sprogpolitik. *Sprogforum* 46, 34–39.

Staunæs, D. (2004) *Køn, etnicitet og skoleliv* [Gender, ethnicity and school life]. Frederiksberg: Forlaget Samfundslitteratur.

Stæhr, A. (2010) Rappen reddede os – Et studie af senmoderne storbydrenges identitetsarbejde i fritids – og skolemiljøer [The rap music saved us – a study of late modern urban boys identity work in leisure and school environments]. Københavnerstudier i Tosprogethed 54. Copenhagen: Aarhus University.

Conclusions

Urban areas in medium-sized linguistic communities are increasingly a product of glocal forces. Glocal forces because they are products of both local forces (the effects of contingent local history in its linguistic repertoire and in its linguistic ideologies) and global forces (digital technologies and huge population mobility increased by transnational capitalism). All these processes are not easy to cope with: there are recurrent cases of intergroup conflict. The intercultural city, where each cultural and linguistic group is recognized and valued is an ideal, still not a reality.

From the eight chapters of this volume, several recurrent aspects can be pointed out.

Multilingualism is pervasive and growing in these medium-sized communities. Generally this multilingualism might be seen as an asset, but also as a hindrance, as an inconvenience or even as a threat.

In cities in post-dictatorial states or autonomous territories (Tallinn, Barcelona, Vigo, València) there is a clear conflict between the former colonial or authoritarian group, and the independent or autonomous local group. A clear distinction can be made, though. For instance the control of the state machinery attributes Estonians in Tallinn a decisive power, allowing to give the local language the main power, whereas in the Spanish regions, Spanish, the dominant language which still is the central state's more valuable language, threatens the local one, dramatically in Vigo and València, more softly in Barcelona. The lack of an own or favourable disposed state, and therefore the lack of the main power associated with it, explains that substitution of the local languages is very likely.

The degree of decentralization in municipalities is very heterogeneous, ranging from the Finnish case, where cities and villages can choose a rather autonomous language policy, to the Spanish case where municipalities have to abide strictly to superior legislation at the national or regional level.

In general, there is a mismatch between linguistic practices at school and outside school. In Spanish cities, for example, at school some recognition of foreign immigrant languages is usually spread whereas these languages are neglected in everyday life. An interplay of language and ethnicity explains this derogatory ideologies towards these minority languages: 'immigrant languages' are used among the lowest paid positions in the work force, whereas 'foreign languages', those spoken by rich residents, are considered to be valuable social capitals.

In all societies, where the local group controls the state, the capital associated to it explains that the local language is normally used in the job market, and in higher education. This hegemony of this local language, however, doesn't entail homogeneity, i.e. an international language (normally English) increasingly pervades many social domains.

In all examined cities, English tends to occupy most domains, above all in imported entertainment, science and research and higher education. Family and everyday domains are still taken over by the local languages. In some societies with an acute internal linguistic conflict, English plays the role of lingua franca (Tallinn), but not in Spain (Barcelona, Vigo, València), where the spread of English is still very limited. Generally English is not perceived as a 'killer language', even though some measures are taken to limit its expansion.

Ethnolinguistic boundaries are very variegated in the analysed urban areas. Whereas in former soviet republics (Tallinn) these boundaries are very sharp between local Estonians and members of the Russian minority group, in Spain, especially in Barcelona, a more integrative, unitarian stance is taken in the political and social area. Most citizens in Barcelona are considered to be Catalans, regardless of their origin. In a very different manner, Brussels exemplifies a dramatic example of impermeability between the two groups in contact: actually there are clear-cut ethnic boundaries between Francophones and Dutch speakers in the Belgian capital having each group separated institutions and organizations. Generally most Dutch speakers are at least bilingual.

Linguistic competition is reflected very differently in the linguistic landscape (signage, labelling in streets). Once again, stateless societies (that is those without an own state or with a non favourable disposed state) are those where linguistic landscape (bottom-up) is mainly in the dominant language whereas some up-down messages are sometimes in the local language, which is protected by local legislation.

These structural patterns are reproduced in or are reproduced by linguistic ideologies. In Tallinn or Copenhagen there are clear manifestations of linguistic authenticity, that is, language is seen related to a given local, more genuine identity. In the Danish capital, for example, linguistic purism and homogeneity is very valued. On the other hand, a specific language such as English can be attributed values of anonymity, that is, can be deethnicized, detached from the exclusive characteristics of a given group.

Language contact in these medium-sized communities can trigger the appearance of playful mixture of languages. In Barcelona, for example, there is a growing number of code-switching phenomena (not reaching the level of language mixing, though) between two neighbouring languages in a non segregated society.

A clear indicator of the social power and prestige of a language is its attraction towards immigrant groups. The minority position of the local population in the three Spanish cities under analysis (Barcelona, Vigo, València) is mirrored in the lack of attraction for immigrant groups from outside Spain. The number of 'new speakers' of the local language is very limited (O'Rourke et al., 2015). Especially in the two latter cities immigrants prefer to learn and use the most powerful language, Spanish.

Another indicator of the degree of intercultural policy in a given city is the degree to which foreign and immigrant languages are recognized and learnt in the local society. In Helsinki, for instance, immigrant groups have the right to reproduce their language in the host country. This Finnish policy is a wonderful example of what we could call 'linguistic and cultural generosity' on behalf of the majority.

All these experiences of urban multilingualism in medium-sized communities show a fascinating heterogeneity, due to their respective history. In any case, an overarching factor behind these differences is the role played by the state (Vila, 2013; Vila & Bretxa, 2013). Without a state, for example, market forces tend to play against the minority language. Without an own state for the minorities, glocal forces (migration, mobility) threaten the weakest languages.

To sum up, the perspective of looking at this intermediate kind of medium-sized languages in urban contexts ameliorates our understanding of how and why languages live and decay, of how intercultural cities, where communities show interest into each other's culture and language, can be better built and encouraged. As Milian-Massana (2012: 17) summarizes, humanity should find an 'equilibrium between the legitimate interest in the State's international competitiveness and the employability of its citizens and the need to maintain and develop the full capacity of expression of mother tongues in as many domains as possible'. We hope these multilingual experiences in urban areas will help to conceive mainstream and non-mainstream groups, not in terms of competition but in terms of cooperation. Common feelings can be incorporated by many different voices.

References

Milian-Massana, A. (ed.) (2012) *Language and Legal Challenges in Medium-Sized Language Communities*. Barcelona: Institut d'Estudis Autonòmics.

O'Rourke, B., Pujolar, J. and Ramallo, F. (2015) New speakers of minority languages: The challenging opportunity – Foreword. *International Journal of the Sociology of Language* 231, 11–20.

Vila, F.X. (2013) Challenges and opportunities for medium-sized language communities in the 21st century: A (preliminary) synthesis. In F.X. Vila (ed.) *Survival and Development of Language Communities* (pp. 179–200). Bristol: Multilingual Matters.

Vila, F.X. and Bretxa, V. (2013) The analysis of medium-sized language communities. In F.X. Vila (ed.) *Survival and Development of Language Communities* (pp. 1–17). Bristol: Multilingual Matters.

Index

Aasland, A., 90
Ag, A., 176
alienation, 90
allochtonous, language, xv, 146
alternation, xvi
Amazig, *see* Amazigh
Amazigh, xii, 159
anonymous language, xv, 43
Arabic, 15, 28, 30, 35, 41, 53, 71, 72, 73, 75, 77, 113, 137
Aronin, L., 50
assimilation, 30, 36, 42, 115, 121, 146
asymmetrical multilingualism, xv, 143
attitude, 13, 33, 39, 40, 44, 45, 56, 57, 87, 92, 94, 100, 102, 103, 134, 136, 145
Augé, M., 140
Austria, 1, 6, 8, 9, 118
authenticity, xv, 25, 40, 42, 43, 45, 85, 86, 94, 95, 97, 98, 101, 102, 103, 105, 150, 187

Backhaus, P., 50
Baetens, H., 144
Barni, M., 50
Bastardas, A., xvi, 105, 146, 157, 164, 165
Ben Rafael, E., 50
Berber, 15, 137, *see also* Amazigh
Bienne, 147
bilingual education, 18, 56
bilingualism, xiii, 27, 28, 30, 31, 33, 39, 43, 45, 48, 53, 54, 66, 67, 77, 79, 82, 97, 108, 147, 150, 152, 153, 158, 159, 160, 161, 163, 165, 167, 185
birth country, 3, 4, 5, 20
Blackledge, A., 50
blaver, 122
Block, D., 50

Blommaert, J., 51, 86, 101
Bodoque, A., 124
Boix-Fuster, E., xiii, xv, 26, 43, 103, 153, 155, 160
Bourdieu, P., 86, 101
Bourhis, R.Y., 57
Branchadell, A., 104
Bretxa, V., xi, xiii, xvi, xvii, 188
Brink, L., 170, 179, 180
Briziç, K., 18
Brussels, xiii, xiv, 10, 12, 13, 14, 15, 18, 22, 25, 26, 27, 28, 29, 30, 31, 32, 33, 34, 35, 36, 38, 39, 40, 41, 42, 43, 44, 45, 46, 47, 48, 49, 72, 147, 187
Budryte, D., 87
Buruma, I., 149
business communication, 32, 33, 80

Calvet, L-J., 32, 145, 146
Carod-Rovira, J.-L., 147
Carson, L., 19
Castellanos, J., 161
Castells, M., 101
Castilian, 52, 53, 54, 55, 56, 57, 58, 59, 60, 61, 62, 63, 118, 120, 121, 125, 136, 137, 138, 149, 143, 148, 154, 156, 161, 162, 166, *see also* Spanish
Castilianization, 120, 121, 123
Castilianized, xiv, 50, 53, 140
Catalan, xiii, xv, xvi, 9, 31, 62103, 104, 105, 108, 11, 113, 117, 118, 120, 122, 123, 124, 125, 126, 136, 137, 138, 139, 140, 143, 147, 148, 149, 150, 151, 152, 153, 154, 155, 156, 157, 158, 159, 160, 161, 162, 163, 164, 187
Catalanist, 122, 147
census, 2, 3, 4, 5, 6, 7, 8, 46, 87, 88, 91, 114, 125, 126, 127, 128, 129,

Centre Universitari de Sociolingüística i Comunicació (CUSC-UB), see University Centre for Sociolinguistics and Communication
Chinese, 7, 71, 72, 73, 78, 137, 140
Chinn, J., 87
citizenship, 6, 7, 74, 87, 88, 90, 93, 169, 175
Clyne, M., 4, 15
commodification, 64
competitive, xiv, 25, 34, 38, 39, 40, 41, 42, 45, 46, 89, 90, 188
cooperative, xiv, 25, 39, 40, 41, 45, 113
Copenhagen, xiii, xvi, 72, 168, 169, 170, 171, 172, 173, 174, 175, 176, 177, 179, 180, 182, 183, 184, 187
Coupland, N., 51
Craen, P. van de, 144
Creese, A., 50
CUSC-UB, see University Centre for Sociolinguistics and Communication, CUSC
Cyprus, 7, 8, 9
Czech Republic, 7, 8, 9, 136
Czech, 136

Danish, xiii, xvi, 150, 168, 169, 170, 171, 173, 174, 175, 176, 177, 179, 180, 181, 182, 183, 184, 187,
De Swaan, A., 32
De Troyer, A., 34, 35
Deboosere, P., 32, 34
Declercq, K., 44, 47
default language, xv, 29, 157
diglossia, 30, 122
dominant language, xiv, xv, xvi, 3, 29, 30, 36, 86, 146, 154, 158, 159, 160, 186, 187
double monolingualism, 27
Dublin, 1, 18, 19, 23, 143
Duchêne, A., 47
Dunlevy, D. A., 58
Dutch Language House (*Huis van het Nederlands*), 34, 35, 38, 41
Dutch, xiii, xiv, 6, 8, 10, 11, 12, 13, 15, 25, 26, 27, 28, 29, 30, 31, 32, 33, 34, 35, 36, 37, 38, 39, 40, 41, 42, 43, 44, 45, 46, 47, 48, 147, 149, 187

Ehala, M., 91, 94, 95
emigration, 33
empowerment, 61, 62

English, xiii, xiv, xv, xvi, 1, 3, 5, 6, 11, 14, 16, 17, 18, 19, 25, 28, 29, 30, 31, 32, 33, 34, 35, 41, 45, 49, 53, 59, 60, 61, 62, 70, 71, 72, 73, 75, 76, 77, 78, 79, 80, 81, 84, 85, 86, 92, 93, 94, 95, 96, 97, 102, 103, 104, 105, 106, 107, 110, 136, 137, 138, 139, 140, 141, 143, 147, 158, 160, 173, 174, 183, 187
Erk, J., 37
Escola Valenciana, 124, 140
Estonian, xiii, xv, 71, 72, 73, 74, 77, 78, 85, 86, 87, 88, 89, 90, 91, 92, 93, 94, 95, 96, 97, 98, 99, 100, 101, 102, 103, 104, 105, 106, 107, 198, 150, 186, 187,
ethnic language, 86, 95, 97, 103
ethnicity, 4, 5, 6, 7, 8, 20, 71, 90, 96, 175, 179, 180, 182, 186
ethnocentrism, 183
ethnocultural identity, 3
ethnolinguistic boundaries, 86, 161, 162, 187
Ethnologue, 13
European Union, xiv, 1, 6, 18, 52, 68, 69, 70
Extra, G., xiv, 4, 5, 8, 9, 10, 11, 15, 18, 19, 21, 29, 50, 71, 74, 172,

Farràs, J., 151
favourable disposed state, 186, 187
Fernández Diaz, A., 158
Finland, xv, 8, 9, 67, 68, 69, 70, 71, 72, 73, 74, 76, 77, 79, 80, 81, 82,
Finnish, 67, 6869, 70, 71, 72, 73, 74, 75, 76, 77, 78, 79, 80, 81, 82, 83, 84, 108, 150, 186, 188
first language, 29, 32, 54, 69, 70, 71, 72, 74, 82, 97, 152, 153, 159, 163
Fishman, J. A., 50
Flanders, 26, 30, 31, 32, 35, 36, 37, 38, 41, 47
Flemish Community Commission (VGC), 34
Flemish, 25, 26, 27, 28, 30, 31, 33, 34, 35, 36, 37, 38, 39, 40, 41, 42, 43, 44, 45, 46, See Dutch
Fonzari, L., 95
France, 2, 6, 8, 135, 148, 149
Francoism, 119, 139, 150
francophone, 26, 27, 28, 29, 30, 31, 33, 34, 35, 36, 39, 40, 43, 44, 45, 46, 47, 187
Freitas Juvino, M. P., 53

French, xiii, xiv, 8, 10, 11, 13, 14, 15, 25, 26, 27, 28, 29, 30, 31, 32, 33, 34, 35, 36, 37, 38, 39, 40, 41, 42, 44, 45, 46, 47, 48, 53, 62, 72, 73, 75, 76, 78, 98, 120, 137, 147, 160, 174
Frenchification, 30, 31
Frenchified, 43
Fribourg, 147

Gal, S., 85
Galicia, xiii, 9, 51, 52, 53, 56, 58, 60, 63, 64, 65, 66
Galician, xiii, xiv, 9, 52, 53, 54, 55, 56, 57, 58, 59, 60, 61, 62, 63, 64, 65, 66
Galiza, 65, *see also* Galicia
García, O., 50
gender effects, 20
ghettoization, 140
Giddens, A., 141
Gimbel, J., 173
Giner, S., 149
Glaesser, E., 112
globalization, xi, xv, xvi 17, 18, 50, 51, 64, 85, 86, 94, 95, 101, 102, 103, 104, 106, 113, 121, 125, 140, 141, 164
Gogolin, I., 17
González, I., 14, 57,
Gorter, D., 4, 8, 9, 50, 102
Göteborg, 10, 12, 14, 15, 18
Gothenburg, xiv
Greek, vii, 28, 133
Grimes, B., 13
Grundtvig, N. F. S., 170

habitus, 17
Haffner, B. von, 173
Hague, the, xiv, 10, 12, 13, 14, 15, 18
Hall, J., 161, 162
Hallik, K., 87
Hamburg, xiv, 10, 12, 14, 15, 18
Hambye, P., xiv, 33, 40, 44,
Harris, M., 148
healthcare services, 75
Heidmets, M., 87
Heinemann, U., 161
Heller, M., 27, 37, 47, 95, 106
Helsinki, xiii, xv, 67, 68, 69, 70, 71, 72, 73, 74, 75, 76, 77, 78, 79, 80, 81, 82, 83, 84, 188
Hernández Dobon, F.-J., xv, 40, 125, 134
Hernández, F. J., xv, 40, 125, 134

historical language, xv, 143, 146, 148, 163, 164
Hogan-Brun, G., 18, 87, 95
home language (HL), xiv, 1, 2, 3, 4, 6, 8, 9, 10, 11, 13, 14, 15, 18, 20, 23, 40
Hungary, 7, 8, 9
hybridism, xv, xvi, 154, 159

identification language, 152, 153
identity conflict, 123, 124
ideology, xiii, xvi, 25, 37, 38, 85, 95, 96, 102, 145, 147, 168, 175, 183, 186, 187
immersion, 46, 77
immigrant language, 18, 28, 64, 186, 188
immigrant minority, 2, 20
immigration, xiii, 2, 3, 11, 13, 18, 20, 30, 33, 53, 63, 73, 75, 103, 114, 119, 135, 136, 137, 156, 157, 162, 172, 173, 175,
Infopankki [Information Bank], 75
Ingendaay, P., 162
inhibition, 130, 131, 133, 134
Institute for the Languages of Finland, xv, 79
institutional communication, 156, 157
instrumental, 40, 47, 93, 95, 136
integrative, 40
intergenerational language transmission, 15, 153
intergenerational transmission, xii, 53, 54
Irish, 9, 18

Janssens, R., 29, 32, 33, 40, 44, 45, 46, 47, 48
Järve, P., 87, 94, 100,
Jaworski, A., 50
Jørgensen, J. N., xvi, 173, 179

Kaiser, R., 87
Kakihara, T., 58
Kirss, L., 94, 95
Kolstoe, P., 87
Kristiansen, T., 171
Kulu, H., 90
Kuntaliitto [Local Finland], 71
Kuo, E. C. Y., 151
Kurdish, xii, 15, 71, 72, 73, 75, 172
Kymlicka, W., 87

Laitin, D., 95
Landry, R., 57
language choice, xiv, 11, 15, 16, 20, 158

language coexistence, 25, 28, 30, 39, 50, 55, 137, 138, 147, 160
language community xiii, xvi, 38, 86, 104, 145, 147, 183
language conflict, xiii, 146, 147, 150, 162, *see also* linguistic conflict
language dominance, xiv, 11, 15, 16, 20
language homogenization, 144
language landscape, 73, 77, *see* linguistic landscape
language maintenance, xiv, 17, 20, 26
language normalization, 143, 149
language planning, 10, 79
language policies, xii, xiii, xiv, xvi, 10, 25, 26, 39, 40, 42, 45, 57, 63, 83
language policy, xi, xii, 17, 25, 26, 27, 35, 38, 39, 40, 41, 46, 58, 59, 61, 79, 80, 83, 84, 87, 104, 106, 146, 149, 160, 162, 163, 174, 184, 186
language preference, xiv, 11, 15, 16, 20
language proficiency, xiv, 11, 15, 16, 20, 21, 94
language shift, xii, 17, 26, 29, 54, 144, 145
language standardization, xi, 121, 143, 148, 183
language use *in vitro*, 146, 159
language use *in vivo*, 146, 159
language vitality index (LVI), 15, 16, 21
language-promotion campaigns, 139
Laponce, J., 30
Larreula, E., 147
Latvia, 6, 8, 9, 18, 101
Latvian, 74, 88, 150
Lauristin, M., 87, 90, 91, 92, 93
legitimacy, 104, 124
legitimate speaker, xii
Lingala, 28
lingua franca xiv, xv xvi, 25, 28, 32, 33, 45, 102, 105, 113, 143, 146
linguistic community, xii, 13, 26, 29, 33, 41, 42, 77, 121, 135, 141, 164, 186
linguistic conflict, 38, 123, 136, 138, 187
linguistic economy 135
linguistic ghetto, 144
linguistic landscape, xiii, xv, 28, 50, 51, 53, 56, 57, 58, 59, 60, 61, 63, 65, 74, 102, 106, 146, 156, 157, 159, 160, 164, 165, 187
linguistic protectionism, 49
linguistic radar, 50
linguistic repertoire, xiii, xv, xvi, 55, 65, 67, 68, 71, 144, 145, 148, 150, 186

linguistic sustainability, xi, xii, 164, 165
linguistic variation, 4, 168, 169, 176, 180, 182
Linz, J. J., 147
literacy, 15, 17, 20, 50, 119
Longueville, E. de, 46, 47
López Docampo, M., 58
Lund, J., 170, 179, 180
Lyon, xv, 1, 10, 12, 14, 18

Mabille, X., 37
Mackey, W. F., 145
Madrid, xiv, 10, 12, 13, 14, 15, 18, 119, 147, 162,
Madsen, L. M., 176, 182
Maegaard, M., xvi, 175, 176, 177, 179, 182
mainstream language/group, xiv, 11, 13, 14, 16, 17, 178, 188
Mandinga, 137
Marí, I., 139, 145
Martin Rojo, L., 50
Masso, A., 87
Mataix, T., 149, 152, 157
MCP, *see* Multilingual Cities Project 9, 12, 17, 18
McRae, K. D., 68, 145
medium language, 49
medium-sized community, 42, 45, 186, 187, 188
medium-sized language community, xvi, xvii, 25, 26, 38, 40, 86, 104, 144, 164, 188
medium-sized language, xv, 32, 85, 86, 102, 108, 188
medium-sized linguistic community (MSLC), 40, 86, 104, 106, 141, 144, 164, 186
migration, 3, 11, 17, 18, 32, 42, 52, 72, 74, 125, 164, 188
Milian-Massana, A., xii, xvi, xvii, 165, 188
minoritized language, xi, xiv, 50, 64, 95
minoritized, 26
minority language, xi, xii, 7, 14, 21, 26, 38, 42, 45, 56, 63, 64, 65, 66, 67, 70, 75, 76, 81, 131, 148, 150, 152, 168, 172, 173, 183, 186, 188
Montreal, 147
Monzó, Q., 150
Moring, T., 79, 80
Moyer, M., 50
Multilingual Cities Project (MCP), xiv, 1, 9, 10, 13, 17
multilingual communication, 113

multilingual image, xiii, 67, 74
multilingual services, xiii
multilingual sign, 61
multilingualism, xiii, xiv, xv, xvi, 1, 5, 10, 17, 18, 35, 41, 48, 50, 51, 64, 65, 67, 77, 83, 104, 106, 108, 143, 144, 145, 146, 160, 164, 166, 186, 188
Myntti, K., 71

Nassauk, J-P., 21
nationality, 2, 3, 4, 5, 6, 7, 8, 11, 32, 172, 175, 176
neofalantes, 53
Netherlands, the, xiv, 6, 8, 9 11, 12, 31, 32
Nicolás, M., xv, 40
Niglas, K., 94, 95
Ninyoles, R. L., 120, 39, 141
Nordberg, B., 71
normal and preferential, 156, *see also* normal and preferred use
normal and preferred use, 156, 157, 158
Nuolijärvi, P., xv, 71, 80, 81
Nyholm, A. S., 74

Ó Murchú, H., 18
O'Donnel, P., 33
O'Rourke, B., 53, 188
Observatorio da Cultura Galega, 56
Occitan, 148, 149
Occitania, 150

Pardines, S., 124
participant observation, 96, 175
passive bilingualism, 97, 163
Paunonen, H., 71
Pedersen, I. L., 169
Pérez Andújar, J., 155
phonetic variation, 177
Piqueras Infante, A., 125, 135
Pitarch, V., 121
pivotal role, 164, 152, 164
Poleshchuk, V., 87, 89, 90, 91, 94
political persecution, 120
Portuguese, 28, 53, 62, 72, 136, 137, 159
primary school children, 11, 12, 13
private communications, 157
productive bilingualism, 160
Pujolar, J., 103, 161
Puntí, J., 155

Quist, P., 176, 177

Rafanell, A., 150
Ramallo, F., xiv, 53
Rambla, F. X., 155
Ramonière, M., 18
Rannut, M., 87
Rannut, Ü., 87, 92, 93
receptive bilingualism, 160
recognition, 12, 31, 36, 37, 38, 39, 41, 45, 63, 113, 122, 186
regional minority language, 7, 14
religious denomination, 5, 7
reported language proficiency, 11
Reuter, M., 74
revitalization, 26, 53, 64
Risager, K., 173
Romani, 14, 71
runaway growth, 141
Russian, xiii, xv, 28, 35, 53, 67, 68, 71, 72, 73, 74, 75, 76, 77, 78, 85, 86, 87, 88, 91, 92, 93, 94, 95, 96, 97, 98, 99, 100, 101, 102, 103, 104, 105, 106, 107, 108, 136, 187
Russophone, 88, 90, 92, 93, 94, 96, 99, 100, 101, 103, 104

Sámi, 71, 77, 79
Sanchis Guarner, M., 113
schooling, 17, 57, 128, 133, 140, 173
Selander, P., 74
self-categorization, 3, 4, 5
Shafir, G., 87
Shohamy, E., 50
signage, xiii, 28, 46, 102, 187
Singleton, D., 50
Skerrett, D. M., 87
Slovenia, 6, 8, 9
Smet, P., 34
social perception, 131
Soler-Carbonell, J., xv, 42, 103
Sorribes, J., 116, 117
Spanish, xii, xiv, xv, 10, 11, 14, 28, 35, 41, 51, 52, 61, 66, 72, 73, 74, 78, 96, 104, 105, 106, 114, 115, 118, 119, 120, 136, 138, 139, 140, 141, 143, 147, 148, 149, 150, 151, 152, 153, 154, 155, 156, 157, 158, 159, 160, 161, 162, 163, 164, 165, 166, 186, 188
Stæhr, A. 176, 182
standard language, 46, 69, 173, 182, 183
stateless societies, 187
Staunæs, D., 176
Steenwinckel, A., 34, 35, 41, 47
Strubell, M., 150,

Subirats, M., 151, 155, 156
subjective ethnolinguistic vitality, 163
superdiversity, 51
sustainability, xi, xii, xiii, xvi, 65, 164, 165
Swedish, xiii, xv, 10, 11, 13, 67, 68, 69, 70, 71, 72, 73, 74, 75, 76, 77, 78, 79, 80, 81, 82, 83, 169, 172, 174
Switzerland, 3, 145, 147, 160
symbolic value, 18, 45, 56, 63
systematic bilingualism, 28

Tallinn, xiii, xv, 78, 85, 86, 87, 88, 89, 90, 91, 92, 93, 94, 95, 96, 99, 101, 102, 104, 106, 107, 108, 109, 186, 187
Tammaru, T., 90
Taylor, C., 38
Thurlow, C., 50
Toebosch, A., 33
Torres, N., 124
Turkish, 2, 6, 7, 15, 28, 35, 72, 73, 75, 172

uniformitarian ideology, 183
University Centre for Sociolinguistics and Communication, CUSC, xiii, xvi, xvii, 86
Urdu, 137
US, 2, 3, 4, 5, 138, 158
USA, *see* US

Vaamonde Liste, A., 54, 65
valencià, 113, 119, 120, 121, 122, 123, 124, 125, 126, 127, 128, 130, 131, 132, 133, 139, 140, 142, *see* Valencian
Valencia, xiii, xv, 9, 112, 113, 114, 115, 116, 117, 118, 119, 120, 121, 122, 125, 127 128, 131, 132, 133, 134, 137, 138, 139, 140, 147, 148, 186, 187, 188

Valencian Academy of the Language [*Acadèmia Valenciana de la Llengua, AVL*], 124
Valencian, xv, 113, 114, 115, 117, 120, 121, 122, 123, 124, 125, 126, 132, 139, 147
Van Parijs, Ph., 30, 33
vehicular language, 34
Velthoven, H. van, 37
Verlot, M., 15
Verschik, A., 87, 94, 95
Vertovec, S., 51
Vetik, R., 87
Vienna, 1, 18
Vigo, 13, 14, 50, 51, 52, 53, 54, 55, 56, 57, 58, 61, 63, 64, 65, 66, 186, 187, 188
Vihalemm, T., 87, 90, 91, 92, 93, 95, 97, 101
Vikør, L. D., 69
Vila, F. X., xi, xii, xvi, xvii, 86, 108, 165, 188
Vilnius, 1, 18, 78
Virkkula, T., 81
Vlaamse Gemeenschap Comissie (VGC), *see* Flemish Community Commission (VGC)

Wallonia, 26, 30, 32, 36, 37, 39, 41
Webber, J., 150
Wellings, M. P., 58
Williams, W., 53
Witte, E., 34, 35, 36, 37, 41, 43, 44, 46
Woolard, K. A., 25, 42, 85, 86, 95, 103, 105, 147, 148, 155, 162

Yağmur, K., 10, 21, 50

For Product Safety Concerns and Information please contact our EU Authorised Representative:

Easy Access System Europe

Mustamäe tee 50

10621 Tallinn

Estonia

gpsr.requests@easproject.com